MAKING STRATEGY HAPPEN

Making Strategy Happen

Transforming Plans into Reality

ARNOLD S. JUDSON

BLACKWELL
Business

The Planning Forum

Copyright © Arnold S. Judson 1990

First published 1990
Reprinted 1993 (twice)

Blackwell Publishers
238 Main Street,
Cambridge, Massachusetts 02142, USA

108 Cowley Road, Oxford OX4 1JF, UK

Library of Congress Cataloging in Publication Data

Judson, Arnold S.
Making strategy happen: transforming plans into reality
Arnold S. Judson.
p.   cm.
ISBN 1–55786 0971
1. Strategic planning.   I. Title.
HD30.28.J83   1990
658.4′012   dc20   89–18583   CIP
The Planning Forum ISBN 0–912841–33–8

British Library Cataloguing in Publication Data

A CIP catalogue record for this book is available from
the British Library.

Typeset in 10½ on 12½ pt CG Times
by Advance Typesetting Ltd, Long Hanborough, Oxford
Printed in Great Britain by
Athenæum Press Ltd, Newcastle upon Tyne

This book is printed on acid-free paper

Contents

Preface   vii

Acknowledgements   x

Part I   Great Plans do not Happy Outcomes Make   1

1   The Implementation Issue   3

2   Why Strategies Fail   12

3   The Anatomy of Implementation   35

Part II   New Uses for an Old Vehicle   41

4   Driving Strategy Implementation with Operating Plans   43

5   Setting the Stage   52

Part III   Three Cornerstone Analyses   63

6   Targeting High-leverage Improvement Opportunities   65

7   Setting the Right Priorities and Objectives   76

8   Assessing Capabilities for Success   88

Part IV   Formulating an Agreed Plan   97

9   Establishing Direction and Focus   99

10   Specifying the Work Required   110

Part V   Ensuring Implementation Success   127

11   Tracking Implementation Progress   129

12   Sustaining Momentum and Focus   150

13   Making Strategy Happen   170

Contents

Appendixes

1 Sample Operating System Characterization 182

2 High-leverage Targets of Opportunity (Prioritized) 200

3 Organization and Management Readiness Assessment
Questionnaire 202

4 Generic Strategy Options 212

5 An Example of a List of Issues to be Addressed by
a Strategy 223

6 Some Typical Obstacles to Successful Strategy
Implementation 228

7 Examples of Action Programmes 230

8 Examples of Tailored Measurement Packages 240

Notes 244

Index 246

Preface

This book is about how to ensure that a firm's strategic plans actually lead to desired tangible outcomes, both in the marketplace and within the organization. I intend this book to fill a void in the growing literature on strategic planning and strategic management, almost all of which focuses on how to formulate sound strategies. Unfortunately, the overwhelming lesson of the past decade is that soundly conceived strategic plans, no matter how brilliant, seldom get implemented.

This gap between intent and accomplishment is the result of many complex factors. Some of these have to do with how plans are formulated; others are associated with the dynamics of individual and group behaviour and of organizational systems; and the remainder have to do with the very nature of the implementation process itself. In order to improve the probability that plans will be implemented effectively, one must first understand the forces that determine or undermine success.

In the first three chapters, I discuss why so many strategies fail to be implemented, and the key factors on which successful implementation depends. These chapters are intended to establish the contextual framework for the rest of the book. Chapters 4 through 12 lay out in considerable detail, supported by illustrative examples, a practical, proven process which can be employed by the management of any for-profit business or not-for-profit institution to enhance the probability that their intended strategies will indeed be realized. This process centres on the formulation of an operating plan as the primary mechanism for ensuring that management address the key factors for successful implementation. In the final Chapter 13, I summarize and integrate the principal themes and points contained in the book.

Once the reader becomes familiar and comfortable with the conceptual framework and rationale presented in the book's first three chapters, s/he can use the rest of the book as a practical manual for applying these concepts. The material in the eight appendixes is offered both as examples of tools and instruments to be used in the process for formulating an operating plan, and as actual illustrative examples of what various management groups were able to achieve by using these tools.

In this book I assume that management have already in mind or articulated on paper, certain strategic business or institutional objectives they want to achieve, along with the strategies that they believe will enable them to realize these objectives. To formulate an operating plan, I advocate the use of a particular group participative process as a key next step in ensuring that the intended strategies are actually implemented. As this process unfolds, questions may be raised about the viability or appropriateness of the previously determined business or institutional objectives and strategies. If this occurs, the organization's strategic management process should provide for a review, reconsideration and possible modification of these objectives and strategies. An effective strategic management process is not linear and sequential, but rather iterative and dynamic.

This book is based both on contemporary concepts of business strategy and organizational behaviour, and on more than forty years of action research on the application of these concepts in hundreds of business and not-for-profit organizations in a wide range of industries and fields. Prior to 1970, my primary focus was on the improvement of organizational effectiveness and productivity. From the start, this required a concern with how large, complex organizational systems can achieve substantial, durable changes in their *modus operandi*. In the early 1970s, I became interested in the emerging practice of strategic planning.

My earlier work caused me to focus equally on two issues: (a) how to develop a high-quality, integrated and credible strategic plan; and (b) how to ensure that the plan is actually carried out. This dual focus resulted in the group approach to plan formulation described in this book. Initially, my colleagues and I applied this group process to the formulation of strategic business plans. Later, we adapted the same approach to the development of operating plans. After applying this process in about a dozen situations, I realized that the work I was doing with clients was highly congruent with the work I had done earlier to help organizations improve productivity.

The process that my colleagues and I have been using to help our clients formulate and implement strategy has evolved substantially since 1970. We are continually refining the tools and instruments we use as well as the processes in which they are employed. We have also added several new elements. Many of these innovations were stimulated by our clients. The process described in this book represents the latest stage in the development of this evolving process.

Because the relationships that my firm and I have with our clients tend to extend over many years, we have had the opportunity to track their strategy implementation progress closely. We have thus been able to match outcomes and achievements with initial intents and plans. As a consequence, I feel confident in the power and effectiveness of the approach I advocate in this book. With this book, I hope to share this experience more widely than has been possible to date.

Arnold S. Judson
Cambridge, Massachusetts

Acknowledgements

B ecause this book represents the accumulated learning of my entire working career, I want to take this opportunity to cite the more important influences that contributed to this learning.

I owe my more than forty years' commitment to improving organizational effectiveness and productivity to my association with Douglas MacGregor and the other faculty involved in the innovative graduate programme in organizational behaviour that he established at the Massachusetts Institute of Technology in 1947. Another strong influence in that programme was Joseph Scanlon.

My interest in strategic planning and strategic management was sparked initially by a former colleague, Robert V. L. W. Wright. Foremost in helping me to develop my thinking about strategic management along with the process described in this book, is my colleague and partner of some thirty years, Daniel H. Gray.

I want to thank my wife, June, both for providing a continuing stimulus for innovation and for taking risks, and for supplying consistent emotional support throughout my career.

For helping me in the development and production of my manuscript, I want to thank Stacy Curtis, Cheryl Greco and Joanne Zukowski and Ralph Moxcey for his design of the book jacket.

Arnold S. Judson

Part I

Great Plans do not Happy Outcomes Make

1

The Implementation Issue

It is hard to believe, in today's complex and uncertain world, that business managers began formally to engage in strategic planning only two decades ago, and that its value is currently an issue of hot debate. Since the early 1980s, an increasing number of journal articles have appeared questioning whether strategic planning is worth the effort. Many giant corporations, noted for sophisticated management practices, have drastically reduced or eliminated their planning staffs. Many other firms, on the other hand, are either just beginning to apply strategic planning, or are struggling to improve their planning processes.

Why is there so much apparent disenchantment with strategic planning, especially by the world's largest firms whose sophisticated executives and managers have had the longest experience with planning processes? Why are so many other firms continuing to introduce strategic planning, or trying to make their planning processes more effective? Is strategic planning just another management fad, going the way of management-by-objectives, sensitivity training and quality circles? What is an executive to make of these confusing trends, when sustaining business success is ever more difficult in an increasingly intense, dynamic and competitive environment?

Great Expectations: the Rise of Planning

Before attempting to make any sense out of management's affair with strategic planning, it is important first to understand the context of its rise and possible fall from grace. The entire history of business planning spans less than a human lifetime. Prior to World War II, whatever planning that occurred in the vast majority of business organizations was concerned typically with physical operations in manufacturing: the design and construction of facilities, the introduction of technologies, processes, tools and equipment, and the like. During the pre-history phase of business planning, the principal planning tool employed was the Gantt chart, developed in 1917 and 1918 to plan war production.

3

Great Plans do not Happy Outcomes Make

True business planning began with the introduction (by E. I. duPont de Nemours & Co.) of general forecasting of economic conditions and detailed proposals for individual projects as the procedural cornerstones for appropriating capital expenditures. The practice of capital and expense budgeting spread first to a few of America's giant corporations by the mid-1920s (for example, General Motors, Standard Oil Company of New Jersey), and was taken up more broadly by business organizations after World War II.

Until mid-century, whatever planning was going on in most firms consisted of the preparation of capital and expense budgets. The main purpose of budgeting, however, was not enhancing management's ability to provide for the firm's future success. Rather, budgeting was focused more on controlling expenditures in the near term. Typically, budget preparation centred on the estimated requirements of each department considered separately (and later, on those of the entire firm), rather than on the needs of each of the businesses in which the firm was engaged. The planning horizon was seldom more than the next year. Budgeting addressed the question, 'How can I ensure that my department will have the funds needed to meet our commitments next year?' Once approved, the budget was then used by both company and departmental managers as a tool for controlling costs (see Figure 1).

After World War II, three major trends began transforming businesses and the way they were managed. Marketing began to emerge as an increasingly important element of doing business. Concurrently, the impact of new technologies was spreading at an accelerating pace, especially in electronics, information, communications and materials. Both of these developments were occurring in a world of expanding market opportunities. Pent up consumer demand, constrained by more than 15 years of economic depression and war, created an almost 20-year period of unbroken growth opportunities for business enterprises. More sophisticated executives recognized the shortcomings of budget planning in coping with these new challenges.

Long-range planning

At first, each department was asked to plan for the next several years, rather than for only the next year. It was assumed that functional specialists at departmental level were best able to anticipate future developments and what it would take to deal with these. It was further assumed that a viable long-range plan for the company could be achieved by aggregating all the departmental long-range plans.

4

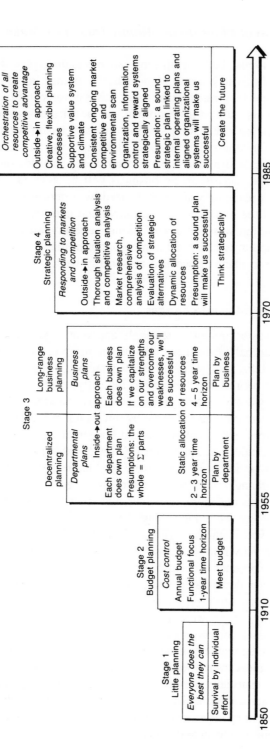

Figure 1 The evolution of business planning.

Great Plans do not Happy Outcomes Make

In the late 1950s, bottoms-up long-range planning gave way in more sophisticated firms to long-range business planning. For the first time, four to five year long-range plans were being developed that focused on a single business, not on a department or the firm as a whole (which might, in fact, be conducting several different businesses). A driving presumption for long-range business planning was, 'If we identify our true strengths as a firm and capitalize on these, and also overcome our weaknesses, the success of the business will be assured.' Thus, long-range business planning was characterized by a perspective that viewed and addressed the marketplace, customers and competitors from within the firm. Winning was a matter of 'doing superbly what we know how to do best.' So long as external market opportunities continued to grow, this approach to planning worked reasonably well.

External and internal changes

By 1970, it was becoming increasingly apparent to business leaders that the world external to the firm was becoming ever more complex and uncertain, and that changes on all fronts were occurring at unprecedented speeds. This world was changing radically. Both competition and opportunities were becoming global rather than national. Many 'foreign' competitors were playing the game by unfamiliar rules, created by more patient investors, more supportive and congenial regulatory and labour relations conditions, and dramatically lower labour costs. Unlike the prior postwar period, when relatively low interest rates, inflation, and monetary exchange rates were stable and predictable, the economic environment became more turbulent and quite unpredictable. Capital and energy costs were increasing dramatically. Also, the regulatory environment was changing, with many new areas subject to regulation (for example, environment, working hours and conditions, minority employment, product safety, truth in advertising, etc.), and many industries being deregulated and/or privatized (for example, trucking, airlines, financial services, telecommunications, etc.).

Concurrently, there were profound changes taking place in social values, consumer behaviour and technology. The rise of minority rights was accompanied by the erosion of traditional family values and relationships. Consumers were becoming more educated and demanding of products and especially services. The rapid development of computing and telecommunications technologies was revolutionizing the availability and management of information. The development of new materials was revolutionizing products and design.

Along with these fundamental changes in the firm's external environment, major changes were also taking place inside organizations – many of them in response to the external changes. Many business firms were growing larger and much more complex. Rather than conducting a single business, many corporations became engaged in many, often diverse businesses. Global competition led to global sourcing and geographic dispersion. Large firms adopted complex multi-business, multi-divisional, multi-layered and multi-national structures. Within firms, many new specialized functions emerged and grew to deal with changes in technology and in the regulatory and social environment (for example, information systems and processing, environmental impact, legal, employee benefits, organizational development, strategic planning, quality, etc.). More, specialized functions meant increased organizational fragmentation. Changes in consumer behaviour coupled with changes in technology led both to the proliferation of products and services to meet specialized market demands, and to shorter product and service life-cycles. The need for organizations more frequently to design, develop and market many more products and services placed unprecedented strains on business firms.

Another major area within organizations that changed was the nature of the workforce. Many firms experienced a dramatic increase in the proportion of women, minorities and professionals (or 'knowledge workers') in the workforce, while the proportion of more traditional 'blue-collar' workers declined. Better educated and more demanding than the typical workforce of the 1950s and 1960s, this 'new' workforce was no longer content to be dealt with as unthinking instruments of production. Rather, they demanded immediate, positive satisfaction from both their work and their working environment. What was formerly viewed as benefits became expected as entitlements.

All these changes had a profound effect on most firms' cost structures. By the early 1970s, relative to the decade and a half following World War II, the proportion of most firms' total costs represented by capital, energy and materials had grown substantially, at the expense of labour costs. But the labour cost portion of total costs had also changed radically. By 1970, the cost of 'white collar', professional and managerial 'overhead' or 'indirect' segment of labour cost had become for most firms a far more significant proportion of total labour costs than the 'blue-collar' or 'direct' segment. For many manufacturing firms, 'direct' labour costs had dwindled to a small fraction (10 to 20 per cent) of total labour costs. Furthermore, the costs of fringe benefits, especially for health care, had risen substantially.

The cumulative impact of all these external and internal changes on management, especially top executives, was enormous. No manager had been prepared, either through education or experience in the 1940s and 1950s, to deal with the levels of external volatility and uncertainty, together with internal complexity, that characterized the business and organizational circumstances of the 1970s. Senior management craved new means and tools to cope. Strategic planning appeared to offer some answers to meet this urgent need.

Strategic planning

Business leaders, initially in the USA and soon after in the UK and Western Europe, realized that they needed more sophisticated information about the firm's external environment as a basis for establishing the direction for the business, setting priorities and allocating resources. Unlike long-range planning which had been based on an inside→out perspective, strategic planning for a single business was based first and foremost on a thorough analysis and understanding of the characteristics of its industry, markets and competition. Internal capabilities were assessed within a framework of industry, market and competitive dynamics. Strategic alternatives were then identified and evaluated. Corporate strategy in multi-business firms was developed by reconciling: (a) the opportunities, threats, intended strategies and promised performance for each of the corporation's separate businesses[1]; and (b) the objectives, priorities and resources of the corporation as a whole. A presumption that drove strategic planning was that 'a sound, well conceived plan will make us successful.'

The extraordinarily rapid and enthusiastic adoption of strategic planning in the 1970s by the managements of the world's largest enterprises was driven initially by management consultants. They provided the conceptual frameworks and analytical methods and tools so necessary to address the complexities of each firm's external environment. The new emphasis on external research and analysis caused the managements of the world's leading corporations to establish large staffs of corporate and business unit planners. To them was delegated the task of formulating business and corporate strategies. Many of these planners were recruited from the very management consulting firms responsible for developing the strategic planning concepts and methods. During the 1970s, consulting in strategic planning grew at an average rate of 25 to 30 per cent compounded annually. By 1981, one survey[2] estimated that about half of the top *Fortune* 1000 firms were actively engaged in strategic planning.

Dashed Hopes: Sobering Up

Starting in late 1979 and continuing with increasing frequency each year of the 1980s, business and management journals (most in the US) published articles critical of strategic planning. These pieces pointed out that few strategies actually achieved their intended objectives (some estimated no more than 10 per cent), and questioned the value of management's affair with strategic planning. Analyzing 31 of these articles, four main themes recur to explain why strategic planning has yielded such disappointing outcomes to date (Table 1). Dominating the criticism is failure to implement the strategy once formulated. A frequent cause for this failure is attributed to the fact that in most companies during the 1970s, strategic planning was in hands of planners, often former consultants, who were focused on theory and analytical methods, and who were far removed from the realities of the competitive marketplace. By the early 1980s, many leading firms had already begun to dismantle their planning staffs and shift the primary responsibility for formulating strategy to line executives. It is too soon to assess the impact of this change.

Table 1 Explanations for disappointments with strategic planning

	Frequency	(%)
Failures in implementation after strategy formulation	17	45
Failures in concepts underlying plan formulation	10	26
Inadequate relevant information/ poor assumptions	8	21
Failures in analysis of information	3	8

Source: Based on 31 business and management journal articles appearing from 1979 to 1988.

For the most part, the criticisms of strategic planning appearing in business journals have, in my view, not adequately explained the causes of the disappointing returns from managements' considerable investment to date. These causes are more numerous and subtle than most articles suggest. It is certainly true that successful implementation is the ultimate test of a strategy. By 'success', I mean achieving the intended strategic objectives. In most instances, managements have failed to carry out their intended strategies. Simply to point this out as a cause for questioning the value of strategic planning provides little help to executives who need to

9

deal more effectively with the problems of increasing external uncertainty and internal complexity. If we are to make any progress in improving implementation success, we must first understand in greater depth the true direct causes of implementation failure.

Underlying causes for implementation failure

In Chapter 2, I discuss the specific multiple causes of implementation failure. I should note that because the longest and most extensive experience with strategic planning has occurred to date in the USA, this discussion draws heavily on this experience. Two broad underlying factors have helped to set the stage for this failure in American firms. Both have to do with some characteristics of the American business culture and the attitudes of American executives and managers.

One of these factors is American managers' tendency to lust after quick fixes. Driven by relentless pressure from the US investment community for continuous, short-term improvements in financial performance, American executives are continuously on the lookout for panaceas both that promise fast relief from their problems and that appear to require only a minimal expenditure of their effort. The result of this syndrome is a history of faddism in American management. The four post World War II decades are littered with examples of promising new 'solutions', enthusiastically taken up, only to be discarded a few years later when the inevitable disappointments set in.

In the 1950s, for example, psychological testing promised vast improvements of the selection, placement and advancement of personnel. Next, management-by-objectives promised dramatic improvements in managerial and organizational performance, resulting from more highly motivated people working more collaboratively in synch with company objectives. Also in the late 1950s, management first became infatuated with diversification (to smooth out cyclical business fluctuations) and with quantitative management (hard numbers are more reliable than intuition and judgement when making decisions).

In the 1960s, sensitivity training and T-Groups (and then the Managerial Grid) promised to enhance management effectiveness. Matrix management, centralization/decentralization, and the notion of con-glomerates also enjoyed widespread favour. The 1970s saw the rise of strategic planning, portfolio management, zero-based budgeting, and quality circles. And in the 1980s, we witnessed just-in-time provisioning, total quality control, restructuring, 'intrapreneuring' and changing corporate cultures.

In each instance, the potential value offered by the prospective new 'solution' was substantial. When positioned carefully and then managed appropriately, each of these innovations could provide major benefits over time. Unfortunately, however, managements' initial expectations tended to be unrealistically high. Also, they had little comprehension of the changes in both organizational arrangements and in their own behaviour required to gain the promised benefits. Moreover, they looked for tangible results in the near term. With such attitudes and expectations, it should be of little surprise that the outcomes were inevitably disappointing.

The other underlying factor that contributed to managements' disillusionment with strategic planning was a set of attitudes and assumptions that was wrongheaded. Strategic planning was initially perceived as an activity quite separate and distinct from the day-to-day management of the enterprise. Managements assumed that soundly conceived plans based on penetrating analyses mostly of quantitative data gathered about the firms' internal operations and external environment could be developed 'off-line' by staff who were experts in planning but who were not necessarily deeply grounded in the details of running the business. Managements further assumed that such soundly conceived plans would present such irresistible logic to those managers and supervisors responsible for implementation, that carrying them out would flow smoothly. With such unrealistic perceptions and expectations, it is little wonder that initially high hopes would be doomed to disappointment.

2

Why Strategies Fail

In an effort to deepen our understanding of why so many strategies have failed in implementation, my partner, Daniel Gray, designed and led in the mid 1980s, a research project.[3] Its focus was on where things most often go wrong in the process of strategy formulation and implementation. This chapter draws heavily on his work as summarized in his article, 'Uses and Misuses of Strategic Planning' (*Harvard Business Review*, Jan.–Feb. 1986).

In this research, he invited a response to an extensive questionnaire from a broad sample of business unit heads, corporate planning directors, and chief executive officers with substantial experience in strategic planning in American multi-business corporations. He also conducted 14 executive seminars to search for remedies. There were 300 respondents to the questionnaire and 216 participants in the day-and-a-half seminars. Of these, 61 per cent were general management line executives either at corporate or business unit level. The remaining 39 per cent were corporate planning directors and staff. Forty-one per cent of the seminar participants were from service businesses, 52 per cent from manufacturing businesses and 7 per cent from government agencies.

In the responses both to the questionnaire and the seminar, almost every participant (87 per cent) reported feelings of disappointment and frustration with his/her experience with strategic planning. Fifty-nine per cent attributed their discontent mainly to difficulties encountered in the implementation of plans. Two out of three trace their implementation problems to the design of their strategic planning systems and the way they manage them. Yet, despite all the frustration expressed, most companies in the sample stated their resolve to continue with strategic planning.

It is striking that most companies remain committed to strategic planning despite the disappointing returns on their investments to date. The reasons for this are rooted in the needs that led firms to adopt strategic planning in the first place (see Chapter 1). Their managements have come to realize that financial controls alone are insufficient to steer the business. Balance sheet feedback is too aggregated, too stripped of connotative information and often too late. If managers are to make more timely and appropriate mid-course corrections in response to external change, financial plans must be augmented and supplemented by strategic plans. Without these, the penalty for inability to adapt along the way is simply too great.

Another reason that companies persist in planning despite disappointment stems from a tendency by managers to separate in their thinking, strategy formulation from strategy execution. If one believes that the strategy was soundly developed in the first place, then subsequent failures in implementation can be blamed on the poor work of those lower down in the organization responsible for executing the strategy. However, when one examines in depth the relationship between strategy formulation and strategy execution, this tendency to view the two aspects of strategy as distinctly separate issues can be seen to be wrongheaded.

Most of the chief executives, corporate planning directors and business unit heads who responded to our questionnaire were later involved in one of a series of executive seminars. In discussing common problems, they appeared to have second thoughts about what was wrong with their firms' planning systems and what was needed to put things right. Two-thirds of what these managers had initially described as implementation difficulties were, on closer scrutiny, attributed to ten factors. Factors 1 through 9 relate to the way strategic plans are *formulated* − well in advance of actual implementation. Only factor 10 relates directly to implementation itself. Yet, the mishandling of each of these factors can have profound, adverse impacts on the extent to which intended strategic objectives are actually realized. In this chapter, each of these factors is discussed in turn.

1   Poor Preparation of Line Managers

In Chapter 1, I noted that since the early 1980s, an increasing number of companies have recognized that the responsibility for formulating strategy belongs to line managers, not staff planners. The latter's role is supportive and facilitative. But in many instances, line executives have been inadequately prepared to assume this responsibility.

EXAMPLE

One of the world's top 100 industrial firms consists of more than 40 strategic business units (SBUs), most of which provide a wide range of industrial products for the chemical, aerospace and automotive industries. After four years' experience with a sophisticated planning system, managers complained that it failed to 'come alive' and that formal business unit plans were lying 'unused in bottom drawers'. Just after making a major acquisition, the company convened their SBU heads to teach them the skills that strategic planning requires, and to identify how their planning system could be improved.

There was a week-long conference in luxurious surroundings. Visiting management gurus were brought in to do star turns. Landmark cases describing classic acquisition assimilation problems were discussed. There were workshops where messages from the participants to the corporate hierarchy could be hammered out. At the end of the week, the chief executive officer (CEO) flew in to talk about his vision of the future.

Total cost: more than $250,000. Result: last-minute watering-down of the messages, a 60-day fade-out of the experience, and no significant change in behaviour.

Line managers need to understand the key concepts and language of strategic planning. It is unlikely that without some help, they will *uniformly* understand the operational meaning of such notions as 'bases of competition', 'strategic issues', 'key success factors', 'portfolio role', and 'strategic management'. Typically, line managers view strategic planning as an additional burden imposed from above, diverting them from 'running the business'. All too often, many line managers adopt a grudging, mechanistic approach to their planning duties. Small wonder that staff planners creep back in to lend a hand and help fill the void.

Another aspect of preparing line managers to become more effective strategy formulators has to do with broadening their perspective. They need to think about the business as a whole rather than only their own function. They need to know how to rise above their specialized frames of reference into a general management view of trade-offs between functions. They also need to know what questions will be asked and what challenges to expect when they submit their proposed business plans for approval.

Improving line managers' understanding and skills in strategic planning through participation in 'quick-fix' management development courses often yields disappointing results. Too much management development training still consists of discussions of generic or hypothetical case materials and packages of received wisdom presented to groups of peers. Such training may provide some value, but it usually falls far short of replicating the real conditions facing the line management strategist.

When line managers can focus on real problems in their own companies, they can enhance their understanding of the strategic context and implications. An opportunity to learn how to think more broadly and how to behave in ways that are more flexible and adaptive should be offered with the explicit understanding that particular changes in personal behaviour are required. This offer should be made to groups representing the various functions and levels whose cooperation is needed to solve problems that are both tough and urgent.

EXAMPLE

A US manufacturer of electronic components effectively upgraded the planning capabilities of its line managers while it successfully addressed an urgent need to offset price declines with cost reductions. The company assembled a group of 25 managers ranging from the level of superintendent to that of divisional chief operating officer. With the help of a process facilitator and with engineering, marketing, and personnel staff on call, the training group was charged to explore the rationale, the feasibility and cost, the potential savings, and the cultural consequences of four options – asset reduction, productivity gain sharing, plant rationalization, and operator training – and then to recommend a remedial action programme. Four of the 12 lowest-ranking members of the group would be chosen for promotion and given training roles in their own or other plants. In the end, the group's plan was accepted, three men were promoted, and divisional operating costs dropped 17 per cent in the ensuing six months.

---

2 Faulty Definition of the Business

How the management of a firm conceives of and defines each of the businesses they are conducting can have a profound bearing on the business's strategic behaviour, its competitive clout and on the strategic options management may choose to implement.

EXAMPLE

One of the largest UK beer companies, Courage Breweries, viewed itself as in the beer business, distributing most of its products through more than 1300 owned pubs. When management was encouraged to consider the assets represented by these 1300 pubs and the land they occupy, along with what takes place in a typical pub (for example, entertainment, gaming machines, food and socializing), Courage's traditional definition of its business came open to question. In fact, beer is fourth or fifth in importance both in the customer's choice of pub (purchase decision), and in source of revenues. Courage Breweries shifted the definition of its business from that of a beer producer and distributor to that of a caterer to people's leisure-time needs. The UK beer industry was an aging oligopoly with excess capacity. Courage's shift from a supply-side mindset to a consumer lifestyle mindset helped break open a stalemated market share equilibrium and improve profits.

EXAMPLE

A US manufacturer of rubber and plastic control devices and assemblies saw its business flatten out under a definition of itself as a company that supplies 'these specific products to these specific industries'. While continuing to make large batches of flow valves and gaskets for automobile and appliance makers, the manufacturer began to diagnose and treat the precision-moulding process control problems of manufacturers in general. To its single-tier, high-volume, production-driven product line the company added an R&D and marketing-driven premium-price line.

EXAMPLE

Any company designing and manufacturing computers has a choice of how to define its business along a broad spectrum. This ranges from a supplier of 'tools' with a wide range of possible applications, to a provider of specific solutions to customers' business and technical problems. Definitions close to the 'tool' end of the spectrum suggest technology-driven strategies with emphasis on hardware design. Definitions closer to the 'solution' end of the spectrum suggest more customer and market driven strategies, focused more on software, and requiring an understanding of customers' specific business problems. When a particular firm's executives do not agree on how to define its business, this can have a seriously adverse effect on their ability to carry out any business strategy successfully.

These examples are meant to illustrate two issues relevant to the connection between business definition and successful strategy implementation. The first issue has to do with 'getting the definition right'. In this context, 'right' means in tune with the marketplace requirements and competitive dynamics. It means the definition which best positions the firm to compete successfully.

The other issue has to do with how similarly each manager and executive perceives and understands the business definition. Successful strategy implementation depends heavily on an agreed business definition among the entire management group. Differences in perception will undermine the effectiveness of strategy implementation.

3 Faulty Definition of the Strategic Business Unit/(SBU)

When a multi-business fails to define its SBUs correctly within its organizational structure, an excellent planning process cannot undo the damage. When strategic planning is newly installed, it is often assumed that the organizational units already in place should handle the planning. Because these units are typically a result of historical evolution, they may owe their boundaries to many factors that make them inappropriate to use as a basis for planning: geography, administrative convenience, the terms of old acquisition deals, product lines, traditional profit centres, a belief in healthy internal competition, or old ideas about centralization and decentralization.

Such rationales for unit boundaries often lead to faultily defined SBUs. Executives who take organizational structure as a given before planning begins seldom realize that their SBU definitions are defective. Organization theory and strategic management hold that the main purpose of organization (both structure and process) is to support the development and execution of strategy. Thus organization should come *after* strategic planning.

EXAMPLE

When the General Electric Company (GE) initially instituted strategic planning in the late 1960s, it did so shortly after divisionalizing its organization on the basis of product lines. This formal restructuring had a significant impact on strategy formulation and consequently on each division's as well as on the Appliance Group's market performance. At first, each division was responsible for developing and executing its own product line strategy. As a result, there was a refrigerator strategy, a dishwasher strategy, a cooking range strategy, a garbage disposer strategy, a washer strategy and a dryer strategy. Each was developed independently of the others. GE's top management believed that having each division pursue excellence independently of and in competition with the others would lead to better overall performance which was measured simply as the sum of the divisions' individual contributions. Defining each division as an SBU proved to be a serious error.

The faultiness of the reorganization logic and its consequences for strategic planning can be attributed to either ignorance or discounting of customer and competitor behaviour in the major home appliance market. Specifically, the product line organization with its associated localized strategic perspective impeded consideration of several important factors that characterize this market. These include:

- *Quality and style*: customers expect that the refrigerator, dishwasher, cooking range, etc., which they purchase be coordinated in terms of quality (materials used, performance, warranties, etc.) and appearance (colour, tones, physical design, features, etc.).
- *Price*: customers expect a pricing policy that unifies the major kitchen appliances within the context of the manufacturer's 'quality and style' philosophy.

- *Competition*: the division responsible for cooking ranges quickly discovered that its competitors and distribution channels were identical to those faced by its sister divisions which manufactured refrigerators, dishwashers, etc. Despite this extensive overlap, each division was waging its own battle with the same set of competitors.

These interrelationships suggest that GE's divisions were in fact a single SBU — a conclusion which GE realized after several unsuccessful quarters.

The following principles should guide the definition of SBUs.

- Let external rather than internal forces shape unit boundaries. If competitive forces require a larger unit than normal spans of control would dictate, go with the larger unit.
- When separate units are strategically appropriate for external reasons but must, for economies of scale, share central facilities and services, let them share, but keep them as separate units.

EXAMPLE

A Texas chemical company decided against combining the planning processes of its generic and specialized businesses. Although they share a common infrastructure, their customers and competitors are so different that the managers of these businesses could never agree on a common strategy.

- Include within the jurisdiction of the SBU all functions and processes the unit head needs for executing the strategy. For example, it may not be wise to require a manager charged with opening up new markets for a cluster of products to buy manufacturing and distribution services from sister profit centres.
- Leave the unit head free to take profits where strategy dictates. Hence nothing smaller than an SBU should be a profit centre.

While the application of these principles of SBU definition is crucial to good strategy development and execution, they can conflict with one another. As a practical matter, therefore, these principles cannot serve as absolutes. In the end, boundary setting is an executive judgement call but not a purely subjective one. The final judgement can be either adaptive, in which case the boundaries line up with the realities of the prevailing strategic game, or wilful, in which case the company accepts the risk of trying to change the way the external game is played.

Failure to address the unit definition question at all or to address it without giving due weight to the external environment can lead to failure in strategy implementation. Looking first at the environment, however, is by itself no guarantee of success. A rule often used in unit boundary setting is one product, one manager. This is meant to ensure direct accountability and single-minded strategic concentration on the fate of the product. The penalty for this approach, however, can be the loss of opportunities for discretionary profit taking, synergistic manipulation of related products, marketing cooperation, and economies of scale. The result is often the creation of too many business units too narrow to compete effectively.

4   Excessive Focus on the Numbers

When in strategic planning there is an excessive focus on financial and other numbers relevant to business performance, the resultant plan is likely to have serious distortions and be of limited value in guiding implementation. A numbers-driven plan is often the result of a short-term, bottom-line mindset on the part of top management. There is also likely to be an excessive focus on the numbers when the staff support function for planning is under the control of the corporate financial function.

When performance numbers govern strategy formulation, SBU managers responsible for carrying out the strategy tend to make arbitrary or constrained strategic choices. Such choices seldom reflect the realities of the industry, markets and competitive environment. Rather, managers select options because they appear to promise the concrete results needed to meet the performance objectives imposed from on high by executives who have only a superficial acquaintance with the business and the environment in which it is operating. When the selection of strategies is force-fitted to meet arbitrarily dictated objectives, the strategies themselves are likely to be seriously flawed, and their implementation is unlikely to yield the desired outcomes.

EXAMPLE

One of Canada's largest multi-divisional manufacturing firms has a well established strategic planning system, widely regarded as sophisticated. At the start of each year's planning cycle, Corporate issues a set of planning 'guidelines' that include explicit numerical performance objectives for growth and profitability with a 5–10 year horizon. These objectives are set uniformly for all Divisions, despite substantial differences in their businesses and competitive circumstances. After each Division submits its proposed strategic plan to meet these quantitative goals, Corporate aggregates both promised outcomes and requested funding. Often, Corporate's analysis of the Divisions' strategy submissions reveals a shortfall between the Divisions' collective promised results and Corporate's expectations. In such instances, Corporate unilaterally reduces funding limits for particular activities (for example, research and development or advertising and promotion), again uniformly for all Divisions. Despite these reductions in funding, Corporate is unwilling to entertain any changes by Divisions in their proposed strategies and projected results. Typically, Divisional management view such Corporate actions as arbitrary and out of touch with reality. The resulting credibility of Divisional strategic plans is seriously undermined, and the promised outcomes are seldom achieved.

When the numbers dominate strategic planning, there is often an imbalance between the quantitative and qualitative elements of the plan. Explanations of what lies behind the numbers and what the numbers really mean are often cursory. How the numbers are to be achieved is seldom described because managers at the SBU level (the only managerial group capable of generating the desired outcomes) are so preoccupied with end results that typically they give short shrift to considering the means by which these results will actually be achieved.

There are at least three adverse consequences of a numbers-driven planning system. First, the quality of the plans suffers because they are shaped more by top management's wilful assumptions than by the realities of the marketplace. Second, the managers responsible for implementation are demotivated with no real commitment to implementation because the plans lack credibility and no longer reflect their best thinking. Third, Corporate executives insulate themselves from opportunities to learn about the firm's various businesses because of their imposition of uniform quantitative objectives and their unwillingness to enter into a debate with SBU managers on the consequences of arbitrary cuts in funding.

To achieve high-quality plans that are both credible and can be 'bought into' by those who must implement them, qualitative issues must receive as much if not more consideration than quantitative ones. No single consideration should dominate the process of formulating strategy in the initial stages. While the external realities of the marketplace and the internal characteristics and capabilities of the organization are primary factors in shaping strategic thinking, specific objectives, strategies and actions, and resource requirements should all be viewed as variables until a 'best fit' strategy is formulated. Only after this occurs should the results in quantitative terms be projected. If these should prove insufficient to meet Corporate's expectations, there should be sufficient opportunity to select and debate alternative strategies and outcomes until a mutually acceptable approach is found.

5 Imbalance between External and Internal Considerations

In Chapter 1, I noted that strategic planning differs from earlier efforts to plan for the long term by its primary emphasis on the firm's external environment. In practice, this means developing an understanding of the firm's industry, markets, customers and competition, and using this knowledge to determine what is strategically relevant when assessing the firm's capabilities, and competitive strengths and weaknesses. Understanding and focusing on externals is crucial in making the strategic choices that will lead to the desired long-term outcomes. I call this focus on externals an outside→in perspective.

The opposite view, an inside→out perspective, occurs when management devote most of their efforts to assessing the firm's capabilities without reference to the realities of the external environment. Typically, they make assumptions about what is going on outside the firm based on fragmentary data and personal impressions. Often these are biased, distorted and/or wrong because they are coloured by personal bias and wishful thinking. An inside→out perspective encourages management to want to 'build on our strengths' and to 'focus on what we know best', and to assume that if they do this successfully, customers will line up readily.

EXAMPLE

When one of the world's largest minicomputer manufacturers attempted to establish a substantial position in the emerging desktop microcomputer market segment, its initial efforts met with costly failure. As part of the process of reformulating its strategy, the firm conducted an internal study and critique of what went wrong. This examination revealed that there were at least eight separate engineering groups engaged in designing and developing products for the desktop computer market. Each of these groups was operating on its own set of assumptions about what customers wanted and needed. No two sets of assumptions were alike. The only commonality was what drove each group's assumptions about the marketplace: personal experience and bias. Although the firm had acquired a great deal of market and competitive information and had considerable in-house marketing expertise, the engineers responsible for developing new market offerings either discounted, ignored or rejected the marketers' inputs.

For a management to have an outside→in perspective, they must first value an understanding of industry, market, and competitive dynamics. Next, they must invest in the research necessary to develop that understanding, and use the knowledge gained to inform their strategic debate and subsequent choices.

What is the appropriate balance between outside→in and inside→out considerations? The answer will vary with the particular business and maturity of its industry. In well-established businesses in mature industries, there is usually a great deal of information about customer wants and needs and about the dynamics of competition. In such cases, business strategy should be formulated with a heavily weighted outside→in perspective. On the other hand, in situations where the firm is in an emerging or rapidly growing industry, and particularly where the firm is creating the market by offering genuinely new products and services, the balance between outside→in and inside→out should be about equal or even skewed toward the latter. This is because customer's wants and needs are largely unknown, market demand is unsaturated and competitors' positions and strategies are highly volatile.

23

6 Unrealistic Self-assessment

There is another element in strategic planning that can significantly influence the quality of the strategic choices and the extent to which a strategy can be implemented successfully. This is the quality of management's analysis of their organization's capabilities to carry out various strategies. Management's assessment of the firm's strengths and weaknesses in the light of possible courses of action is an important consideration in the choice of strategic options. Further, this assessment is an important input to the definition of the work required to implement the selected options.

The quality of management's assessment of internal capabilities has two dimensions. One of these is strategic relevance. Organizational attributes are essentially neutral − they represent neither strengths nor weaknesses in absolute terms. A particular characteristic can be either a strength or a weakness depending on the strategic context. Depending on the firm's competitive position in its industry, the nature of the competitive 'games' being played, its strategic objectives and intended strategies, a particular organizational characteristic is either a strength if it is likely to contribute to the successful implementation of that strategy, or a weakness if it is likely to undermine implementation.

The other dimension to the quality of management's self-assessment is the weight and magnitude assigned to each strength and weakness. How 'good' or 'bad' a particular organizational characteristic is deemed to be is, in the final analysis, a subjective judgement. Such judgements are extremely vulnerable to personal bias, ignorance, wishful thinking and cultural beliefs. Unrealistic assessments can seriously undermine strategy implementation.

EXAMPLE

The leading competitor in the very fragmented American paint industry was a highly regarded, century-old firm, widely known for its excellent quality products. Yet, this firm's market share of less than eight per cent had been eroding slowly for several years. Repeatedly, market studies were reporting that consumers no longer were able to distinguish the market leader's high quality paint from paint offered by scores of local and regional manufacturers − at substantially lower prices. In the eyes of the consumer, paint had become a commodity. Technology in the paint industry had become well understood and widely shared with the result that almost every one of the hundreds of

---

EXAMPLE continued

paint manufacturers were offering products of at least acceptable quality. Yet the market leader refused to believe the market studies. For as long as anyone could remember, this firm produced the best quality paint in the industry. Laboratory tests verified this. The company's culture perpetuated the belief that premium quality was synonymous with the company's name, and that this fact called for a premium price. Despite the slow erosion of the firm's share of market, and despite all of the information about changes in consumer buying behaviour, management stubbornly refused to change its strategy.

The quality of management's assessment of their firm's strengths and weaknesses can be improved both by paying more attention to the strategic relevance of each attribute of the firm's capabilities, and by striving for greater objectivity. Both these actions can be facilitated when there is greater emphasis on an outside→in perspective, because it is the marketplace that defines relevance and fosters objectivity. The latter can also be strengthened when the assessment is made jointly by a group of managers representing all key functions. For example, a perceived strength by R&D may be regarded by Marketing as a weakness. The opportunity to debate such differences often yields more realistic conclusions.

7 Insufficient Action Detailing

Implementation is bound to go awry if strategy formulation goes no further than defining general thrusts and end-point goals.

EXAMPLE

A US electric utility adopted a strategy of 'energy conservation, high earnings, diversification and excellence'. These four goals were so general that the person in charge of managing each one was unwittingly at cross-purposes with the others. Field personnel cuts made to improve earnings eliminated the very people needed to run a new diversification venture aimed at saving energy through home and factory audits and retrofits. At the same time, the pursuit of engineering 'excellence' led to the purchase of materials that were too durable to mesh with the utility's plan for capacity replacement.

About seven out of ten companies in our study do not carry the formulation of strategy much beyond some general statement of thrust such as market penetration or internal efficiency and some generalized goal such as excellence. Having only generalizations to work with makes implementation very difficult. Targets don't mean much if no one maps out the pathways leading to them. After this kind of half-baked strategy is handed over for execution, subordinates who have not been in on the formulation of the strategy are left to deal with its cross-impacts and trade-offs when they bump into them. For example, if told only that the name of the strategic game in an industrial product business is high quality and prompt delivery, various people in the organization — designers, salespeople, inspectors, schedulers, fabricators and assemblers — may each reconcile these two factors differently. Subordinates' efforts are often parochial and improvisational; the way they carry out an undefined strategy is often unsatisfactory — if they elect to complete it at all.

The cure for half-baked strategy is action detailing, but this task often baffles and irritates many executives. Only one in three of the companies in our study has a process or a forum for the interfunctional debate and testing of unit strategies. Their procedures for action detailing and other kinds of reality testing are often nonexistent or merely rudimentary. Action detailing of a sort is carried on in some places as a part of operational planning, but it usually follows strategic planning and takes the strategy as given. Planning in detail should be used as a further test of a strategy's feasibility.

One way to combine operational and strategic planning is to begin an action planning advocacy process as soon as preliminary agreement on strategic options has been reached. An interfunctional task group is set up for each strategic option — with strong representation from middle management. Each group first can identify and analyze the issues that must be resolved for implementing a particular strategy. Then they can rough out the major action steps or pieces of work necessary to resolve each issue and thus implement the strategy. The group then presents its proposed action programme to the unit strategic planning team. Each task group's job is to explain and defend what it considers the best way of bringing the strategic option to life.

After the planning team has heard, debated, modified and validated each of the proposed action programmes, they deal with time frame, risk analysis, allocation of responsibility, resource requirements, organizational obstacles, performance measurement and monitoring devices. In mapping out and testing strategic options, managers begin to think explicitly about assumptions, alternatives, contingencies, and what competitive reactions to expect. Failure to come to grips with these details can undermine the execution of the strategy.

When senior executives are invited to try their hands at action detailing, they often find it an uncomfortable exercise. They tend to offer as action steps what are really no more than wishes or desired results: such as 'upgrading front-line supervision', 'introducing services that appeal to the customer', or 'eliminating wasteful practices'. Good action detailing, however, requires the participation of middle and lower management and supervision. Top management knows the direction; those below know the terrain. Not only is lower-level participation essential to working out practical steps, but it is also highly desirable. Through such participation, managers and supervisors generate the kind of understanding, ownership, commitment and motivation necessary for successful implementation. Such widespread understanding and commitment among those most critical to carrying out the strategy creates a kind of 'critical mass' within the management group and greatly enhances the likelihood of successful implementation. The alternative, which is to try to push strategic planning out into the organization and down through the ranks by exhortation and other forms of one-way 'communication', has only minimal effect.

Companies trapped in half thought-out planning may lack the information and motivation necessary to good strategy execution. These companies may avoid the front-end costs of participation, discussion, and explicit detailing, but they pay the cost of not seeing their options and not reaching their goals.

8 Insufficient Effective Participation Across Functions

Throughout this chapter, I have implied that strategic plans are of better quality and are more likely to be implemented successfully when the plan is formulated by a team of executives and managers working together in 'real time'. This team should include the SBU general manager, the functional heads who report to this executive and middle-level managers selected for their ability to contribute usefully to the debate. In addition, the planning team should include other functional executives and managers outside the SBU who are responsible for providing strategically significant resources and supporting services to the SBU.

The purpose of involving such a broad range of participants in the planning team is twofold. First, it ensures that all functions required to carry on the business are brought together to discuss alternative courses of future action and determine which one should be pursued. This ensures that the collective knowledge of the business, its external competitive environment and internal operations, are brought to bear on the strategic debate. The resulting decisions are thus likely to be of better quality (that is, more sensitive to the external and internal realities) than they might otherwise be without the benefit of certain expert inputs.

The other purpose served by using a multi-functional team to formulate strategy is that the plan is far more likely to be implemented successfully. This is because all members of management responsible for carrying out the plan will have participated in its formulation. They will therefore understand in detail the intended direction and its supporting rationale. They will also be committed to the plan's implementation because they will have developed some degree of ownership in the plan through their involvement in the formulation process. When key functions are left out of this process, implementation suffers.

EXAMPLE

A large North American life insurance company was organized into six 'lines of business' or SBUs: individual life, group life, accident and health, etc. Each business unit had its own dedicated marketing, sales, underwriting, policy issue, claims and actuarial functions reporting to a business general manager. All SBUs were supported by a group of centralized corporate functions: Systems Design and Data Processing; Human Resources; and Finance and Administration. Each SBU formulated its proposed strategic plan which was then submitted to Corporate for review and validation. The proposed plan was formulated by a team comprised of all the functional heads in the SBU and the SBU head. None of the supporting corporate functions was involved in the SBU planning process despite the fact that all SBUs depended on them. This was especially true of Systems Design and Data Processing which represented from 25 to 40 per cent of each SBU's annual budget. As a consequence, the systems and data-processing support required to execute each SBU's strategy was invariably several months late and substantially over budget, thus seriously undermining strategy implementation. By not including representatives from this key corporate group, SBU management were unable to benefit from their expert, reality-based inputs to the discussion of alternative options. Furthermore, Systems Design and Data Processing did not learn about each SBU's strategy until after it had been validated and formalized. Thus, their perception of the plan was that it lacked credibility. Their commitment to providing the needed support was minimal.

---

9 Poor Management of the Corporate Face-off

In a multi-business corporation, even when all the steps in the strategy development process are taken according to the principles of best practice, strategic plans can be ruined and the whole system undermined at the final corporate review stage. The issue here is how good is the design and management of the planning cycle when the SBUs' proposed plans hit the corporate screen. I call this crucial encounter the corporate face-off.

The face-off is a moment of inevitable, healthy conflict. Not only do all the units' resource requests often exceed what Corporate is prepared to provide, but also their aggregate performance promises are often less than the Corporate requires. Performance requirements typically come from an analysis of capital markets. On the other hand, performance promises arise from strategies for dealing with each SBU's particular environment. Thus, conflict is to be expected.

What should happen at the face-off is reconciliation. This often involves queuing, downsizing, redirection and recycling. What actually does happen is often rather primitive: exhortation, backdoor dealing, across-the-board cost cuts, moving the goalposts, and mandated promises. In other words, the SBUs' plans are force-fit in various ways into the corporate plan (remember the example of the Canadian manufacturer cited earlier in my discussion of excessive focus on the numbers).

When Corporate must deal with many, diverse SBUs, the single common denominator is the numbers. Thus, Corporate normally focuses its attention more on the numbers in each SBU's proposed business plan than on the strategies. This typically causes a similar effect within the SBUs.

EXAMPLE

One general manager responsible for an aging product described scaling down his profit projections after a rival company had increased its market share by 4 per cent in five months with a generic commodity substitute. This manager's boss, however, ordered the higher profit figures restored and asked him how he expected to win the marketing wars with 'negative thinking'.

Unfortunately, this example is typical. Numbers are often altered at the face-off so as to close the gap without any discussion of the need to revise the risk assessments, competitive reactions, probability estimates, and other problems lying beneath the numbers.

Assume that all units have done their strategic planning very well up to the time of final review. Think of the consequences for the next round of planning if they are directed to tack new financial projections arbitrarily onto strategies whose predicted effects in a particular competitive environment have already been calculated to be lower. The obligatory promise that Corporate extracts from an SBU may appear to close the gap for a while, but it will undercut and degrade the next round of planning and budgeting. The force-fit at the face-off is an invitation to play games. It sends a clear signal that scrupulous planning is considered a waste of valuable time.

Only a small minority of the companies we studied (13 per cent) say they have a satisfactory process for managing the face-off. A little over one-third report some attempt at 'rigorous trade-off analysis among business units'. Among corporate controls, strategic planning is often the 'new kid on the block'. Some executives see strategic planning as challenging financial controls and think of the face-off as the place where financial management supersedes strategic management. In these companies, financial strategy is not reconciled with other strategies but rather pre-empts them as the final arbiters of corporate resource allocation.

Multi-business strategic planning clearly calls for both centralization and decentralization. No strategic corporate portfolio management and resource allocation rationale can exist without bringing the family of SBU heads together at the centre to debate alternatives. Similarly, differentiated unit strategies cannot be executed in varying business environments without a process for local advocacy and local discretion in execution. In short, the planning process demands both integration and differentiation. These terms may be more useful and revealing than centralization and decentralization. They leave strategic planners free to decide what needs to be integrated at the centre as well as what needs to be differentiated on the periphery, and free to set up whatever organizational arrangements best facilitate strategy development, reconciliation, execution, and adaptation.

10 Conflicts with Institutionalized Controls and Systems

The foregoing nine factors describe flaws in the 'upstream' strategic planning process that can undermine 'downstream' strategy implementation.

This tenth factor is the only one directly applicable to the implementation process. A strategic planning system can't achieve its full potential until it is integrated with other control systems such as budgets, information, and rewards. The badly designed, poorly managed face-off is a manifestation of a deeper problem — compartmentalized thinking which treats various existing control systems as freestanding and strategically neutral. When this is the case, there is a high probability that conflicts will arise between the requirements and organizational impact of each SBU's intended strategies, and the requirements of institutionalized control systems. These are usually far more deeply rooted in the organization's culture than strategic thinking and planning. When conflicts occur, the existing control systems prevail and strategy implementation suffers.

While most executives who have adopted strategic planning see it as an indispensable tool, they tend to treat it at first as just another addition to an array of control devices. Before long they may discover that one control is at odds with another. Then the notion of linking these different controls arises, and that is as close as most companies in our study have come to a concept of integrated control. The three linkage problems they frequently identified have to do with plans and budgets, plans and information systems, and plans and reward systems.

Plans and budgets

The conflict between strategic plans and budgets is the most commonly perceived area of dissonance. Managers tend to view the annual planning and budgeting sequence as logically connected but not integrated in fact. A budget should be derived from the strategic plan. Yet in many firms, strategic planning is so divorced from budgeting that budget preparation precedes strategy formulation. The best strategic planning is systemic, involving the integration of all the relevant functions. It starts from an environmental analysis and then works in the unit's ability to respond. Budgeting, on the other hand, focuses on each function, and usually proceeds by making incremental adjustments to the previous year's internal departmental budgets. This practice allows the momentum of last year's (possibly obsolete) business strategy and this year's functional strategies to determine the funding of this year's business unit plan.

The absence of strategic action planning often thwarts those who want to integrate plans and budgets. Not until a company has formulated explicit action steps can it cast fixed capital, working capital, operating expense, and revenue and head-count implications in the form of

31

strategy-based budgets (see Chapter 11, pp. 143–4). Most CEOs yearn for such budgets so that they can see how their strategies, not just their departments, are doing. But the same CEOs often report that they are told such budgets are not possible without disrupting the whole accounting system.

Plans and information systems

Many strategic planners in the units and at the top of multi-business corporations express concern about the adequacy of their planning information bases and decision support systems. They worry about linking poor information bases with sophisticated computers. Even accurate, timely, and accessible information will not help the planner if it leads to an inappropriate strategy.

EXAMPLE

An American manufacturer of components for automobiles, appliances, medical equipment, and the like once developed a sophisticated data base for manpower planning that it can no longer use. The company's well-stocked management information system displays on demand how many machinists – white and black, male and female, high-school educated and not – live within 30 minutes' commuting distance of its plant in New Jersey. The trouble is, the competition has changed, so that the company cannot be globally cost-competitive unless it bases its production in Europe or Asia.

Like many businesses, this company based its strategy on data that had accumulated in response to questions raised in the past by its financial managers and its technical and professional specialists, whose expertise was too narrow. The information system drove future strategy instead of the other way around. Strategy is what makes a fact relevant or irrelevant, and a relevant fact significant or insignificant.

Corporate CEOs and their SBU heads are the ones who must raise the issues, ask the questions, and formulate the business definitions, missions, objectives, and strategies that will drive their decision-support systems. With today's information technology, it is possible to move in the right or the wrong strategic direction with great speed.

Plans and reward systems

When companies design reward systems as separate, freestanding controls, they may overlook the fact that such controls are not strategically neutral.

EXAMPLE

A strategy for competitive survival required a US manufacturer of temperature control devices to put expensive new assets in place to bring out a new version of a fading product. Its management had less than a year to realize the six-figure bonuses they would receive under a payout formula based on a three-year average return on investment. The head-on collision of a strategy that increased the asset base at the expense of reducing executive bonuses delayed the strategy's implementation for five months.

Many companies have witnessed the quiet destruction of a two- or a three-year strategy while their executives protected their first-year profit-sharing bonuses. It is folly to appeal to managers' self-interest with rewards for behaviour other than the kind the strategic business plan calls for, and it is naive to expect them to override the powerful incentives that reward systems evoke.

11 From Strategic Planning to Strategic Management

No organizational arrangement, control system, or productivity programme is strategically neutral. Strategic planning becomes the device for consistently lining up such factors.

Among companies exploring the problem of integrated control systems, the idea is taking shape that strategic planning can serve as the core control instrument of a business enterprise, with other controls adjusted and adapted to facilitate the execution of strategy. Why this emphasis on strategic planning? Because of all control devices, it is the one that is driven by the business environment. Strategic planning comes before the final results are known, determines whether profit will be taken now or later, and decides which facts are relevant. While financial controls are obviously indispensable, the feedback they give is often too aggregated, too homogenized, and too late − not to mention too conservative of past business practices.

With strategic planning, the concept of integrated controls goes further than the reconciliation of budgets, rewards, and decision-support systems. As the unifying role of strategy in running a business becomes clear, we see that getting control over the productivity of a business is not strategically neutral either. It is apparent that in embryonic and growth industries productivity should refer to such things as market-response time and market penetration, even if the price of these achievements is some internal inefficiency or postponed profit.

Seen as part of strategy, productivity is not exclusively concerned with physical input and output ratios or even with current net revenue. Productivity is keyed to the intended outcome of a business plan. Sometimes the intended outcome is profit today, in which case productivity may mean moving down the experience curve. Sometimes the goal is profit tomorrow, in which case productivity may mean pre-empting rivals and buying market share for future payback.

From this line of reasoning it is a short step to the conclusion that *strategic planning is really just an aspect of strategic management*. From this perspective strategic planning should be viewed as integral with strategy implementation. The two are not separate activities, but rather are parts of a continuum. Clearly from our earlier discussion, *upstream flaws in the planning process cause downstream implementation failures*.

Managements should no longer regard strategic planning as a separate task, distinct from strategy implementation and managing the business day-to-day. Rather, they should address strategic planning as the 'front-end' element of strategic management − the core process for managing the business. Their mindsets, their plans, their practices, and their overall controls must be coordinated and fit together harmoniously. In the most effective companies I've observed, strategic management is no longer an added managerial duty. It is a way of thinking about a business and how to run it.

3

The Anatomy of Implementation

Now that we have examined the relationship between strategic
planning and implementation and seen how flaws in the planning
process can undermine implementation (Chapter 2), let us focus more
closely on the dynamics of the implementation process itself. What is it
basically that makes the difference between implementation success and
failure?

The bases for success or failure in implementation are subtle and
numerous. These include the ten flaws in the planning process discussed
in Chapter 2, along with the extent to which the plan itself is soundly
conceived. Additional contributing factors to implementation success
stem from the fact that almost every strategic plan calls for major changes
in how organizations work. The successful achievement of these changes
requires durable and far-reaching changes both in how the organization
works *as a total system* and *how individual departments and people
behave* in that system.

Required Changes in the Existing Operating System

Consider first the demands made on an organization by a typical strategic
plan. Most strategies are aimed to improve business performance: faster
growth, more share of market, better returns, higher profits, etc.
Typically such strategies call for the organization to operate differently.
I mean the organization as a whole, each of its component departments
and the people in each department. For example, one strategy may
require new products and services that better meet customers' needs,
brought to market in half the customary time. Another strategy aimed at
improving customer satisfaction requires substantial improvements in the
quality of market offerings. A third strategy may press for more
aggressive pricing, enabled by greatly reduced costs.

Successful implementation of such strategies often requires fundamental changes in the behaviour of the existing organization or its
operating system. This includes all the functions, people, technology,
workflows, policies and procedures and institutional systems (e.g.,

planning, information (including performance measures), control, rewards, communications) and the way these interact to carry on an existing business. Each operating system has its own culture and performance capabilities (strong and weak), including an inherent ability to resist change.

One element in any operating system is exceptionally powerful in perpetuating established behavioural norms. This element is the set of performance measures institutionalized at function or departmental level. These measures provide the day-to-day indices by which each department's managers and employees both determine the objectives and priorities for allocating personal time and effort, and assess the adequacy of both individual and departmental performance.

As with any living organism the elements of any operating system interrelate in extraordinarily complex and subtle ways. It is difficult to anticipate accurately how any changes required by a business strategy will impact the operating system (e.g. changed functional roles, orientations, responsibilities and actions, changes in how functions must interact, changed priorities, new technology, etc.). Only extraordinary managerial effort informed by an understanding of what drives successful implementation will achieve the desired changes.

Action Steps

In a well conceived strategic or operating plan, the changes required of an operating system to implement a particular strategy are outlined in the form of a sequence of action steps. Each action step specifies the scope of work to be done, the nature of the 'deliverable' when the work has been completed, the resources required including the key individuals who will be working on the task, the person accountable for meeting the commitment, and the date of completion (see Chapter 10). Implementation of an action programme (and by implication, the strategy) is monitored and measured by relating actual progress against the completion of the tasks in the action programme.

But completing an action programme does not necessarily mean that the strategy has been successfully implemented. Achieving an action usually marks only the start of a change in the operating system. Fully realizing the intent of that change by making it operational over a sustained period of time is another matter. For example a plan's action steps might call for the installation of work cells in a manufacturing process, the development of new skills, or the redesign of a new-product introduction process. Once these actions have been achieved, a monitoring procedure based only on the plan itself would signal that implementation was complete. Yet, in actuality, the gains intended by such actions would not be realized until a subsequent consistent change in the way the operating system works had been achieved over time. Thus, full implementation of a strategy requires the completion of two phases: (a) initial *installation* of changes to the operating system specified by actions in the plan; and (b) making these installations *operational* over time. My notion of implementation is meant to include both the installation and operational phase.

In my experience, the key to successful strategy implementation by an organization or operating system lies in its ability to focus on a relatively few key issues and to maintain this focus for a substantial period of time − long enough to achieve the required resolutions after the completion of the installation phase.

Changes in Personal Behaviour

At the level of individual manager, supervisor and employee, successful strategy implementation often requires durable changes in personal behaviour. These changes typically require each individual to replace familiar, well-established activities with modified or new ones. Often, new skills must be learned. The impetus for such changes in behaviour are altered priorities and the need to develop and sustain focus on a few key issues and tasks.[4]

In my work with clients, I find repeatedly that even when there is a strong, widely-shared commitment to carry out a strategy, initial good intentions quickly fade. Implementation breaks down as normal day-to-day pressures and crises cause people to shift their priorities and diffuse their efforts. What begins as an attempt to carry out a particular set of actions to implement a strategy, soon degenerates into business as usual. Only some actions get installed and those that are apparently complete, never see full realization in the operational phase.

Departmental Measures

Typically, departmental measures tend to reflect the manager's view of what constitutes excellent performance. Unfortunately, this may or may not be relevant to what constitutes excellent performance in the entire system because a department is only a single component of that system.

For example, cutting costs in one department may create more costs in another department.

In most organizations, any department may have to respond to a variety of measures instituted by such functions as Finance, Materials, Quality, and Human Resources. These measures are typically developed and administered in isolation of one another. Thus, a department manager might have to deal with a quality report one day, a report on costs for Finance the next day and an output report every day. Because such measures are often applied individually in isolation of the others, there is no integration or balance among them to reflect strategic and operational priorities at departmental level. A collection of such functionally-driven measures is more likely to undermine rather than help successful strategy implementation by the operating system.

Once established, departmental measures tend to remain in force. When new measures are added, old ones are seldom dropped. Thus, at any point in time, there is unlikely to be much congruence at departmental level between the measures in force and those indices relevant to the effective implementation of the current business strategy. Only when departmental measures are reviewed and deliberately aligned with the current strategy, do they act as a positive force to keep intended implementation on course.

Key Issues

The more effectively a management addresses five key issues, the more successful it will be in achieving substantial and lasting changes in how the whole organization and its operating systems work.

1 How thoroughly does everyone affected by or involved in carrying out the strategy *understand*:
   - The needs of their customers?
   - What is to be achieved, and why?
   - How is the strategy to be accomplished, and to what timetable?
   - What resources will be applied? and
   - What specific changes in behaviour are required of each person involved?

2 How strong is the *commitment* (initial and ongoing) of relevant managers and employees to implementing the strategy successfully?
   - How credible do they find the objectives and strategy?

- To what extent do they 'own' the objectives and strategy?
- To what extent have they participated directly in analyzing options and formulating the strategy?
- How can commitment be sustained throughout the implementation period?

3   How completely have the *resources* required to implement the strategy been identified and provided (including funds, tools, skills and time)?

4   How systematic a process has been instituted for *tracking* implementation progress and for making mid-course *corrections*?

- What gains are projected and how will these be measured, monitored and communicated?
- How will actual experience be matched against forecasted results, and how will timely revisions be made in the implementation plan to reflect developing experience?

5   How consistent and credible a *climate of accountability* is maintained throughout the implementation period?

- How clearly do those who have made commitments believe they must make good on their promises?
- What are the consequences when groups and individuals succeed or fail; how congruent are rewards with success and failure?
- How visible and consistent is leadership behaviour?

If management is to address these five key issues effectively, it must begin doing so *at the very outset of the planning process* both in developing the business strategy, and immediately following in formulating more detailed operating plans. Typically, business strategizing involves senior executives from Marketing, Sales, Finance, Operations and Technology. Operational planning involves more middle managers from these same functions, with particular emphasis on Operations and support functions.

Direct Involvement by Management

I have already emphasized in Chapter 2 that the managers in an operating system who are key to strategy implementation, should participate directly in and contribute to its formulation. By being involved, they are more likely to own the strategy, understand and be committed to its successful implementation. Furthermore, their collective contribution to the analysis and choice of options will improve the quality and credibility of the plan itself. This is because each organizational function relevant to the business strategy and operating plan will be able to make inputs to the debate considering the operating system as a whole and how its function will be affected before making the final choice of option.

When management fail to address the question of implementation until after the business strategy is determined, they miss a golden opportunity both to enhance the credibility of the plan and to build the understanding and commitment so crucial to successful implementation. Moreover, when all the key organizational players participate in formulating both the business strategy and operating plan, no important consideration and input is overlooked before the course of action is decided. Also, there will be a more realistic and thorough identification of the resources required, and a better estimate made of the probable gains along with the means to track progress.

By waiting until after the plan is set to address its implementation, senior management put themselves in the position of having to *sell* the plan to other managers who must implement it. Achieving the necessary understanding, credibility and commitment at that point is much more difficult than it would have been if the key implementers were involved in the strategy decisions.

Once a management recognizes the advantages of coupling its consideration of implementation with strategy formulation, it enhances the probability that the strategy will be implemented successfully. This approach is the most powerful way to ensure that the five key ingredients to effective implementation will be set in place.

Part II

New Uses for an Old Vehicle

4

Driving Strategy Implementation with Operating Plans

In Chapter 3, I suggest that successful strategy implementation is a matter of first specifying and then installing whatever changes are required of the organization and its operating system to implement the business strategy. Then, to ensure that the organization sustains the focus and momentum needed to carry out each strategy's action plan over time, the changes installed in the operating system must be made operational on a continuing basis. The remaining chapters describe how all this can be achieved.

In my experience, the operating plan is the most appropriate vehicle both for specifying what changes need to be made in the operating system, and for directing management how these are to be installed. Operating plans differ from strategic plans in at least three important respects. The strategic plan is orientated primarily to the firm's external environment. An effective strategic plan typically lays out the moves the firm wants to make in the marketplace in order to improve its position both financially and with respect to its customers, channels, and competitors. In addition, such a plan will outline whatever internal organizational actions are needed to support the external strategy. The time horizon for a strategic plan will vary with the industry, but is often at least five years. The rationale underlying the strategic plan is found in an extensive analysis of the firm's industry, markets and competitive dynamics.

By contrast, operating plans are orientated primarily to the firm's internal environment. A useful operating plan lays out in considerable detail the work required to change how things are done within the organization in order to support the achievement of the firm's strategic business objectives. The strategic plan provides the rationale and priorities for the operating plan. Operating plans typically have two- to three-year time horizons, considerably shorter than those for strategic plans.

Determining the Number of Operating Plans

In large organizations with thousands of employees working in many different facilities, it is desirable for management to formulate at least one or more operating plans to support each SBU's strategic plan. The number of operating plans should be determined by the need to address the special characteristics of each facility or group of facilities (see the discussion of scope determination in Chapter 5, pp. 52–6). Operating plans should be formulated immediately following the development of the strategic plan. By working out in detail the internal actions required to implement the business strategy, senior management can test the practicality and viability of their earlier choice of strategic options. When the development of the operating plan(s) raises serious questions about the credibility of the strategic plan, senior management can rethink its choices and make any required modifications.

In smaller organizations with hundreds of employees working in a single facility, the operating and strategic plans can be integrated into a single plan. The same group of managers can develop first the business strategy and then the operating plan in a single integrated process. Whether or not to develop a separate operating plan(s) depends on the size and complexity of the SBU.

How the Operating Plan Addresses the Five Key Issues

In Chapter 3, I suggest that successful implementation depends on how effectively management deals with five fundamental issues associated with changing the operating system in order to carry out the business strategy. These issues have to do with:

(a) understanding;
(b) commitment;
(c) resources;
(d) measuring and monitoring; and
(e) a climate of accountability.

Management can use the operating plan as an effective mechanism to address all these issues except (e). A well conceived operating plan contains the information needed to engender understanding, specify the resources required, and lay out the process for measuring and monitoring implementation progress. Further, because a good plan will answer many questions those affected might have, it helps both to allay any fears that might encourage resistance to the intended changes and to establish credibility. Thus, the two most significant obstacles to commitment are minimized.

Driving Strategy with Operating Plans

Earlier, I suggest that the most effective way to develop both strategic and operating plans is through debate by groups of knowledgeable senior and middle managers who are key to carrying out the work required. Participants in such a process are able to develop an in-depth understanding of both the rationales underlying the option choices and the specification of the work required for their realization. Concurrently, because the choices are theirs, they develop the enthusiasm and commitment to making the strategies happen.

Of the five key success factors to effective strategy implementation, only a climate of accountability cannot be achieved through the operating plan. The climate required first to instal the changes to the operating system and then to make these operational, depends on the quality of top-level leadership and middle and lower management throughout the implementation period. I discuss this issue in greater detail in Chapters 11 and 12.

The strategic business plan, supporting operating plan(s), and institutionalized systems together comprise the three elements of strategic management for an SBU (Figure 2). Successful implementation of both business and operating strategies depends on how close an alignment and congruence management can achieve among all three elements. The business strategy should initially drive the 'fit' of the operating plan(s) and institutionalized systems. However, as the latter are developed, it may be necessary to revisit the business strategy and modify it in order to achieve a 'best fit' among all three elements.

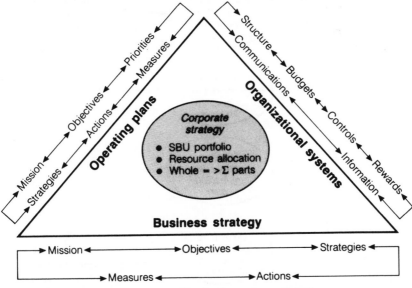

Figure 2   Strategic management.

Formulating an Operating Plan: a Model

A model for formulating operating plans is shown in Figure 3. In Chapters 5 through 11, I discuss each element of the model in detail with particular emphasis on how a planning group can effectively apply the model. The model is intended to provide an overview of the entire process, so that the relationship among each of the elements is clear. The numbers associated with each element suggest the recommended sequence for each step in the process.

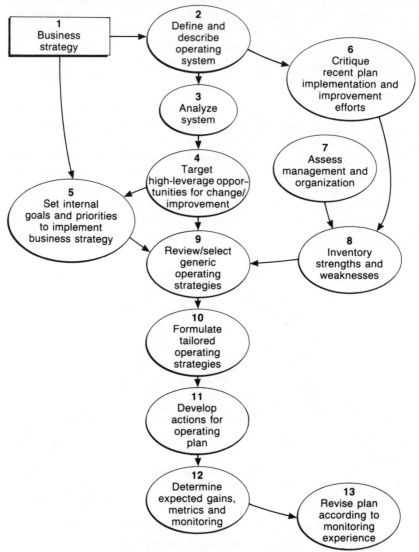

Figure 3   A model for formulating operating plans.

Our model presumes that a preliminary strategic business plan has already been formulated for an SBU. This preliminary plan cannot be made firm until after the operating plan(s) has been developed. As the planning group consider in detail what changes are required within the operating system to implement the business strategy, and how these are to be achieved, they may raise questions about the viability or practicability of the business strategy as initially conceived. In such instances, the preliminary strategic business plan may require modification.

The foundation of any operating plan is the few (no more than six) operating strategies that lay out the major action programmes on which the organization must focus over a two- to three-year implementation period. The choice of these operating strategies (steps 9 and 10 in Figure 3) determines how resources will be applied to achieve the desired outcomes for the business strategy. Thus, the choice of where to focus the operating plan is crucial.

A group of managers who are key to carrying out the plan are much more likely to agree on appropriate option choices when they make three preliminary analyses. The first of these aims at identifying a few potential high-leverage targets of opportunity, which if addressed successfully, will achieve durable changes in the operating system required to carry out the business strategy (step 4 on our model). By 'high-leverage', I mean those elements of the operating system where the application of resources will generate a disproportionately powerful impact in changing the entire system in the desired direction.

EXAMPLE

A 300-employee firm designs and manufactures electromechanical devices used on aeroplanes and missiles to actuate the various control surfaces used for in-flight guidance. For a number of years, sales were flat because costs were higher than those of key competitors and because delivery promises were met erratically. Several internal factors contributed to both these problems. Inventory levels were excessive overall, but there were spot shortages of critical components (because of capacity limitations, the firm purchased many components from a variety of small machine shops). There was a high level of regularly scheduled overtime and rework, along with high levels of employee absenteeism and turnover. In formulating their operating plan, the planning group identified the need to control material flow as a high-leverage target of opportunity. By analyzing the workings of their operating system, they concluded that if they could improve their ability to control material flow from suppliers through internal production and delivery all the factors mentioned earlier would be impacted favourably, thus reducing costs and improving delivery reliability.

To identify the potential high-leverage targets of opportunity, the planning group must first define and describe the internal operating system that supports implementation of the business strategy (steps 1 and 2). Once the boundaries of this operating system are clear (which organizational functions, workflows, processes, procedures, etc. are included), the planning group must then analyze how it actually works (step 3) in a systematic and comprehensive way. This is to identify which causal factors contribute the most to those operating problems most likely to be blocking or undermining the achievement of the desired strategic business outcomes. These causal factors are the potential high-leverage targets of opportunity.

A second analysis that improves the choice of the operating plan's strategies determines which priorities should be assigned to the fundamental strategic imperatives that drive the operating system (step 5). For example, what is the relative importance of such imperatives as lowest total costs, appropriate quality and delivery reliability? Assigning priorities requires the planning group to understand what the business strategy requires of the operating system. They must also assess where the gap is greatest between the business strategy's imperatives and the operating system's ability to respond. Once priorities are established, they can be applied to the potential high-leverage targets of opportunity to determine which potential targets should be addressed. These become the primary goals for the operating plan.

A third analysis is required to make appropriate strategy choices for the operating plan. The planning group must assess the operating system's capability to deliver what is required to implement the business strategy...in short, an inventory of strategically relevant strengths and weaknesses (step 8). To ensure that this assessment is both comprehensive and reasonably objective, two prior steps are useful. By identifying recent efforts to improve the working effectiveness of the operating system, and then analyzing the extent to which and why these efforts were either successful or disappointing (step 6), the planning group can gain useful insights about the capabilities of the operating system as a whole. Step 7 refers to a separate analysis of the operating system using a questionnaire described in Chapter 8. By considering the business plan's strategic imperatives (already identified in step 5), the planning group can test each potential strength and weakness for strategic relevance before the final inventory is defined.

Once the planning group have determined the goals for the operating plan by applying the priorities to the potential high-leverage targets of opportunity, and have agreed on the strengths and weaknesses of the operating system to address these goals, their next step is to select the strategies for making the required changes to the system (steps 9 and 10). Any operating system has a finite number of generic options available to improve its effectiveness (I have identified about 33 which I discuss in Chapter 9). By considering these options in light of goals and system capabilities, the planning group can choose those few strategies on which to focus their operating plan. These strategies describe the major programmes or thrusts for the ensuing implementation period.

Step 11 in our model requires the specification in some detail of the work required to implement each strategy. Each action programme includes a description of each task, its outputs, the resources required, the person accountable and start and completion dates. The action programme for each strategy should be sufficiently detailed to lay out the full scope of work required to implement the strategy.

Once the action programmes are specified, the next step (12) is to project the gains expected from successful implementation, and to determine how these gains will be measured. In addition, a plan and procedure for monitoring implementation progress should be developed. The formal implementation progress review meetings should include a process for revising and updating the operating plan (step 13) as experience with carrying out each strategy accumulates.

An Operating Plan is a Plan to Improve Productivity

When an operating plan is developed using our model, management will also have formulated a strategy for improving productivity. The meaning of productivity has changed fundamentally since the early 1960s. Productivity must be redefined because of the changes both in the nature of organizations and in their external environments noted in Chapter 1.

Despite these changes, traditional ways of thinking about productivity persist, especially at topmost organizational levels. In a study I conducted in the early 1980s of more than 500 top-level executives in 340 mostly large companies,[5] four out of five regarded productivity improvement as a problem, particularly in manufacturing and operations. They equated productivity gains with reduced costs and increased output from skilled and unskilled workers in these departments.

These senior executives expect gains to come from better machinery and processes, more efficient work methods, and possibly from incentives to increase personal motivation. They set goals and expect that these improvements will be achieved by unrelated, short-term efforts, yielding immediate, measurable results. Typically, they delegate oversight responsibility to middle-level plant or department managers.

Until the late 1950s, this traditional 'quick-fix' approach to productivity improvement worked, and the United States led the world in industrial as well as agricultural productivity. So long as most of the work force was in manufacturing and agriculture, with most physical assets and costs in machinery and factory operations, the traditional approach made sense.

But four decades of change have made this definition of productivity obsolete. Today when management deals separately and sequentially with each company function or department, they miss the really high-potential, interfunctional opportunities for improvement. These occur in such areas as: waste caused by unresolved conflicts in departmental priorities; duplication of effort, and rework caused by uncoordinated interdepartmental efforts; and mismatched local systems and procedures.

Managements must broaden their definition of productivity to encompass the performance of their organizations as a whole in achieving strategic *business* objectives. All efforts, whether devoted to developing, producing, marketing, or delivering a product or service, and all support systems for information, communications, planning and rewards belong under the concept of productivity.

This definition of productivity does not centre on any single function, but rather on the entire operating system of functions and supporting activities required to conduct a business. No other concept is so capable of enhancing the company's competitive edge. This definition redirects the quest for productivity gains into marketing, engineering, research and development, sales, finance, accounting, systems development and data processing, and employee relations – and into their interconnections as well. It focuses attention not only on how effectively all company functions operate, but even more importantly, on how they work *together*.

The greatest opportunities for productivity gains are where functions touch. This is where the business does or does not get integrated into a profitable, competitive whole. The old view of productivity looked to the parts and trusted the whole to come together spontaneously.

This broader, more systemic approach to productivity makes possible an integrated strategy that addresses fundamental causes of dysfunctions. True management excellence calls for sharp, difficult trade-offs where functions like marketing, product design and operations come together. Such an integrated strategy is identical with the operating plan, when this plan is developed using our model.

Productivity gets its true meaning from the strategic priorities of the SBU, not from the parochial interests of a single department. With this concept, top management can get far greater leverage by linking productivity efforts directly to the priorities of the business plan.

When productivity improvement is pursued by addressing the operating system as a whole, the effort must be led by the executive responsible for the entire business. When this senior executive creates and sustains a climate that makes productivity improvement everyone's business, there is a continuous alignment of priorities between the productivity improvement effort and the business plan.

5

Setting the Stage

B efore a planning group can convene to formulate an operating plan, three interrelated steps must be completed to set the stage. First, it is necessary to define the scope of the operating system which will be addressed by the operating plan. Once determined, the scope will suggest who might participate in the planning group. The scope will also help to identify the senior executive who is accountable for the effective implementation of the operating plan and the achievement of its intended outcomes. Once designated, this individual whom I shall call the Sponsor, must validate the definition of scope and approve the makeup of the planning group. In this Chapter, I discuss each of these stage-setting steps in turn.

Sadly, there are no clear rules or formulae for making the decisions required to define scope, designate the Sponsor and the planning group participants. Each of these decisions requires consideration of a number of different, often conflicting criteria. The resulting decisions depend on considerable judgement and, in the end, inevitably represent some compromise. I can offer only some guidelines intended to help improve the quality of these judgements. Their quality impacts significantly on the ultimate success of plan implementation.

Defining Scope

Defining the scope of an operating system may require a two-stage process. First, one defines the entire operating system relevant to a single SBU. If this scope proves to be so large and complex as to be unmanageable, then a second-stage analysis is required to unbundle the 'macro' system into more manageable subsystems.

Initially, determining the scope is a matter first of setting the boundaries of the macro system, and then establishing what must be addressed within these boundaries. Boundaries should be drawn to include all organizational functions, activities, workflows and supporting processes, systems and procedures required to carry out the strategy for a single SBU. This determination is straightforward and simple when dealing with a relatively small firm (less than 1000 employees) that is a single SBU operating out of a single facility. In such an instance, the operating system is simply the entire organization with all its functions and supporting systems.

However, when the firm is a large multi-business operating out of a number of different facilities, the problem of defining the operating system for a single SBU is often difficult, because there is seldom a direct correspondence between each SBU and the formal organizational structure. Furthermore, when the SBU is large, involving a number of different facilities, the problem of determining scope becomes even more complex. Let us consider several examples before suggesting some guidelines for scope definition.

EXAMPLE

A manufacturer of various components for the worldwide aerospace industry was organized into six quite autonomous divisions, each modest in size, and all located in widely separated towns in the northeastern USA. All but one of these divisions had been an independent company prior to acquisition. The acquiring firm maintained the autonomy of each division by encouraging it to be quite self-sufficient with regard both to human and financial resources.

Each division had the full complement of functions required to carry on its business (four small divisions were in single businesses; each of the two larger divisions was conducting a principal business and one or two different, small businesses).

A field salesforce served all divisions and reported separately to Corporate. Corporate maintained a small staff consisting of two senior executives for human resources, a senior corporate planning and development executive, a chief financial officer and his staff, and the chief executive and chief operating officers. Each Division president and his staff were expected to formulate and be accountable for divisional strategy.

Each division had a single divisional operating plan to support the divisional business strategy. The scope of the operating system was defined in each division to include the entire divisional organization plus a segment of the field sales organization. Because dependence on Corporate was minimal, confined to financial reporting and planning guidelines and human resources counsel, the scope of the operating system was not extended to include any corporate functions.

EXAMPLE continued

This way of defining scope was relatively straightforward. Yet there were some compromises. The largest division with about 1000 employees working in one large facility and three small satellite plants was actually conducting one principal business and two small different businesses. In this division there were in fact three SBUs with four facilities. Yet, management chose to define a single operating system that supported the three SBUs because it was not feasible to identify discrete functions or segments, or even individuals who worked exclusively for the smaller SBUs. Also, management chose not to define separate operating systems for the small satellite facilities because their scale and characteristics did not warrant separate treatment.

EXAMPLE

The Construction and Maintenance Department (CMD) of one of America's largest electric utilities uses an operating plan to guide the activities of its 5000 employees, each of whom are based either in one of three geographically-defined divisions or in a headquarters office. The scope of this operating plan includes all functions within CMD plus its interactions with other relevant groups within the utility. These include CMD's internal 'customers':[6] the departments and individual plants responsible for nuclear, fossil and hydro power generation, and power distribution and transmission. Also included in the scope are CMD's interactions with Design Engineering, Procurement, and such Corporate service functions as Human Resources, Finance, and Information Systems.

This functionally-centred operating plan supports the utilities' overall business strategy. Because of CMD's large size and significant differences among its three Divisions, each Division develops its own locally specific operating plan after CMD's macro operating plan has been formulated.

EXAMPLE

A US manufacturer of moderate-sized jet engines operates a single facility employing more than 10,000 people. They are engaged in three distinctly different businesses: engines for military applications; engines for commercial aircraft; and a service business providing after-sale engine maintenance and overhaul.

This company's organization structure does not reflect these three businesses. Although many of those conducting the service business are housed in their own building adjacent to the enormous main facility, spare parts are scheduled, manufactured and controlled by the same people, equipment and processes used to produce the engines for military and commercial customers. Furthermore, no distinction is made organizationally between the military and commercial business.

Although this firm pursues three distinctly different business strategies, there is no way to define distinct operating systems that support the separate businesses. For the most part, the same people, processes, equipment and workflows are involved in all three businesses. Thus, a single macro operating plan must serve three different business strategies. To enhance the implementation of this macro operating plan, each major department develops its own functionally-centred operating plan that addresses an operating system defined to include interactions with principal internal 'customers' and other relevant Corporate groups as described in the prior electric utility example.

With these examples in mind, I now want to suggest some guidelines for defining the scope of an operating system sufficiently unique to require its own operating plan.

1 Begin with a single business or SBU. Identify all functions, workflows, systems, people, processes, policies and procedures, etc. required to carry out the business strategy.

   (a) If these functions, workflows, people, etc. are dedicated to the support of a single business, and the numbers of people and operating complexity involved appear to be relatively manageable by a single operating plan, then 1 above will define the scope of the operating system.

   (b) If 1 above supports more than a single business, and it is not possible to identify those functions and people dedicated to each business, a compromise is necessary: the entire operating system must be addressed, but viewed in relation to each of the businesses it supports, considering possible differences in priorities.

(c) If the size of 1(a) is such that the system is unmanageable by a single operating plan, consider a macro operating plan coupled to several sub-operating plans formulated to address sub-operating systems centred on functions or workflows.

2 When 1 above involves multiple locations and physical facilities, consider the size and uniqueness of each location/facility.

(a) If the locations/facilities are relatively small and similar in terms of workflows, technology, process and culture, they can be addressed together as elements of the same operating system.

(b) If the locations/facilities are large and different from one another, especially with respect to culture and technology, then each of these should be addressed as the nucleus of a distinct operating system, ensuring that relevant interactions with Corporate and other functions are included.

3 When an operating system is centred on a major organizational function or location/facility, that system should include all other company functions or locations that represent internal 'customers' or significant influences on the performance of the nucleus function or location/facility.

Seldom in my experience have I encountered a perfect situation where a single facility of manageable size and complexity was conducting a single business. Typically, defining an operating system requires compromise among the criteria to be considered. When compromise is required, management should recognize where this is occurring, so that they are aware of the trade-offs.

Forming the Planning Group

Once the scope of an operating system has been defined, a planning group should be assembled to formulate the operating plan. This group can range in size from 15 to 30 members. The group should contain the collective knowledge and understanding of all significant components of the operating system and how these work together dynamically. Typically, each member of the planning group will initially be familiar with only part of the entire operating system. Yet, each person will have perceptions and assumptions (many of them biased and distorted) about the other elements of the system which are less familiar. Yet the group should collectively be able to reach a relatively common understanding of the system in its entirety and assess its operating capabilities and effectiveness.

Every major function and element of the operating system should be represented in the planning group by the most senior functional manager. The ranking member in the planning group should be the general manager with accountability for the greatest number of relevant functions in the operating system. Lower-level middle managers should be included when they represent a key area of functional, process, technological or system expertise. Finally, there should be some representation from first-line supervision.

A few first-line supervisors should be included in the planning group for two important reasons. The group of supervisors immediately responsible for directing the workforce is often key to the successful achievement of any durable changes to the way the operating system works. This lowest layer of management is especially critical to making such changes operational once they are initially installed (Chapter 3, p. 37). Yet, when first-line supervisors feel a low sense of empowerment and excluded from the management group, they frequently regard senior managers' statements of intent and calls for action with scepticism. Successful implementation of most strategies ultimately depends on the wholehearted support and active buy-in by first-line supervisors. By including a few of them in the planning group, management will find it easier to gain credibility and support with supervisors throughout the organization.

A second reason to include supervisors in the planning group is their expertise. Because they are the part of management closest to where the work is actually done, they can contribute practical, down-to-earth critique and suggestions to any discussion of the strategic options under consideration. Their detailed knowledge of how the operating system *really* works at the level where things get done is especially valuable in formulating action plans to support each strategy.

For these reasons, a planning group should include two to four first-line supervisors. They should be selected with three criteria in mind. First, they should be articulate. Second, they should be outspoken, not readily intimidated in the presence of more senior managers. Finally, they should be regarded by their peers as leaders and/or credible spokes-persons for their group. In my experience, when operating plans are developed by planning groups containing some first-line supervisors, the quality is unfailingly better than plans formulated without the benefit of inputs from this level of management.

Decisions about the size of the planning group are a trade-off among:

(a) manageability;
(b) ensuring that all important elements of the operating system are sufficiently represented; and
(c) including as many as possible of those managers who are key to implementation success.

Clearly, it is generally easier to work and gain consensus with a group of 12–18, than it is with a group of 25–33. Yet, I believe that it is better to form a large planning group that includes both the collective knowledge about the operating system and those who must improve its operating effectiveness, than to keep the group small in the interest of manageability. The process described in this book is designed to work effectively with relatively large groups. I frequently work with groups of up to 35 participants with excellent results.

Sponsorship

The third stage-setting step prior to the start of work by a planning group is the designation of a Sponsor for the operating plan and the definition of the Sponsor's role in formulating and implementing the plan. The Sponsor is the person best positioned in the organization to launch the planning group, to validate its recommended plan, and to establish and sustain the climate of accountability required for its successful implementation over time.

In most instances, the Sponsor is a senior-level *general* manager with direct authority for the greatest number of key functions in the operating system. In smaller organizations, the Sponsor is typically the chief executive officer, managing director or chief operating officer. In larger organizations, the Sponsor may be a group or divisional president or director, or an SBU general manager. When the operating system is centred on a major corporate function, the Sponsor may be the head of that function.

I want to discuss here both the behaviour required of the Sponsor, and the point of view that should influence that behaviour. The Sponsor may or may not actually participate directly as a member of the planning group. In smaller organizations where the Sponsor is likely to be a member of the planning group, the relationship is direct, informal and continuous. Thus, many of the issues that arise are resolved immediately, in 'real time'. In larger organizations, the Sponsor is often one or two steps removed from the operating system and unlikely to be a member of the planning group. In these instances, the relationship is more formal and episodic, and requires structuring.

With these distinctions in mind, the Sponsor in both small and large organizations has an important role to play in setting the stage for formulating the operating plan. First, the Sponsor must validate the definition of the operating system. The Sponsor must ensure that all key functions, processes, systems, workflows, interactions, etc. are included within the boundaries of the organizational territory to be addressed by the operating plan. The Sponsor should also determine whether a single operating plan is sufficient and manageable, or whether more than one operating plan will be required, and if so, how to subdivide the macro operating system.

Once the operating system(s) has been determined, the Sponsor should decide which functions, activities, systems, etc. must be represented in each planning group, and validate the prospective members. Such decisions depend on judgements about the relative importance of each element of the operating system in the context of likely required changes. Once individuals are selected to participate, the Sponsor should establish a supportive climate for their involvement.

Planning group members need to know what is expected of them, the broad context of the work they are about to undertake, and its importance, especially if a group process approach to plan formulation is new to the organization. Furthermore, as their involvement in the planning group is a part-time assignment in addition to their normal duties, members need to understand its priority. The Sponsor is well positioned to answer such questions, and should do so before the planning group begins its work.

A formal brief written guideline statement preceded by a short introductory briefing session are useful vehicles for the Sponsor to establish the context and define expectations for the planning group, and to legitimize the investment of time and effort by its members. Both the briefing meeting and the follow-on guideline statement should include the following:

- an overview summary of the probable changes required of the operating system to implement the business strategy;
- what is meant by the operating system, how this is being defined, and why (if so) more than a single operating system is being addressed;

- the importance both of aligning the operating plan to support the business strategy, and considering the business imperatives as primary in shaping the operating plan;
- any constraints the Sponsor believes important for the planning group to consider;
- the need for the planning group to pay equal attention both to *what* changes are required in the operating system, and *how* these changes are to be achieved;
- wherever improvements in the way the operating system works are required, the general magnitude of the improvements sought (at this point the Sponsor should refrain from laying down concrete objectives because such objectives may be either beyond reach and thus potentially demotivating, or too modest because the system is capable of achieving more);
- the importance of active participation by planning group members in debating the choice of strategy options and other aspects of the operating plan, and the need for consensus on the conclusions reached;
- should the planning group identify any issues beyond their reach that require resolution to enhance operating plan implementation, these should be presented to the Sponsor for action; and
- the desired format for the operating plan proposed by the planning group.

When the Sponsor participates in the planning group, the emerging plan is in effect validated as it is developed. When the Sponsor is outside the group, validation occurs after the proposed plan is submitted for review. After a proposed plan has been validated, the Sponsor plays a critical role throughout the implementation period. This is discussed further in Chapter 12.

To be effective both in setting the stage for formulating the operating plan and supporting its implementation, the Sponsor's point of view is crucial. It must be appropriate to the process I am advocating. The more a Sponsor believes in or at least feels relatively comfortable with the following four fundamental concepts, the more effective will be the climate established both for the work of the planning group, and later for plan implementation.

1   The key to successful implementation of any business strategy is to achieve appropriate changes in the way its operating system works. This requires a carefully conceived, comprehensive and integrated approach. An operating plan is a primary mechanism for articulating

60

and communicating such an approach. The key to success is defining the issue as a systems problem and addressing it accordingly.

2 Improving the performance of large, complex operating systems is a matter requiring investment decisions with entrepreneurial risks. One such investment is the time and effort required to formulate a sound, credible plan.

3 A sound, credible plan is more likely to be developed when the key, knowledgeable managers participate in vigorous, open debate before key choices and decisions are taken.

4 A foundation for successful implementation is best established when the managers who are key to carrying out the plan are directly involved in its formulation. This is the best way to ensure their understanding and commitment.

Once the territorial boundaries for the operating system have been defined, the Sponsor designated, and the planning group formed and briefed, they are now ready to go to work. One remaining pre-work issue requires resolution. Who will actually lead the planning group in their working sessions?

Choosing the Planning Group Leader

The process described in Chapters 6 through 11 works best when the discussion leader is *neither* the Sponsor nor ranking member of the planning group. Frequently, there are substantial initial differences of opinion among group members. Yet consensus on the key elements of the plan is a critical aim. Neither the Sponsor nor the ranking member of the group is likely to have the objectivity and group process skills required to resolve differences and achieve consensus. There is a third important requirement for the leader. This is the ability to be provocative and act as devil's advocate in the interest of ensuring that the group:

(a) deal with difficult issues;
(b) think more broadly, integratively and creatively; and
(c) sustain a perspective that is systemic and continuously references the strategic *business* imperatives as the framework for reaching conclusions.

Leaders with the requisite perspective and skills are most likely to be found outside the operating system, probably at corporate rather than at a business operating unit level. Such individuals often reside in departments such as Planning, Organizational Development or Human Resources. In my experience, a planning group's initial effort to formulate an operating plan is most effectively led by an outside consultant who can simultaneously train an internal person who will then lead subsequent iterations.

Part III

Three Cornerstone Analyses

6

Targeting High-leverage
Improvement Opportunities

When the planning group meet for their initial working session, where should they begin to work in the process? Probably, it will be the first time that the participants will have been together in the same room. Each member will be knowledgeable about a relatively small part of the operating system and unfamiliar with most of the other elements. Yet, lack of understanding seldom prevents a person from having opinions about what is going on outside his/her immediate area of experience and why certain things are working either well or poorly. So long as members of the planning group continue to hold mistaken assumptions and misperceptions, they will have difficulty in reaching agreement on objectives and courses of action.

A fundamental prerequisite for gaining consensus in any group is to establish a uniform understanding of what constitutes present reality. A common, shared data base that describes the characteristics of the operating system helps to reduce dramatically different assumptions and perceptions held by group members. This compelling need points to step 2 in our model for formulating operating plans (Figure 3, page 46) as the most appropriate starting point for the work of the planning group. This step, a comprehensive description of the operating system, begins the process of systems analysis aimed at identifying the high-leverage opportunities for improving the performance of the operating system.

In Chapter 5, I suggested some guidelines for determining the organizational boundaries for the operating system 'territory'. This territory must now be mapped in some detail so that the planning group can form a common understanding of the system's components, how these interrelate and interact dynamically, and how the system as a whole performs.

A comprehensive understanding of any operating system requires knowledge not only of each element shown in Figure 4, but of how these elements interact dynamically. The system's performance depends on each element's characteristics and how they combine to form a working system. In Figure 4, note that three elements in the northwest quadrant (General social/economic climate, Government regulation, Customer

Three Cornerstone Analyses

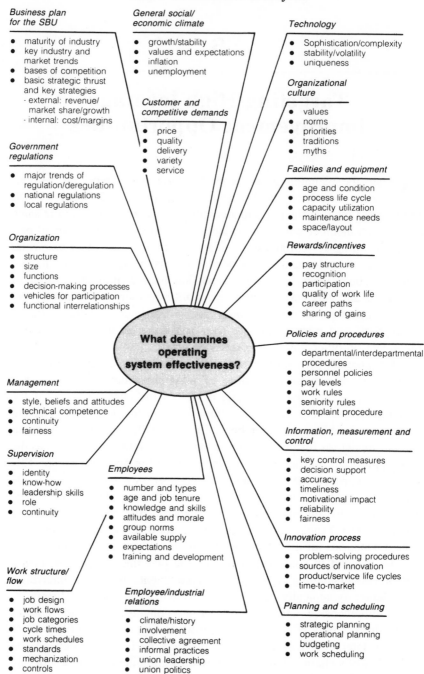

Business plan for the SBU

- maturity of industry
- key industry and market trends
- bases of competition
- basic strategic thrust and key strategies
  - external: revenue/ market share/growth
  - internal: cost/margins

Government regulations

- major trends of regulation/deregulation
- national regulations
- local regulations

Organization

- structure
- size
- functions
- decision-making processes
- vehicles for participation
- functional interrelationships

Management

- style, beliefs and attitudes
- technical competence
- continuity
- fairness

Supervision

- identity
- know-how
- leadership skills
- role
- continuity

Work structure/ flow

- job design
- work flows
- job categories
- cycle times
- work schedules
- standards
- mechanization
- controls

General social/ economic climate

- growth/stability
- values and expectations
- inflation
- unemployment

Customer and competitive demands

- price
- quality
- delivery
- variety
- service

Employees

- number and types
- age and job tenure
- knowledge and skills
- attitudes and morale
- group norms
- available supply
- expectations
- training and development

Employee/industrial relations

- climate/history
- involvement
- collective agreement
- informal practices
- union leadership
- union politics

What determines operating system effectiveness?

Technology

- Sophistication/complexity
- stability/volatility
- uniqueness

Organizational culture

- values
- norms
- priorities
- traditions
- myths

Facilities and equipment

- age and condition
- process life cycle
- capacity utilization
- maintenance needs
- space/layout

Rewards/incentives

- pay structure
- recognition
- participation
- quality of work life
- career paths
- sharing of gains

Policies and procedures

- departmental/interdepartmental procedures
- personnel policies
- pay levels
- work rules
- seniority rules
- complaint procedure

Information, measurement and control

- key control measures
- decision support
- accuracy
- timeliness
- motivational impact
- reliability
- fairness

Innovation process

- problem-solving procedures
- sources of innovation
- product/service life cycles
- time-to-market

Planning and scheduling

- strategic planning
- operational planning
- budgeting
- work scheduling

Figure 4   Elements of operating system effectiveness.

66

and competitive demands) are external to the operating system and essentially givens. Although these elements cannot be changed by management, they must be understood as part of the framework within which the operating plan is formulated. The SBU's business plan is also part of this external framework, but management may modify it as a result of what they learn while developing the operating plan. Technology is both external and internal to the operating system. All the other elements shown in Figure 4 are internal to the operating system, and can be changed by management's actions.

Developing a 'Straw-person' Characterization of an Operating System

In order to develop a comprehensive description of an operating system, answers are required to the following questions. Each of these relates to a discrete dimension of the system, both internal to it and relevant to its external context.

What is the scope of the SBU's business and operating system?

- What business is the SBU conducting?
- What functions, workflows, systems and other resources are supporting this business?
- What is the organizational position of the SBU and its operating system within the company as a whole?
- What key services support the operating system from elsewhere in the company, and what demands are made on the operating system by other SBUs and Corporate departments?

What is the business context for the SBU?

- What's happening to the industry (broad overview)?
  - Growth rate
  - Structure
  - Technology   } Major industry trends
  - Prices
  - Capacity
  - Financial operating characteristics

- What are the competitive dynamics in the SBU's marketplace?
  - Major competitive games being played
  - Major drivers for competition
  - Principal bases for competition
- What is the SBU's current competitive position and recent trends?
- What is the SBU's recent and current strategy?
- What results were achieved by the SBU's recent and current strategy?
- What strategic imperatives are required of the operating system by the SBU's strategy?

What is the role/mission/charter of the operating system?

What organization structure is in place?

- Basic type (e.g. functional, divisional, matrix, etc.)
- Geography
- Number of levels
- Other significant characteristics

What management characteristics predominate?

- Age and tenure of management (senior level; middle level)
- Management style/behaviour (differentiate by level, if appropriate)
  - Overall style
  - Perceived priorities
  - Ratio of managers/managed
  - Allocation of time (by broad categories)

What cross-functional collaboration exists?

- Extent
- Mechanisms
- Characteristics

What are the characteristics of first-line supervision?

- Ratio of supervisors/supervised
- Allocation of time (by broad characteristics)
- Background profile
- Style/behaviour

What are the characteristics of the workforce?

- Age/seniority distribution
- Employees by job category and function
- Change in the workforce (trends)
- Levels of skill/competence

What is the nature of training and development?

- Training and development activities/needs ⎫ Management and
- Upward movement (career paths) ⎭ workforce

What are the characteristics of the work climate?

- Motivators/demotivators
- Morale level/trends

What is the nature of planning/scheduling?

- Long-range/strategic planning
- Shorter-term tactical planning and scheduling

What are the characteristics of management information within the operating system and between it and other corporate departments?

- Quality/relevance/timeliness/effectiveness for decision support
- Supporting systems
- Automation

What performance measures are in use?

- Nature of measures/indicators in use; what is being measured
- Behaviour encouraged
- Relevance to strategy implementation

What is the nature of communications within the operating system and between it and other corporate departments?

- Mechanisms used
- Characteristics (e.g. top→down, bottom→up, lateral)
- Effectiveness

What rewards and compensation are used?

- Characteristics of compensation system structure
- Comparative levels of compensation – internal and external to company
- Relationship to performance
- Non-monetary rewards/recognition

What is the operating system's relationship with other corporate departments?

- Objectives
- Services provided to and by the operating system: focus
- Effectiveness
- 'Customer' satisfaction

How would one characterize the performance of the operating system?

- Overall assessment
- How measured (service quality, productivity, etc.)
- Recent trends (external and internal indices)

What are the characteristics of the operating system's culture?

- Beliefs that influence decision choices
- Norms that influence behaviour

How do such questions get answered? How can a planning group with as many as 30 members work with this information to form a consensus on the high-leverage target opportunities for improving the operating system's effectiveness?

The Importance of Research in Understanding the Operating System

The information required for the planning group to have a comprehensive description of the operating system, a prerequisite for their analysis of that system, can be developed through research. Four methods for conducting this research should be used together:

(a) individual interviews;
(b) small group interviews;
(c) review of documentation; and
(d) observation of physical facilities and arrangements, and meetings.

Individual interviews

Individual interviews of about one to one and a half hours each are appropriate with senior and middle-level managers, ensuring that every function and significant sub-function has been covered. These interviews should first elicit the manager's description of how the operating system actually works, particularly that segment most familiar to her or him. The manager should be questioned both about what goes on within the function, and how that function interacts with other relevant functions. It is particularly important to develop an understanding of how the work flows through the organization. The areas of inquiry are suggested by the questions noted earlier in this chapter. Later in the interview, the manager can be invited to comment on which aspects of the operating system work well, which do not, and why. In these interviews, each manager should be encouraged to critique how effectively the operating system has responded to any changed requirements stemming from the business strategy or any other factor in the external environment. Each interview should close with the manager's views on what needs changing (in priority order) in the operating system.

The view of any operating system developed from interviews with its senior and middle-level managers will inevitably be coloured by wishful thinking and whatever frustration these managers may be experiencing. In larger organizations, these upper-level managers may be two to four levels removed from the level where most of the work in the system gets done. Consequently, many of their perceptions may be based more on assumption than fact.

Small group interviews

To develop a more accurate characterization of how the operating system is actually functioning, it is essential to understand what takes place day-to-day at the working level. This information can be gained by conducting a series of interviews with small groups (each with six to nine members)

71

representative of key occupations. Thus, one small group might contain first-line supervisors, another clerks, another salespeople, another factory workers, and another engineers or technicians.

Each small group interview takes about one to one and a quarter hours. This interview can be introduced by a brief explanation of the purpose of the research and an assurance that as the interviewer is interested in group, not individual views, no names will be taken. I have found that an effective way to begin is with a very general question such as, 'What is it like to work here? I am interested in your comments about what you find satisfying, and what you find frustrating.' Typically, someone will respond and others will soon join in, either in support of or in disagreement with the comment. The interviewer should continuously check with the group to determine whether an individual comment is widely supported and thus truly representative, or whether it represents an individual viewpoint.

Group interviews should be conducted after the individual interviews with upper-level managers so that the interviewer already has formulated some notions about how the operating system is *supposed* to work. Thus, the interviewer can test any questionable points with the small groups. Also, the interviewer will be better positioned to interpret the very concrete remarks that are typical in these small group meetings.

Reviewing documentation

A third method for generating information about the operating system is reviewing relevant documentation. In the course of the individual interviews with senior and middle managers, an effort should be made to gather a range of written documents: strategies and plans, project and implementation status reports, tables of organization and staffing, reports about operating system and functional performance, and significant memoranda. When such documents are studied in the light of what has already been learned from the individual and small group interviews, additional insights can be gained about the behaviour and effectiveness of the operating system.

Observing facilities, arrangements and meetings

A fourth research technique that I have found useful is observation of the physical facilities, arrangements and if possible, typical management meetings. A tour of each facility can reveal characteristics of the work environment such as layout, amenities, and the value assigned by management to physical surroundings. I try whenever possible to conduct the individual interviews with managers in their own offices. This not only enhances opportunities for direct observation, but also facilitates the identification and collection of relevant documents. When I have been able to observe management meetings, I have gained a more accurate understanding of management styles, interaction norms, and approaches and skills in resolving conflicts, developing consensus and making decisions.

Developing a Straw-person Characterization

From the data gathered through all four of these research methods, a 'straw-person' characterization of the operating system is developed for presentation to and validation by the planning group. It is important not to present the characterization of the operating system to the planning group as definitive. Rather, it should be positioned as tentative (hence, the term 'straw-person'), with an invitation to the members of the planning group to review, discuss, modify (if necessary) and validate. This approach enables the planning group to enhance the accuracy of the characterization. While they do this, they also internalize the information.

In many years of taking this approach, I have found that the most effective way of presenting the straw-person characterization is to format the data about the operating system in a number of individual, free-standing statements. Each of these should be descriptive of an aspect of the operating system, related to one of its dimensions (see Appendix 1 for an example of a straw-person characterization). Each statement is self-contained, focused on a single aspect of the operating system, and free of any cause–effect implications. Each statement is presented as clearly and succinctly as possible so as to minimize any misunderstanding by the reader. Statements may be presented as 'facts' or perceptions (i.e. 'Many middle managers believe that . . .').

Collectively, the statements describe the operating system comprehensively: its context, parts, totality, dynamics, interrelationships and performance. In most situations I have found that an operating system can be characterized reasonably well with from 90 to 140 such statements. Formatting the data about an operating system in this manner is like constructing a complex picture puzzle comprised of more than a hundred irregularly shaped pieces. Each piece has an integrity of its own, but when fitted together with all the other pieces, a number of pictures can be discerned. These pictures are analogous to potential high-leverage target opportunities.

Validating the Operating System Characterization and Identifying High-leverage Target Opportunities

With such a formatted straw-person characterization of an operating system, a process is required by the planning group to validate and agree on a system description, and to achieve consensus on a list of potential high-leverage target opportunities. Two alternative but equally effective approaches can be taken. One approach is to present the straw-person characterization on a series of flip charts. For each statement, the planning group is invited to respond. If the statement is presented as a 'fact', anyone in the group can challenge its accuracy. When this occurs, if the objection cannot be addressed to the challenger's satisfaction within a few minutes by modifying the wording, the statement is erased. Statements presented as perceptions may be discussed but not changed or rejected. Whether or not a perception is accurate, it exists and must therefore be dealt with. As the planning group discusses and validates each statement, anyone in the group can nominate a potential high-leverage target opportunity. If there is consensus in the group to support the nomination, it is recorded on a separate flip chart.

This process typically requires from about 8 to 11 hours of work by a planning group with about 20 to 30 members. At the conclusion of this process, the planning group will have achieved two critical goals. First, they will have reached a common understanding of the operating system's salient characteristics. Individual differences in perspective, misperceptions, lack of knowledge and bias are inevitable among planning group members at the outset of their work together. By the conclusion of this process, these differences will be substantially lessened. Members of the planning group will be able to discuss issues and options for addressing these from a shared data base. The planning group will also have achieved a list of from twenty to forty potential high-leverage target opportunities that might be addressed by the operating plan. These can then be prioritized by inviting each member of the planning group to mark his/her first, second and third priority choices on the flip chart (see Appendix 2, for example).

An alternative approach to accomplishing these same two goals also requires from 8 to 10 hours. In this approach, the statements characterizing the operating system are recorded on index cards, one statement to a card, arranged in random order. Each member of the planning group is given a deck of from 90 to 140 cards. First, the group considers each card in turn, applying the same rules described above for 'fact' and perception cards. In the first pass, the group proceeds through the entire deck setting aside (but not discussing) those 'fact' cards that are challenged. Also individuals are asked to mark each card that strikes them as particularly significant, for whatever reason. In my experience, seldom more than 20 to 25 per cent of the cards are challenged. The group then reconsiders and discusses the challenged 'fact' cards. If a satisfactory rewording cannot be achieved within a few minutes' discussion, the card is discarded.

Once the planning group has agreed on a validated deck of cards, the full group breaks for about two hours into several smaller groups (each with from five to eight members, constituted to contain a heterogeneous mix of functions and avoiding direct reports being in the same group as their managers). Each small group is directed to work with the cards, paying particular attention to those considered by the group to be particularly significant. Each group's objective is to develop four to five 'posters' centred on a single or a cluster of related 'significant' cards. Each poster should display the relevant cards (with interconnecting arrows drawn on the poster to show the interrelationships), and feature a headline or caption that sends a message that each group wants the planning group as a whole to receive. The completed posters are 'hung' on walls of the planning group's meeting room.

Every member of the planning group is invited to study all posters produced by the small groups. Each planning group member is then given two to three blank index cards and asked to write (one to a card) the two or three most important high-leverage target opportunities to be addressed by the operating plan. Each person is then asked to prioritize his/her choices.

In the final step of this process, each planning group member is asked to read out in turn, his/her nomination for the top-priority high-leverage target opportunity. These are recorded on a flip chart. After the top-priority choices are registered, a round of second- (and then third-) priority choices are read out and recorded. As successive nominations resemble those already recorded, marks are made on the flip chart to indicate frequency of choice. This process will typically yield from five to ten high-leverage target opportunities, prioritized by frequency of nomination.

Thus, in an evening and following day's work, a planning group with as many as 30 members can achieve a common understanding of the important characteristics and dynamics of an operating system. Further, they can reach consensus on the five to ten most critical high-leverage target opportunities for improving the way this operating system works so that the intended business strategies can be more successfully implemented.

7

Setting the Right Priorities
and Objectives

The purposes of an operating plan are both: (a) to describe what changes are required of the operating system to enhance its support of the SBU's business strategy; and (b) to outline how these changes are to be achieved (Chapter 4). For an operating plan to achieve these purposes, it must be closely aligned with the business strategy. This means that the strategic imperatives or demands required of the operating system by the business strategy need clear articulation. Further, these strategic imperatives must drive the focus and objectives of the operating plan. A useful and easy to apply vehicle for achieving a tight linkage and alignment between business strategy and operating plan can be derived from the concept of operating system priorities.

Consider the consequences in three situations where operating system priorities were misaligned with the requirements of the business strategy.

EXAMPLE

A division of a leading US manufacturer of electrical products makes and sells kitchen disposers. Because its none-too-strong market position was eroding, the division's objectives were to regain and increase its share of a very competitive market. The disposer business was identified as essentially commodity-like, with price the principal basis for competition. The company's business strategy called for more aggressive product pricing based on lowering total costs.

Within the division, however, substantial investments were being made in programmes that ran counter to that strategy. Considerable effort was directed to improve quality and add new features. Because the effect on costs was directly opposite to what was required by the business plan, erosion of market share continued.

How can such a mismatch occur? In this instance, operations and engineering management both had copies of the business plan. Yet their involvement in its development was minimal. They were focusing on what they believed to be important, without reference to the business strategy's imperatives.

EXAMPLE

A leading Canadian manufacturer of large transformers for electric utilities was marketing two distinctly different product lines. In effect, these constituted two different businesses, with different strategies. In the very large, expensive units, this firm held a dominant market position. Customers valued the high quality and reliability of the products, most of which were designed to meet each electric utility's unique requirements. The company's strategy for this business was designed to maintain its high market share and profit margins.

In its medium-sized, more moderately priced product line, the company's competitive position was considerably less strong. In a vigorously competitive market with many vendors, price was the paramount consideration. The company's business strategy was to improve its market share through more competitive pricing. But because the company's operating costs were excessive, its share of the market was deteriorating.

This company's operating plan emphasized improving product quality and reliability, and increasing the mechanization of production operations to reduce manufacturing costs. However, management failed to differentiate their operating system improvement efforts for the two businesses. The priorities governing improvement were geared primarily to the demands of the very large unit business.

Major opportunities for reducing product and operating costs for the medium-sized transformers were being missed. By applying the large-unit design criteria to all transformers, the medium-sized units were over-designed for the market. In effect a Rolls-Royce product was being offered to a market that was satisfied with Fiats. Many opportunities for cost savings in both materials and labour were being overlooked. Many of these could have been realized by better relating engineering design to manufacturability. Such issues were relatively unimportant for the low-unit-volume large transformers, but extremely relevant to the high-volume middle-sized transformers.

Management's differentiated business strategies were not reflected in their operating plan. This fitted only the business strategy for large transformers.

EXAMPLE

The leading North American paint manufacturer cited in Chapter 2, p. 24, was gradually losing market share in what had become a commodity business. Management stubbornly continued to pursue a business strategy based on the premise that because their paint's quality was superior, customers would be willing to pay a premium price. As its market share steadily eroded, most of this company's many manufacturing plants were operating at less than 75 per cent of capacity. A strategy appropriate to the dynamics of the industry and the company's position and objectives would have called for an aggressive pricing policy to recapture and increase market share.

This firm's operating plan called for substantial investment in its plants to improve productivity. These efforts focused mainly on cost reduction, and took the form of further mechanization, methods improvement, and experiments with employee involvement. Yet, a modest increase in capacity utilization would have had far greater positive impact on plant productivity than any of the incremental improvements sought by the operating plan. Management's investment in these productivity improvement efforts was misapplied.

When management finally acknowledged the commodity-like nature of the paint business, they changed their business strategy, and dropped prices substantially. Because the company's products had an excellent reputation, the new strategy resulted in a rapid increase in unit sales which increased capacity utilization in the plants. The result was immediate improvement in productivity which reduced the cost of paint. This more than offset the reductions in margins caused by the drop in selling prices. Further investment in other efforts to improve plant productivity was curtailed. In a relatively short time, both revenues and profits increased.

All three examples demonstrate the need to align operating plans closely with business strategy. When these are mismatched, any gains from investments to improve operating system performance may prove modest and disappointing. Worse, a misalignment may cause the operating plan actually to undermine the business strategy.

Some Key Issues in Achieving Alignment

Several important issues must be addressed to ensure a correct alignment of operating plans with business strategies.

- *The operating system priorities required by a business strategy are not necessarily understood at the operating unit level.* Often, business strategy is determined by senior executives in marketing and finance (with help from strategic planners). Typically, operations and technical managers are involved peripherally if at all. Yet when most company assets and a substantial portion of the payroll are in operations and in technical functions, these often develop their own sense of priorities and momentum, which are often at odds with the business strategy.

- *Cost reduction is not necessarily the only or even the primary objective of an operating plan.* Cost reduction should have top priority only when the business strategy requires a reduction in operating costs or the cost of goods and services sold. However, when the business strategy requires product or service improvement, or increased flexibility so that the organization can respond more readily to changes in market conditions, operating plans should focus more on meeting these demands than on cost reduction. An operating plan aimed at improving quality or organizational responsiveness will be substantially different from one aimed at reducing costs.[7]

- *When a single operating plan serves two or more businesses, each with its own strategy, differentiated priorities must reflect any different strategic imperatives.* Each business strategy must be supported by an appropriate operating plan that addresses its special requirements. The Canadian transformer manufacturer's business strategy for its medium-sized units required programmes aimed at reducing costs. Its large, expensive unit business strategy required an operating plan focused on maintaining both product quality and responsiveness to customer-required design changes. Business strategies are seldom valid for long, often less than two or three years. They must be revised to meet changes in competitive and economic conditions. When business strategy changes, so too must the operating plan.

- *When operating priorities are implicit rather than explicit, they are seldom understood uniformly among key executives and the entire management and supervisory group.* Often, in the press of day-to-day operations, little explicit attention is given to overall priorities and objectives. Priorities are frequently determined by individual managers, applying their own best judgement. Disagreement about priorities is natural. Yet, a *uniform* understanding of operating and improvement priorities by all executives, managers and supervisors is critical for the successful implementation of any operating plan.[8]

How to Ensure Alignment

It is crucial that the management group responsible for implementing an operating plan share a common understanding of the business strategy they are supporting, its strategic imperatives for the operating system, and the implied priorities. First, these managers must recognize the *need* to achieve this uniform understanding. Once this occurs, I have found that when they employ a process of systematic analysis and discussion few management groups have difficulty in reaching consensus on operating system priorities. Their consensus can then be made explicit, communicated broadly throughout the operating system, and incorporated into day-to-day decision making.

I have used a four-step process for developing consensus about operating system priorities. First, operating system managers need to make explicit whatever perceptions they have about the priorities that are actually driving current decisions. Second, the planning group reviews the current business strategy to identify the strategic imperatives for the operating system. Third, in light of these strategic imperatives and the capabilities of the operating system to perform against these imperatives, the planning group discusses and reaches consensus on what the operating system priorities should be, in order to support the business strategy. Fourth, the planning group compare their consensus with the perceptions of current actual priorities. The nature and extent of any difference will determine the actions required to reorient and redirect all managers and supervisors in the operating system.

The Operating System Priorities Worksheet (Figure 5) is an instrument that my colleagues and I have developed and use to support the process for redefining priorities. This instrument is based on a single premise. Any operating system, whether it supports a business based primarily on goods, services, or some combination, must be responsive to only two or three out of seven possible strategic imperatives called for by any business strategy:

1 Low total cost
2 Consistently providing appropriate quality as defined by customer requirements

3 Meeting delivery commitments reliably
4 Responding nimbly to very short-term unexpected, relatively minor changes in demand volume
5 Utilizing fixed assets effectively
6 Flexibility in changing capacity to meet major changes in demand volume
7 Flexibility in meeting market requirements for new products and services in the shortest possible time.

Typically a particular business strategy will demand an emphasis on two or three of these strategic imperatives for the time period required for its implementation. Often, one of these imperatives is paramount. When the business strategy changes, the imperatives will also shift.

However, the priorities for the operating system are derived only in part from these strategic imperatives. The other consideration is any gap that may currently exist between the system's actual capability to respond to each strategic imperative, and the level of system performance required to execute the business strategy successfully. When the gap is substantial, a second or third ranking business strategy imperative may become the top priority for the operating system. This occurs when the relative need to improve operating system performance is far greater for a second- or third-order business strategy imperative than it is for the top-ranking one.

EXAMPLE

A moderately sized British company producing electro-mechanical components for the worldwide aerospace industry was pursuing a business strategy aimed at increasing its share of an expanding market. This company was one of many employing a well-established technology in a highly competitive international industry where the primary basis for competition was price. The top-priority strategic imperative for the operating system was low total cost. Yet, an analysis of how the system was actually functioning revealed that serious performance gaps existed in its ability to meet the business strategy's second- and third-ranking imperatives: the need to meet delivery commitments and quality requirements. Both of these capabilities were out of control. Low yields caused extensive rework. This in turn caused added costs and exacerbated an already serious materials flow problem, forcing the company both to maintain a large work-in-process inventory and to require many employees to work 60-hour workweeks regularly. Delivery reliability was poor. Thus, although total cost was the highest priority demanded by business strategy, the top priorities for the operating plan were quality and delivery reliability. Gains in these two areas would reduce total costs.

Priority description	Business I		Business II	
	Is now	Should be	Is now	Should be
• Produce and deliver products and services at the lowest possible total cost (fixed plus variable)				
• Produce and deliver products and services at consistent levels of quality and reliability that are recognized as excellent by customers				
• Meet promised customer delivery commitments consistently over long periods of time				
• Meet unexpected changes in customer requirements that call for nimble responsiveness in the form of short delivery cycles (e.g., day-to-day)				
• Contribute to higher return on investment by optimizing utilization of fixed assets (facilities and equipment) and capital				
• Respond flexibly to required significant capacity changes in response to changes in demand volume (up or down)				
• Respond flexibly and rapidly to required changes in products and services mix and design				

Instructions:

For each separate business:

1 Reflect current existing priorities by, distributing 100 points among the seven possible operating system priorities in the 'Is now' column. There need not be a number in every box.

2 Indicate what you believe the operating system priorities should be by distributing 100 points among the seven possible priorities in the 'Should be' column. It is not necessary to have a number in every box (if you believe the priority is not relevant).

Key: Business I: _____ Business II: _____

Figure 5   Operating system priorities worksheet.

Setting the Right Priorities and Objectives

Prior to the initial meeting of the planning group, each manager within the operating system is asked to complete anonymously an Operating System Priorities Worksheet (Figure 5). Worksheets from groups of managers can be coded if there is any value in identifying differences (either by organizational level, or by function). For each separate business supported by the operating system, each manager's perception of current priorities (as reflected in actual operating behaviour) is recorded by distributing 100 points down the 'Is' column. Similarly, to identify any desired changes in priorities, the manager distributes 100 points down the 'Should be' column.

Individual responses are summarized and analyzed for convergence or divergence of views, both for each coded group and for the entire operating system. These results are fed back in the initial planning group meeting as part of the discussion on the business strategy's strategic imperatives and the consequent priorities for the operating system. If the planning group's consensus proves substantially different from the priorities currently perceived, they develop an action plan aimed at ensuring that managers and supervisors in the operating system understand uniformly what the priorities should be.

Typically when many managers first register their views on current and 'should be' priorities, there is little agreement. The range of difference in their responses tends to be far more striking than any convergence. Yet, when they apply the above process to reach consensus on what the operating plan priorities should be, I find that they often achieve agreement within an hour's discussion. How can this be when initial views are usually so divergent?

Individual perceptions are seldom based on any consideration of the requirements of the business strategy, even when this strategy is well understood (an all too rare circumstance, I regret to report). Rather, these perceptions usually reflect the functional bias of the manager. Thus, marketing managers tend to focus on priorities for quality or for product/service flexibility, while operations managers tend to focus on priorities for low costs or delivery reliability. Technical managers tend to seize on the new-product priority, while financial managers are drawn to the asset-utilization priority.

When these managers focus on understanding the business strategy and its strategic imperatives, they develop an external, common reference point, outside their functional domains. It is then difficult for them to resist the logic of translating business strategy imperatives into operating system demands, and then assessing the gap between each demand and the current level of operating system performance. By going through this process together and discussing each step thoroughly, convergence of view develops and consensus forms.

Some Guidelines for Setting Appropriate Priorities

A few generic concepts can be useful to test how appropriate the proposed operating system priorities are to current business strategies. The Sponsor (Chapter 5) can use these concepts both to review and validate an operating plan, and to allocate resources among several operating plans in order to fund those strategies with the highest potential for leverage in changing the operating system.

There is a widely accepted notion that an entire industry, like the market offerings within it, progresses through a life cycle (measured in terms of total revenues generated). Such cycles can range from less than a decade to more than a century depending on the industry. One can divide each lifecycle into four phases: embryonic, growth, mature and aging. In general, most businesses in mature and aging industries pursue strategies intended to maintain market position and maximize profit and cash generation. Their operating plans focus internally on improving operations both to lower total costs, and improve utilization of material, energy, capital and people.[9]

On the other hand, businesses in embryonic or growth industries will typically pursue strategies aimed at increasing market share by exploiting combinations of new products and services for existing and new markets or through market penetration. Their operating plans focus externally to improve quality, delivery reliability, and operating-system flexibility so as to allow changes either in capacity, or in products and services. Optimizing asset utilization is a focus typical for businesses whose industries are in the late growth or early mature phases of their lifecycle.

The appropriate focus of an operating plan corresponding to different business strategies can be illustrated by a series of generic relationships (Table 2). Such relationships can be considered normative. An operating plan that deviates from the norm would require special justification, and should be carefully reviewed.

Table 2   Relating the focus of an operating plan to the business strategy

Business plan thrust	Operating plan focus
If the basic thrust of a business plan is:	Then the corresponding focus of operating plan should be:
1 Flexibility in market offerings • manoeuvring for position	Design and development of market offerings: response time
2 Quality of market offerings • establishing/surviving	Quality assurance and control; redesign of market offerings
3 Market penetration • taking share	Selling capability; service; price; distribution; response time bringing new capacity on stream
4 Internal rationalization • cost reduction and control	Standardization; automation; cost control; information flow; efficiency
5 Diversification • broadening the base	Coordination among units
6 Selling share • milking, harvesting	Administration of detail throughout the system; vigorous cost reduction; pruning
7 Renewal of the business	Development of new market offerings

Using Operating System Priorities to Determine Operating Plan Objectives

Once the planning group agree on what the operating system priorities should be, they can apply these to the list of potential high-leverage target opportunities identified in the process of validating the operating system description (Chapter 6). When first generated, this list is an undifferentiated collection of nominations for possible targets to be addressed by the operating plan. These nominations must now be re-examined to identify those with the greatest relevance to achieving the changes in the operating system most crucial to the success of the business strategy.

The task for the planning group is now to identify the *highest*-leverage target opportunities. They must sort through 20 to 40 possible high-leverage targets of opportunity to identify the 4 or 5 with the most promise for serving as the basis for the operating plan's objectives. The process is essentially one of screening each nominated target against the priority criteria. For example, if the agreed top priority for the operating system is low total cost, the question is asked of each potential target, 'to what extent will addressing this particular potential high-leverage target contribute to lower total cost?' Those targets judged to contribute the most in the interests of the top priority can be designated with an 'A';

those targets judged to contribute the most towards the second and third priorities can be designated with a 'B', and all others designated with a 'C'.

In Figure 6 is a list of 19 high-leverage target opportunities. These were identified by a planning group concerned with an operating system focused on the engineering design/development and manufacturing functions producing microcomputer-based desktop systems for one of the world's largest computer manufacturers. This group agreed that the top operating system priority at that time was the system's ability to bring 'appropriate' new products to market in the shortest possible time. A close second priority was low total cost, and a more distant third priority was conformity with customers' quality expectations. This consensus on the operating system priorities led the planning group to apply an A−B−C analysis to the 'raw' list of potential high-leverage targets. The results can be seen in Figure 6. Only five targets were assessed as top-priority, with an additional seven targets assigned a second-order ranking. The planning group then generated the objectives for their operating plan from the higher-priority targets. These are shown at the bottom of Figure 6.

The process I have described enables a management group to derive operating system priorities from both business strategy imperatives and operating system performance capabilities. These priorities are then applied to develop operating plan objectives. This process is the primary mechanism for ensuring that any operating plan meets two vital criteria. One is close alignment with the business strategy. The other is a focus on a few critical areas for improving the performance of an operating system. The better an operating plan meets these two criteria, the more powerful a contribution it will make to ensuring the successful implementation of the business strategy.

Operating system priorities

Priorities	Rank	%
Lowest total cost	2	35
Optimize make/buy inventory Pipeline & Capital Utilization		
Required quality/reliability	3	20
Response to short delivery cycles		
Consistent delivery commitments		5
Volume flexibility		
Product change flexibility (including time-to-market)	① Timeliness	㊵

High-leverage targets of opportunity

Priority

Ⓐ • How to achieve a quantum reduction in time-to-market?
C • How to improve management of information regarding introduction of new products . . . cross-functions; cross-geography?
B • How to improve supply/demand management process for new products?
Ⓐ • How to get in-house component 'vendors' to regard our engineering and manufacturing groups as a customer (treating internal suppliers like external ones . . . i.e., cost benchmarking)?
C • How to get our engineering groups to leverage improvements in customer satisfaction on existing products? (Metrics?)
C • How to institute a more formal process for making sourcing decisions? (Open, participative, discipline?)
B • How to clarify geographic roles and responsibilities within manufacturing for product and business management?
C • How to use manufacturing and engineering to leverage the company's worldwide market presence?
B • How to achieve lowest competitive cost/order?
Ⓐ • How can engineering and manufacturing improve collaboration? (Joint goals?) (CAD tools and design service?) (Metrics that are more reflective of engineering and manufacturing contributions?)
B • How to achieve more standard systems and narrow range of product offerings?
B • How to achieve more standardized components?
B • How to achieve an integrated systems strategy for manufacturing?
C • How to improve effectiveness of first-line supervision?
Ⓐ • How can product specs be nailed down earlier in phase review process to improve time-to-market?
B • How to get more credible business plans for new products?
C • How to improve leverage of resources (overhead, systems) worldwide?
C • How to capitalize on our relationship to the desktop computer business?
Ⓐ • How to leverage new product services to improve time-to-market?

Operating plan objectives

1 Shorten time-to-market.
2 Reduce total costs by addressing both product designs and every aspect of operations.
3 Increase customer satisfaction by providing systems that better meet their needs.
4 Improve organizational arrangements to support objectives 1–3.
5 Improve information systems and management to support objectives 1–3.

Figure 6 Applying operating system priorities to high-leverage targets of opportunity to identify operating plan objectives.

8

Assessing Capabilities for Success

In order for a planning group to select the most appropriate strategic options as the basis for an operating plan, they need first to agree not only on the objectives for that plan (Chapters 6 and 7), but also on the capabilities of the operating system to make the required changes in its *modus operandi*. These can be determined through a series of analytical processes referred to in Steps 6, 7 and 8 on our model for formulating operating plans (Figure 3, Chapter 4). A planning group can apply these processes to form a consensus on a comprehensive, relevant and objective inventory of the operating system's capabilities (or strengths and weaknesses) in responding to efforts to improve its performance.

Before any planning group decides where and how to invest resources to improve a system's operating effectiveness in supporting the implementation of a business strategy, they need to assess how likely it is that the system can successfully make the required changes. This means anticipating what characteristics of the system can be counted upon to support the desired changes, and what characteristics are likely to undermine or defeat any efforts to introduce changes. I consider the former, strengths, and the latter, weaknesses.

Strengths and Weaknesses

Anyone who has ever been engaged in planning is familiar with the exercise of identifying an organization's strengths and weaknesses. All too often, however, the results of such efforts seldom prove useful. When making this analysis, management groups frequently fall into one or more of three potential traps. One common error is to view strengths and weaknesses as absolutes. Another is to overlook important factors. The third trap is wishful or biased thinking, often coloured by cultural beliefs and by misinterpretation of past experience.

In the context of an operating system's responsiveness to management's efforts to introduce significant changes, almost no system characteristic is *consistently* a strength or a weakness. Rather, whether a particular characteristic is a true strength or weakness, or is irrelevant, depends on the nature and extent of the desired change, and its timing. The same characteristic can be a strength in some circumstances, and a weakness in others.

EXAMPLE

The Construction and Maintenance Department (CMD) of the large US electric utility described earlier in Chapter 5, p. 54, grew substantially from the mid 1960s to the late 1970s when it was called upon by corporate management to build a series of nuclear generating stations. Operating more like an independent engineering/construction firm, than a corporate department, CMD successfully built several nuclear plants at costs dramatically below US national averages. CMD's excellent performance was attributed to their skills in managing very large projects, their ability to operate independently from most of the other parts of the company, and their strong commitment to doing top-quality work. CMD's managers viewed these three attributes as major strengths. When the utility's nuclear plant construction programme stopped about 1980, CMD was directed to provide plant and equipment maintenance services not only to the nuclear stations it had built, but also to the utility's many fossil fuel and hydro generating stations. Effective maintenance services require skills in managing small projects, highly flexible planning and scheduling, cost-effective responsiveness, and a close, collaborative and interactive relationship with internal 'customers'. The strengths that served CMD so well in the past now became weaknesses.

Any useful assessment of an operating system's capabilities must be comprehensive. Each element of the system needs to be considered methodically in the light of intended changes. Answers should be sought to the question, 'Is this system characteristic likely to enhance substantially the success of the intended change, defeat it, or is it irrelevant?' A systematically thorough analysis is the key to assuring comprehensiveness.

Wishful and biased thinking is the third enemy of useful analyses of operating systems' capabilities. Tenaciously held cultural beliefs can prevent objectivity. Remember the example of the leading paint company whose management stubbornly refused to acknowledge that their superior-quality paint no longer could command a premium price (Chapter 2, p. 24, and Chapter 7, p. 78). This example provides an additional illustration of a former strength becoming a weakness. Wrong lessons learned from prior experience also contribute to biased thinking.

EXAMPLE

A medium-sized regional US insurance company attributed stalled growth and falling profits to the quality of its field salesforce. The 'evidence' for this major 'weakness' was very high salesperson turnover and an extremely high lapse rate of insurance policies within the first year of the sale. Closer examination revealed that both symptoms of the 'weak' salesforce were consequences of several other factors. This company's insurance policies offered few competitively advantageous features. Further, they were priced high, to reflect the historically poor lapse rates. The firm's business strategy was unfocused and offered little direction to salespeople and their managers. The resulting low compensation levels and apparently weak leadership in the field caused the high turnover and lapse rates.

In assessing an operating system's capabilities, there is one critical question. How can a planning group generate an inventory of system strengths and weaknesses that are comprehensive, relevant to the required system changes, and as objective as possible? I have found that two 'warm-up' exercises can be helpful in conditioning and stimulating the thinking of the planning group as they approach this task.

Learning from History

The first 'warm-up' exercise focuses the planning group on recent examples of efforts to achieve major changes in the way the operating system works. The group are asked first to critique these efforts, and then to draw some generalized lessons from these critiques. When the group re-assess specific examples of change efforts from recent company experience, they often develop more accurate and objective insights about the system's capabilities for responding to change.

To begin this process, the group identify from six to ten examples from the past two years of company history, when management invested substantial resources to achieve major improvements in operating system effectiveness. The planning group are then subdivided into four to five small groups each with five to six members representing multiple functions. Each small group is asked to address one or two examples of past change efforts, to work together to answer the following three questions, and to report on their conclusions.

1 In light of what the planning group have identified as high-leverage target opportunities and objectives for the operating plan, how relevant is the particular change effort we are examining?
2 How would we now assess the success of this particular change effort?
3 How would we explain the reasons for the successful or disappointing outcomes of this change effort (with particular attention to how management went about trying to make the change)?

When the full planning group reassemble to hear the conclusions reached by each small group, they are invited to reflect on whether there are any patterns common to most of the individual case analyses. When a generalization can be made about correlating management's approach to making changes with the degree of success achieved, conclusions reached by the group are recorded on a flip chart for further consideration.

This simple yet powerful process is often effective in helping a group learn useful lessons from the firm's past experience in trying to effect major changes in the operating system. These lessons help to stimulate fresh, more objective thinking about system strengths and weaknesses. An example of the lessons drawn by one planning group from a critique of past improvement efforts can be seen below.

EXAMPLE

A critique of past operating system improvement efforts (Consensus reached by a planning group)

Results achieved and relevance to business strategies
- **Past change efforts yielded mixed results; major efforts tended to be less successful than more modest ones.**
- **Change efforts lacked focus: somewhat scattershot; some relevant, many missing the mark.**

Lessons learned
- **When successful, effort was focused, led by a dedicated champion who first developed and demonstrated a prototype and then worked to achieve a broad buy-in − all with modest resources.**
- **Disappointing results occurred when there was no clear champion and when cooperation was required among many different groups with different agendas and concerns.**

EXAMPLE continued

- Change efforts were less successful when there was: (a) insufficient understanding of the need for the change and of the potential benefits; and (b) differing perceptions of the priority of the change effort.
- Change efforts were more successful when those impacted had an opportunity to participate in the process and contribute to shaping the change.

A Systematic Assessment of Management Beliefs and Organizational Arrangements

There is a second 'warm-up' exercise that a planning group can use to stimulate thinking prior to generating an inventory of operating system strengths and weaknesses. This exercise makes use of a questionnaire that my colleagues and I developed to test the readiness of any operating system to undertake particular operating system improvement strategies. We call this questionnaire OMRA (Organization and Management Readiness Assessment).

We developed this questionnaire to deal with a persistent problem we encountered when working with various organizations to improve the effectiveness of their operating systems. In a number of instances, we found that management were unable to implement successfully an improvement strategy they had selected as desirable. Often, their failure did not become evident until after many months of effort. In retrospect, the failure could be attributed to specific aspects of management's mindset and characteristics of the operating system itself. Dismayed by the resources squandered going down blind alleys, we wanted a way to sound an early warning signal that would question the wisdom of pursuing certain courses of action *before* any choices were made.

Three concepts underlie OMRA. It is possible to sort all the internal dynamic elements of an operating system into two independent clusters, each of which can be characterized by a spectrum of possible behaviours. One cluster includes such key organizational arrangements as:

(a) the extent of management delegation and where and how decisions are made;
(b) the nature of such systems as information, rewards, communication, planning and control;

(c) the nature of first-line supervision;

(d) the nature of employee—management and labour relations; and

(e) mechanisms and processes for inter-functional collaboration and conflict resolution.

The other cluster includes the key beliefs that influence the choices made by management. These beliefs can be characterized along a spectrum ranging from traditional to avant-garde. Similarly, organizational arrangements can be characterized along a spectrum ranging from undeveloped/traditional to highly developed and sophisticated.

For example, an organizational system can be considered highly sophisticated when decisions are made at the lowest appropriate level and functional managers are encouraged to sort out any differences with the aid of various mechanisms such as task forces and process facilitation. Similarly, management beliefs can be considered avant-garde when most members of management believe that decisions should be made at the lowest appropriate level, that information about the business should be shared widely, that employee involvement is a powerful means to stimulate innovation and enhance the success of improvement efforts, and that interfunctional collaboration is key to solving problems and improving strategic management.[10]

A second concept underlying the OMRA is that implementation of any operating plan will be more successful when management's beliefs are congruent with organizational arrangements, and will be more prone to failure when these two variables are incongruent. Congruency in this context means that both variables are at a similar level of development or sophistication.

A third concept driving the OMRA is that higher levels of development and sophistication in both management's thinking and organizational arrangements are required to implement successfully certain strategies in the operating plan, while many other strategies can be effectively implemented even when levels of sophistication/development are relatively low. For example, several of these strategies depend to varying degrees on interfunctional collaboration, employee involvement and/or union—management cooperation. Successful implementation of these strategies requires more advanced thinking from managers and more sophisticated organizational arrangements (i.e. information, communication, reward and control systems and mechanisms for interfunctional collaboration) than many other strategies. Organizations of a more traditional and less developed nature are unlikely to be successful when trying to implement these more 'demanding' strategies (see Figure 8, p. 103).

Using the OMRA Questionnaire

For a planning group to make use of these concepts, they must first locate themselves and their operating system on an OMRA Grid (Figure 7). The analytical instrument for doing so is the OMRA Questionnaire (Appendix 3). Each member of the planning group individually and anonymously completes Forms A, B, C and D of the OMRA Questionnaire. Directions for scoring the questionnaire responses and relating the results to the OMRA Grid are also provided in Appendix 3.

If the results of this exercise position the operating system solidly in the northeast quadrant of the OMRA Grid, the planning group should feel unconstrained in their consideration of all the possible strategy options for the operating plan (Chapter 9). This is both because management's beliefs are congruent with organizational arrangements, and because both variables are sufficiently developed to be able to pursue even the most demanding strategy options. If, on the other hand, the position on the grid proves to be in the southwest quadrant, the planning group should

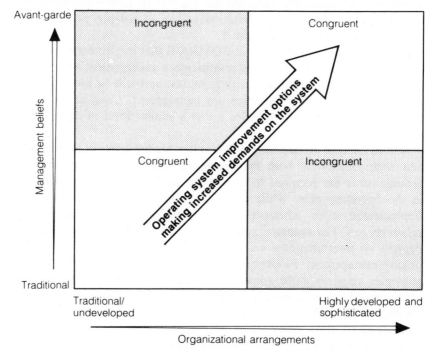

*Organization and Management Readiness Assessment

Figure 7   OMRA grid.

94

approach the more demanding strategy options with caution. When the position on the grid is in either the northwest or southeast quadrants (both 'incongruent'), the planning group should ensure that the operating plan includes a strategy to move towards congruency. Achieving congruency is a top priority objective because this is a prerequisite for successful implementation of all other strategies in the operating plan. The degree of demand made both on management and on the organizational arrangements by each of the generic operating plan strategy options is shown in Figure 8, Chapter 9.

The planning group can also use the OMRA Questionnaire to identify potential operating system strengths and weaknesses for discussion. The group's responses to each of the questions in Form A and B are analyzed to identify which ones reflect large majority agreement (I look for at least two-thirds of the responses in either columns one and two or four and five). These results are reported to the group and discussed. It is important to view the questionnaire results as suggestive, to be explained and validated only after discussion by the group.

The function of the entire OMRA exercise is to improve the quality and usefulness of the inventory of operating system strengths and weaknesses generated by the planning group. The OMRA exercise improves the comprehensiveness of the inventory by engaging the planning group in a systematic examination of key aspects of the operating system. The exercise also tends to improve the group's objectivity. Furthermore, by raising questions about congruency and levels of sophistication, the exercise helps to condition the group's choice of strategy options for the operating plan (Chapter 9). Finally, when there is a need to improve the degree of congruency, the specific reasons for incongruency can be pinpointed, suggesting the ingredients for the strategy to improve the situation.

Generating a Useful Inventory of Operating System Capabilities

After completing the two 'warm-up' exercises, the planning group are ready to apply what they have learned, and develop consensus about the capabilities of the operating system to implement improvement strategies. The objective is to develop two lists: one of strategically relevant, significant strengths that will contribute to implementation success, and the other of strategically relevant, significant weaknesses that could defeat or undermine efforts to improve operating system effectiveness.

With the results of the two 'warm-up' exercises in mind, the planning group are invited first to nominate possible strengths and weaknesses. This process is conducted in a 'brainstorming' mode, with individual ideas put forward without discussion and recorded on flip charts. The second step is for the group to revisit each list. For each item, the group are now asked to vote by a show of hands whether they agree that the nominated strength or weakness is truly significant and relevant. Only those nominations validated by a substantial majority remain in the final inventory.

In generating the list of weaknesses, it is important that the group take some pains with the specification of each weakness. The more concrete its description, the more useful this will be in suggesting what must be addressed in the operating plan to lessen or neutralize its impact. Thus, 'weak first-line supervision' offers a few clues for remedial action. A more useful specification is, 'many first-line supervisors see themselves more as part of the workforce than as members of management, take few initiatives and spend most of their time helping employees do the work'. Similarly, 'poor management information' could be improved by specifying that, 'managers and supervisors are overwhelmed by data, but are provided little accurate, relevant information in time to improve the quality of their decisions'.

With the completion of the inventory of strengths and weaknesses, the planning group are ready to choose the few strategies on which to base the operating plan. As they consider the full range of generic options, their thinking will be influenced by the consensus they have reached on three fundamental points: high-leverage targets of opportunity for improving operating system effectiveness; operating system priorities and plan objectives; and the capabilities of the system to implement any major improvements successfully. The analyses which led to these conclusions were focused primarily on current and past considerations. The group must now focus on the future, and specify the work required to achieve the desired outcomes, given the realities of the current situation.

Part IV

Formulating an Agreed Plan

9

Establishing Direction and Focus

In their consideration of the operating system, the planning group have reached consensus on high-leverage opportunity targets and priorities, improvement objectives, and an assessment of the system's capabilities to make any required changes. They are now ready to select the strategies for the operating plan. By strategy, I mean the specification of the particular route management want to take in order to achieve certain operating plan objectives. Often, a desired outcome can be reached by more than a single pathway. Each route or strategy tends to focus on particular elements of an operating system, thereby providing leverage for achieving desired performance improvements.

The object of the strategy selection task is the achievement of consensus among the planning group's 20 to 30 members regarding the 3 to 6 strategies on which to base the operating plan (steps 9 and 10 in our model for formulating operating plans, Figure 3, Chapter 4). This choice is crucial, for it determines the focus of the operating plan and consequently where and how management will apply resources to improve the operating system's performance in support of business strategy implementation.

At first blush, this task may seem well nigh impossible. How can anyone consider an apparently enormous number of strategy options and narrow the choice to so few? Furthermore, how can such a large number of managers agree on any choice?

In fact, this task is eminently achievable. In my work with hundreds of planning groups, I have never experienced failure by a group to agree on the selection of a few strategies. There are three reasons for this. One is that the range of generic options is finite and far more limited than one might initially imagine. Another reason is that before any group address the problem of narrowing their choices, they have already established a framework for guiding their selection. This framework consists of the three reference points on which the group have already reached consensus:

(a) the high-leverage opportunity targets;
(b) priorities and objectives; and

(c) an assessment of the operating system's capabilities or readiness to make the required changes.

The third reason is the systematic process used by the planning group to reach consensus on their strategy choices.

In Chapters 6, 7 and 8, I describe how a planning group can establish the framework for making their strategy selection. In this chapter, I discuss the finite range of strategy options and the process that a planning group can apply to reach consensus on the few options appropriate to their situation.

The Finite Range of Strategy Options

In enumerating all the possible generic strategy options that an operating system's management can employ to improve support of the business strategy, the resultant number turns out to be both finite and relatively small. This is because there are only a limited number of operating system elements that management can act upon to achieve substantial, durable improvements in total system performance. These elements are the ones offering the greatest leverage in influencing overall system performance.

Consider first the dimensions of total system performance that relate to desired outcomes. I have worked with hundreds of organizations of widely varying sizes in many different businesses providing both goods and services in not only the private but also the public sectors. In all this experience, I have identified only nine distinctly different outcomes for improved system performance.

1 Improved conformance to customers' quality requirements
2 Better utilization of fixed assets
3 Improved flexibility in responding to market requirements/ opportunities for product/service innovation
4 Lower costs
5 Improved flexibility in responding to market requirements/ opportunities for changes in volume/capacity
6 Better consistency/predictability in meeting scheduled delivery commitments
7 Improved capability to respond nimbly to customers' day-to-day demands (very short cycles)
8 Improved utilization of materials
9 Improved utilization of people

Each of these outcomes can be used to define a major thrust or theme for an operating plan. A more detailed description of each of these major thrusts can be found in Appendix 4.

The first seven of these thrusts are identical to the operating system priorities discussed in Chapter 7. Thrusts 8 and 9 do not appear in the list of priorities because they are not driven by the business strategy's demands on the operating system. Rather, they are more internal to the system itself and are means to the ends described by the operating system priorities.

Typically, an operating plan will address no more than two or three of these major themes. To attempt more would risk losing focus, thus reducing the likelihood of successful implementation. In their approach to strategy selection the planning group first need to determine which of the nine possible major generic themes should be addressed in the operating plan. Once they make this choice, it becomes easier to decide which specific strategies will best support the major thrusts.

Each generic strategy option suggests a particular focus for the work required to carry it out. This work is specified in a sequence of action steps or tasks, which collectively describe the true meaning of the strategy. An operating plan can be likened to a building. The design criteria are provided by the high-leverage opportunity targets, the operating system priorities and plan objectives, and the operating system's capabilities for achieving the desired changes. The foundation of the building is the strategies. And the superstructure is the action steps. Action detailing is discussed in Chapter 10.

In my experience, any operating system's management have no more than about 33 generic strategy options from which to choose for improving the system's performance in supporting the business strategy. Each of these options suggests a focus for the investment of resources. The 33 options are described in Appendix 4. Almost all of them are as applicable to service businesses as they are to goods businesses. Most of them are equally applicable to private-sector competitive businesses and public-sector not-for-profit and government organizations. Although all the options are applicable to situations where unions are involved, two options, in particular, address the union−management relationship.

Using the Generic Strategy Options

This set of generic strategy options is intended to be only suggestive, to stimulate thinking and discussion by a planning group as they wrestle with the task of developing consensus on the strategies that are to be the basis for their operating plan. Typically, a planning group will seldom make use of any of the 33 strategy options in its 'pure' generic form. Rather, the planning group identify a set of generic options only as a starting point. The generic choices are then refocused, reshaped, tailored and sometimes clustered and combined to form the situationally specific strategies on which the operating plan is based. The generic strategy options are intended only as a *means* to the end of strategy selection, not the end itself. In the next section of this chapter, I discuss how the planning group can make effective use of these generic strategy options.

In Chapter 8, I suggest that the OMRA Grid (Figure 7) can be used as one of the several reference points in the strategy selection process. Once the planning group position their operating system on the OMRA Grid, questions can be raised for discussion about the readiness of both the organization and management to undertake particular strategies with a high probability of success. In Figure 8, I suggest the relative demands made on any operating system by each of the 33 generic strategy options.

For example, strategies 1 through 9 are essentially quite traditional in nature. Each of these strategies can be implemented by direct management actions. Success does not depend significantly on employee involvement, union−management cooperation, or an unusually high degree of interfunctional collaboration. Furthermore, these strategies present no stringent demands on any of the organizational systems (e.g. planning and control, information, reward, communications, etc.). Strategies 1 through 9 can readily be implemented successfully by an organization with relatively traditional modes of operation and un-sophisticated management processes and systems, and by a management with conventional beliefs about managing.

On the other hand, strategies 26 through 33 make special and stringent demands on any operating system. For successful outcomes, each of these strategies depends heavily on employee involvement, union−management cooperation and/or interfunctional collaboration and organizational integration. Furthermore, they require highly developed organizational systems. If the planning group have not positioned the operating system well into the northeast quadrant of the OMRA Grid, they should approach strategies 26 through 33 with extreme caution, because the probability of successful implementation will not be high. Strategies 10 through 25 are positioned at various intermediate points on the operating system demand spectrum.

As with the generic strategy options, the OMRA Grid and Figure 8 should be regarded only as tools for stimulating thought and discussion, in the interests of more considered and 'appropriate' strategy choices. These tools are not intended to provide answers. Rather, they are meant to be used by the planning group to reach better-quality answers.

Traditional demands ⟷ *Unusual/special demands*

1 Simplify product/service line
2 Upgrade existing plant/facilities
3 Improve equipment and process technology
4 Increase mechanization
5 Increase capacity
6 Optimize make/buy mix
7 Improve vendors' quality
8 Improve distribution
9 Improve energy/utilities efficiency

10 Reduce materials losses
11 Improve work methods and procedures
12 Improve equipment utilization
13 Increase standardization in operations
14 Improve information handling

15 Improve product/service design
16 Improve MIS, financial and operating systems, controls and reports
17 Apply rewards and penalties
18 Improve communications
19 Develop a workforce with multiple, flexible skills
20 Improve manager/supervisor/employee selection, training and development
21 Reduce lost work time

22 Redesign jobs
23 Improve departmental performance
24 Change organizational design/focus
25 Improve integration among departments/functions

26 Improve union–management relations and chip away at workforce-related productivity
27 Shorten time-to-market for new products/services
28 Shorten order-to-delivery time for existing products/services
29 Shorten provisioning time
30 Engage in productivity bargaining
31 Establish total quality control programme
32 Encourage employee involvement
33 Institute employee involvement with productivity gains-sharing

Figure 8 Spectrum of demand on the operating system by operating plan strategy options.

A Process for Developing Consensus on Strategy Choices

The tools described in the preceding section of this chapter are most effectively used by a planning group as a part of a systematic, somewhat structured process. This consists of four steps and is depicted in Figure 9. The process is designed to serve two purposes simultaneously. One is to encourage the planning group systematically to consider a broad range of strategy options before they select the particular strategies for their operating plan. The other purpose is to facilitate the achievement of consensus by the planning group.

In this approach a planning group have led through a sequence of thought processes. Conceptually, the overall design is like that of a funnel. The sequence of four steps drives a planning group along a course starting with an initially global view of the situation and a choice of a very limited number of very broad options. They then move through progressively narrower ways of viewing the situation, each with an increasing number of more detailed and concrete options. The first three steps deal with generic options. Each step concludes with the planning

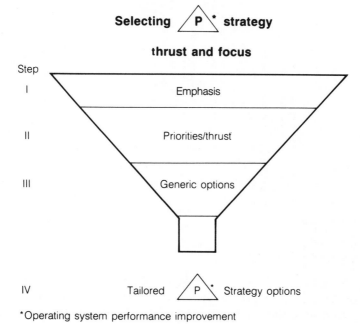

Figure 9   Strategy selection process.

group choosing a few options. The decisions made by the planning group at the end of each step influence the choices they make in the succeeding step. Step IV requires the planning group to translate their prior choices in steps I through III into a specific articulation of the operating plan strategies tailored to their particular circumstances. Thus the process moves the planning group from the general and generic to the specific and particular. As they do so, consensus tends to build.

As a prelude to the strategy-selection process the planning group review the three reference points they have developed: the operating system's high-leverage target opportunities, priorities and objectives, and capabilities for change. Each member of the planning group is then provided with a deck of index cards. This deck contains the options detailed in Appendix 4 (one option per card) and is divided into three sections: 3 emphasis cards; 9 thrust cards; and 33 strategy option cards. An additional blank 'wild' card might be included to enable any manager who wants to do so, to write in a different proposed strategy option if s/he finds the 33 generic options insufficient. It may be useful to colour-code each of the three sections of the card deck.

Emphasis and thrust

After reviewing the three reference points, the planning group's first choice is to select the single emphasis card out of the three options that they believe best characterize what they think should be the emphasis of the operating plan. Initial selection is done individually. Then by a show of hands, the initial results are tabulated on a flip chart. Those who selected each of the options are invited to explain the reasons for their choice. If there is no clear majority, further discussion may be required and a second vote taken. If a majority select the 'Mixed External and Internal Emphasis' card, that group are asked to make a second-order choice among three options:

(a)   more external than internal;
(b)   about evenly divided; and
(c)   more internal than external.

It is not necessary at the close of this initial discussion to end with a clear consensus, before proceeding to the next step. It is important, however, to discuss sufficiently the rationale driving particular choices so that everyone in the group understand the thinking behind the various choices.

In the next step of the strategy-selection process, the planning group consider the nine thrust or theme cards. Each member individually selects the three thrust cards that best describes what s/he believes the major thrusts of the operating plan should be. The three choices are then prioritized. Each member of the planning group records his/her three prioritized choices on a matrix such as the one shown in Figure 10. The planning group then discuss the results.

Members who have made minority choices are invited to explain the reasons for their choices. Often, particular words or phrases on the card will attract a choice because of the particular significance or meaning invested in them by the individual. When these rationales become clarified in the discussion, it is often possible to relate the minority choices to the majority ones, and work towards a consensus. It is important, although not essential, for the planning group to have achieved consensus by the end of the second step in the selection process. Again, the discussion following the initial choices is the most important element of each of the first three steps, because each discussion illuminates and influences the choices made in the succeeding step.

Generic and tailored strategy options

In the third step of the selection process, each member of the planning group selects the five strategy option cards s/he believes should form the foundation of the operating plan. These choices are prioritized and then recorded on a second matrix (on a flip chart, for all to see) such as the one shown in Figure 10. Again, as in the previous step, there is an extensive discussion. Those making minority choices are invited to explain what words on the card attracted them to select it as one of the five. Efforts are made to relate minority to majority choices and move towards consensus. Often, several choices can be clustered around one of the thrusts or themes identified in the prior step.

In the fourth step of this strategy-selection process, the planning group apply everything they have learned from the previous three steps and come to an agreement on the specific tailored strategies that will serve as the operating plan's foundation. This requires relating the choices of thrusts or themes in step two, to the more concrete generic strategy options in step three. When there are clear majority choices in both instances, moving from the generic to the particular is essentially a matter of tailoring the language of each strategy statement to reflect the specific emphasis and focus appropriate to the circumstances. A first draft strategy statement can often be formulated in a discussion by the full

Establishing Direction and Focus

(A) Matrix for recording choice of thrust

Thrust	Top priority	2nd priority	3rd priority
1 Quality			
2 Asset utilization			
3 Product change flexibility			
4 Reduce cost			
5 Volume change flexibility			
6 Meet schedule commitments			
7 Short-cycle delivery			
8 Material utilization			
9 People utilization			

(B) Matrix for recording choice of generic strategies

Strategy options / Priority	I	II	III	IV	V
1 Simplify product line					
2 Facilities					
3 Equipment technology					
4 Mechanization					
5 Make/buy mix					
6 Capacity					
7 Vendor quality					
8 Distribution					
9 Energy efficiency					
10 Material loss					
11 Methods					
12 Equipment utilization					
13 Standardization					
14 Information handling					
15 Product design					
16 Management information					
17 Rewards/penalties					
18 Communication					
19 Flexible workforce					
20 Mgmt/employee selection/ training					
21 Lost work time					
22 Redesign jobs					
23 Department performance					
24 Organization design					
25 Functional interaction					
26 Union-mgmt relations					
27 Time-to-market					
28 Order-to-delivery time					
29 Provision time					
30 Productivity bargaining					
31 Total quality control					
32 Employee involvement					
33 Gains-sharing					

Figure 10   Recording matrices.

planning group. More refined wording can be developed later as part of the action detailing work described in Chapter 10.

In the second and third steps of the process, when none of the planning group's generic choices constitute clear majorities, I have found it useful to subdivide the planning group into four or five small groups. Each group, structured to represent a heterogeneous mix of functions, is asked to discuss the generic strategy option and thrust choices made earlier and form a consensus on their recommended operating plan strategies. Each group then present their conclusions and supporting rationale to the full planning group. In such instances, a pattern of agreement typically emerges. This approach seldom yields any clear strategy statements *per se*. What does result is a consensus on the general nature of each recommended strategy together with some language to suggest its major components. The material can then be reworked into more concise strategy statements in the action planning process discussed in the next chapter.

EXAMPLE

A planning group of 27 members represented the major functions in an operating system that was responsible for the design, development and manufacture of desktop computer systems (see Figure 6, Chapter 7).

They employed the four-step process described above to select the strategies for their operating plan. At the end of step two, there was overwhelming agreement on two generic thrusts: product change flexibility and low costs. Three other thrust choices attracted a substantial number of 'votes': People Utilization; Quality; and Short Cycles.

In the discussion, it developed that those attracted to choosing short cycles did so because they interpreted the card as referring to shortening time-to-market. In the third step, only two generic strategy options attracted substantial majorities: Improve Product Design; and Shorten Time-to-Market.

Two others combined also represented a substantial majority: Improve Organizational Design; and Improve Functional Integration. The option card, Improve Management Information received a significant number of votes, but slightly less than a majority.

Several other options received considerable attention, but substantially less than a majority: Reduce Material Losses; Improve Make/Buy Mix; Shorten Order-to-Delivery; Shorten Provisioning Time; and Improve Work Methods.

EXAMPLE continued

After breaking into four small discussion groups and considering the conclusions reached, the planning group formed a consensus on the following four tailored strategies:

1 Improve Engineering/Manufacturing collaboration to develop and co-implement product criteria for lower total product costs, faster time-to-market, and higher levels of customer satisfaction and functionality.
2 To meet the market share and profitability goals of the micro-systems business, reduce total product costs, including manufacturing costs, material costs, warranty costs, distribution costs, cost per order, plant costs, and overhead costs.
3 Optimize the microsystems business objectives through effective planning, linkages and accountabilities between our business unit and other SBUs and organizations within the company.
4 Develop/improve existing information processes to provide management tools that achieve:
   (a) the conveyance of management information (not data) for timely decision making;
   (b) consistency in our data definitions and quality of data used in our management/reporting processes; and
   (c) operational effectiveness of information processes through standardization, make vs buy, hardware technology, and flexibility.

None of these strategies is a direct descendant of any single generic strategy option. Rather, each of these strategies represents an integration and a focusing of the generic choices made earlier in the strategy selection process.

When a planning group agree on a framework for considering a wide range of strategy options (high-leverage opportunities, priorities and objectives, and the system's capabilities for achieving change), and systematically apply the above process for selecting generic thrusts and strategy options, they can readily achieve consensus on fewer than five or six tailored strategies on which to base the operating plan. This choice is crucial, for it determines the focus for the plan. But this decision represents only the beginning of plan formulation. The true substance and meaning of the plan is in the superstructure: the specification of the work to be done in order to implement each of the strategies, along with the resources and time required. How this can be accomplished is discussed in the next chapter.

10

Specifying the Work Required

When a planning group select three to six strategies on which to base their operating plan, its foundation and focus is established (Chapter 9). This choice is crucial to the plan's effectiveness in achieving the desired changes to the operating system. Yet if the planning group regard their work as complete at this point, their plan will be of little value. It is the superstructure of detailed action programmes built on the foundation of the strategies that invests an operating plan with true meaning and worth. These action programmes specify the work that must be done, by whom, with what resources and accountabilities and to what timetable, in order to make the strategies actually happen. Without action programmes, a plan is nothing more than a wish or a statement of intention.

The Purpose of Action Programmes

A well conceived set of action programmes serves at least four different purposes. First, by articulating the scope and nature of the work along with the resources required to implement each strategy, a planning group can validate their strategic choices. Not until they specify action programmes, can a planning group be reasonably certain that their selected strategies are in fact achievable and likely to have the desired impact. If after developing an action programme, a planning group find a disappointing relationship between invested effort and resources on the one hand, and expected returns or gains on the other, they may want to reconsider their initial strategy choice.

EXAMPLE

The leading American manufacturer of composite cans for frozen juices located its many highly mechanized production plants adjacent to major customers throughout North America. The business strategy was to increase market penetration by more aggressive pricing. To support this, one of the larger, high-performing plant's management chose to base their operating plan on a strategy of employee involvement with gains-sharing (generic option 33, Appendix 4). When the planning group developed a supporting action programme for this strategy, they found that the potential gains resulting from successful implementation would be insufficient to provide the required incentive to motivate employees' contributions to productivity improvement. Further, the effort and time required to implement this strategy would be excessive in relation to any returns. These realizations caused the planning group to reject the gains-sharing strategy in favour of improving functional integration and automation.

A second purpose served by action programmes is that management are provided with a detailed roadmap for strategy implementation. When tasks are described with defined outputs (or 'deliverables'), with specified accountabilities and dates for task completion, management have a control document for directing and tracking implementation. Everyone involved knows what is expected, and management have the means for monitoring implementation progress and holding the appropriate people accountable for expected results.

Third, good action plans provide the Sponsor with the detailed information needed for review and validation of the proposed operating plan. Without such detail, it is difficult for the Sponsor to understand the full scope of proposed strategies. Only when the work required to implement a strategy is described in some detail, can a Sponsor feel satisfied that a high-leverage target opportunity is being addressed effectively, and that the time and other resources required for implementation are realistic.

> **EXAMPLE**
>
> A hard-driving chief operating officer of a leading American paper products company was the Sponsor for an operating plan submitted for his approval by one of the firm's major divisions. Because the division's management were pioneering the participative process for plan formulation described in this book, the Sponsor was following closely the development of the proposed plan. He insisted on reviewing the planning group's strategy choices before any action programmes were formulated. The Sponsor had recently been appointed chief operating officer after having served as president of that division for several years. His initial reaction to the proposed strategies was dismissive: 'These strategies are little more than motherhood.' Later, when he reviewed the completed plan with its proposed action programmes, his response was entirely different. Although the proposed strategies were no different from the ones he sneered at earlier, he now saw them as 'on-target' and 'well conceived'. The more detailed articulation of the scope and the work required changed his response to favourable and supportive.

A fourth purpose served by action programmes is that of a primary communications and orientation vehicle. Of all the elements of an operating plan, it is the action programmes that convey the most meaning about strategic direction and the work that must be completed in order to execute the strategies. In Chapter 3, I noted that successful improvements in the way operating systems work depend heavily on the extent to which everyone concerned understand the strategy, how it will be accomplished, and what will be expected in terms of individual commitment and changes in behaviour.

Action programmes are the principal means for answering these questions for those managers and supervisors within the operating system who did not participate directly in the planning group. Others in the entire organization who need to understand the strategies and the work required to implement them are managers and professionals outside the operating system whose support is required. Action programmes are also valuable for orienting and 'bringing up to speed' any new or replacement managers in the operating system who join the organization during the strategy implementation period.

Clearly, action programmes are the most useful component of an operating plan. Yet, as I have noted in Chapter 2 (pp. 25–7), action detailing is often one of the most poorly done elements of strategic business and operating plans. When well thought through action programmes are so critical to successful strategy execution, why do so many plans fall short in this respect?

Reasons for Failure

In Chapter 2, I noted that a major cause for poor-quality action programmes is the lack of detailed working knowledge of operations by the relatively high-level executives who typically formulate strategic plans. However, even when middle- and lower-level managers from the appropriate functions are involved in the planning process, they must overcome two major and one minor obstacle to developing truly useful action programmes.

One obstacle stems from the fact that the nature of action detailing is quite different from that of strategy selection. The latter is essentially an exercise in deductive reasoning. Thus, once the boundary conditions (e.g. high-leverage opportunities and organizational capabilities) are established, the objectives set, and the options for their achievement understood, option selection is a matter of determining best fit among these fixed and variable factors. Seasoned executives and managers are generally well skilled in such rational processes. Indeed, these skills are typically a requirement for advancement in the managerial ranks.

Action detailing, on the other hand, is an exercise in creative thinking. In this task, the boundary conditions are less clear, and the options are extensive in number. Once the general pathway (strategy) is articulated, the planning group members are faced with a blank sheet of paper with no guidelines. What are the principal areas where work must be done to implement the strategy? What is the nature of this work? Where to begin? What is the best sequence of tasks? How long will each task take to complete, and what does 'complete' mean? What resources will be needed? How will accountability be established and who will be accountable? In general, I find that managers have much more difficulty responding to the demand for this kind of creative thinking than they do to requirements for deductive reasoning. The free-wheeling, spontaneous ability to generate imaginative ideas so characteristic of small children often becomes inhibited in adults. Yet, good action programmes depend on this ability to be creative.

The other major obstacle to action detailing stems from personal reluctance to make commitments to which one may later be held accountable. In action detailing, the more concrete the task and its specification of the 'deliverable', and the more clear the assignment of accountability, the better will be the quality of the action programme. It is hardly surprising that managers may balk at specifying and making such commitments, especially if they must do this in full view of everyone with an important role to play in the operating system.

The minor obstacle is finding a workable answer to the question, 'What is the optimum level of detail in specifying individual actions or tasks?' In truth, action detailing can be pursued almost endlessly to an ever more refined and detailed specification of tasks. At the 'macro' end of the task spectrum are chunks of work that require major programmes taking months or even a year or more to complete. At the 'micro' end of the task spectrum are discrete actions that may be completed in a single meeting. What then, is the appropriate positioning on this spectrum of the tasks to be specified in the action programme?

Although these three obstacles are formidable and have defeated many managements in their efforts to develop strategic plans, they are not insurmountable. How effectively a management group deal with these will determine the degree of success achieved in plan implementation.

A Practical Approach to Action Detailing

Consider first the knowledge required to develop useful action programmes. This is somewhat different from the knowledge needed to formulate broad strategies. Strategy selection depends first and foremost on a broad understanding of the operating system as a whole within its external context of the business strategy and its competitive environment. The kind of thinking required is systemic and dynamic. The knowledge needed is broad-based, centred on business processes and inter- rather than intra-functional activities. Understanding what goes on at the workforce and first-line supervisory levels in an organization is not of primary importance. The development of high-quality action programmes, however, does require considerable knowledge of intra-departmental, workforce and supervisory detail. Understanding these gritty activities often makes the difference between plans that are romantic and wishful, and those grounded in practical reality.

The knowledge required to formulate high-quality action programmes is more likely to reside in the heads of lower-level middle managers and first-line supervisors than in the memory cells of more senior managers. Yet, the character of the memory banks in which this detailed, specialized knowledge of operations is stored is likely to be compartmented and fragmented. In order to identify, position, prioritize and integrate the 'bits' of information relevant to a particular strategy, at least one manager with a broader, more strategic perspective also needs to be involved in the creative thinking required to develop an action programme.

The nature of the action detailing task initially requires a creative brainstorming approach set within a broad strategic context but drawing on the collective detailed operating knowledge of those involved. The resultant work specified for each strategy must then be integrated into a coordinated master plan which takes account of task interdependencies and specifies the time and other resources required for implementation. After experimenting with many different approaches, I have found that action detailing is most effectively accomplished in five phases (Figure 11).

Phase I: create proposed action plans

In Phase I, a designated member of the planning group forms a small task group with three to five other members to formulate a proposed action programme for a single strategy. Some of the other members of this group may be drawn from the planning group, but most will be recruited from lower levels of management and supervision. They are probably not members of the planning group but have the detailed operating knowledge relevant to the assigned strategy. The task group work together in a series of three to four half-day meetings to develop a proposed series of action steps or tasks which when completed will execute the strategy. Each strategy has a uniquely selected task group to formulate a proposed action programme. Each group focus only on specifying the work required to implement the assigned strategy. Issues of the time and other resources required, and accountabilities are taken up later in Phases III and IV.

Phase II: review, modify and validate

In Phase II, each strategy's task group present in turn their proposed sequence of action steps along with their supporting rationale to the planning group for review, modification and validation. In the discussion that follows each presentation, the planning group typically enhance the quality of the proposed action plans by adding steps and sharpening the specification of each task. After the planning group have validated the proposed action steps, an individual member of the planning group is designated to work on an interim task assignment for each action step (Phase III).

115

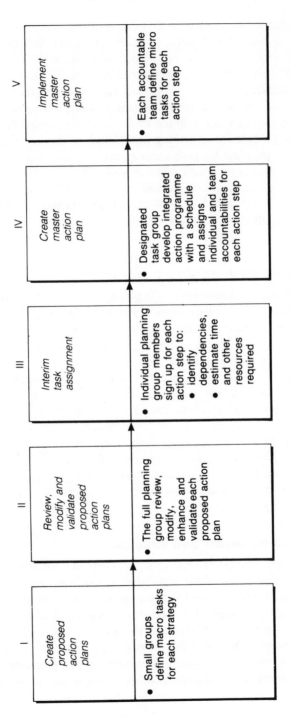

Figure 11 Phases of action detailing.

Phase III: assign interim tasks

Phase III may be performed by the designated individual alone, or by that individual working with anyone else s/he wishes to enlist. There are three elements to the task:

(a) identify any dependencies on the completion of any other action step that supports other strategies;
(b) estimate the time required to complete the assigned action step; and
(c) identify the people and other resources needed to complete that action step.

This information is provided as input to a group formed to create a master action programme (Phase IV).

Phase IV: create the master action plan

A small group of mostly senior managers are selected to consider the inputs from the interim tasks in Phase III and create a master, integrated action programme for all the strategies that comprise the operating plan. As a first step, the group develop a preliminary master schedule for all action steps that support the operating plan's strategies. This is done by relating each action step to a time line of 24 months or more, taking into consideration any identified dependencies and estimated times for completion provided from the work in Phase III. The preliminary master schedule is laid out displaying the work that can be done in parallel and the work that must be sequenced, and how long it will take to implement fully each strategy.

In the next step, the group review the preliminary master schedule to test its sufficiency and credibility with questions such as the following:

- Are the times allowed for completion of the larger tasks realistic? What adjustments are needed in the time allowed?
- Is the total time required for implementing a particular strategy within the bounds of initial expectations and feasibility? If the time required appears to be more than anticipated, what can be done to accelerate implementation?
- Have all the interdependencies of the action steps been taken into account? Are the dependencies justified?
- How soon will any tangible gains from the strategies become apparent? If the time required to realize a visible benefit or gain seems excessive, what can be done to achieve some 'quicker fixes'?

117

- In reviewing the entire action programme for each strategy, are there any significant omissions? If so, what additional tasks should be specified?

Depending on how the group answer these questions, they adjust the preliminary master schedule. Once the group are comfortable with the adjusted schedule, starting and completion dates are entered for each action step.

Finally, the group designate at least one manager as accountable for each action step. In addition, the group may assign other managers, supervisors and professionals to each action step to signal the need for particular functional inputs and involvement. In making these assignments, the group consider questions such as the following:

- Who in the organization is the 'natural owner' of this task by virtue of his/her formal responsibility?
- Have we ensured that every function with important inputs to make and/or with a special interest in this task is represented by an assigned person?
- In making assignments, is anyone unreasonably overloaded?
- Have we taken care to spread the work to middle- and lower-level managers, thereby providing opportunities for career development and for establishing a broad base of managers collectively committed to successful strategy implementation?

In my experience, I have found it desirable prior to assigning people to tasks, to identify for each action step, a group of individuals who are particularly interested in working on that task. This expression of interest should be registered prior to Phase IV, so that the designated group of senior managers responsible for formulating the master integrated action programme can make assignments of people to tasks with the benefit of this knowledge. An appropriate time for members of the planning group to register their interest in working on particular tasks occurs at the end of Phase II. Once the planning group have validated the proposed action steps, all of these can be displayed on a series of newsprint sheets taped on the walls of the meeting room. Planning group members are then invited to write their initials under those action steps on which they would like to work. If an individual enters her/his name under more than one step, first choice preferences should be noted.

Phase V: implement the master action plan

In the final Phase V of action planning, further detailing of the actions is required to implement the macro tasks specified in the master action programme. Earlier in this chapter, I noted that typical action programmes are comprised of a mix of specific, narrowly focused micro tasks that can be executed in a matter of a week or two, and broad, more programmatic macro tasks which require months to complete. As a first step in implementing these macro tasks, the assigned team develop a more detailed action plan for that task. This can be accomplished by applying the approach taken by the small groups who develop the proposed action plans for an entire strategy in Phase I of the action planning process. The process of formulating a sequence of micro tasks to specify how a macro action step will be executed serves two purposes. First, the team responsible for implementation clarify how they plan to proceed. In addition, by developing their work plan together, they ensure that each member of the implementation team has the understanding and commitment necessary for successful execution.

Improving the Quality of Action Detailing

Formulating an action programme, whether it be for an entire strategy or for one of its macro steps, is most effectively accomplished by a small group whose collective knowledge of operating detail is relevant to the task. As the nature of this task is creative, the group's process must stimulate and support creative thinking. Group 'brainstorming' techniques are particularly useful and appropriate. These include making a deliberate effort at the outset to focus on idea generation, postponing critical assessment of each idea until a later phase. At first, each member of the group directs his/her energy towards accessing subjective thoughts and feelings, free-associating to one another's verbalizations and building on each other's ideas. These are recorded without any attempt to critique or assess their merit. Group evaluation and selection occurs only after the members are satisfied that they have devoted sufficient time to uncritical idea generation.[11]

Creative thinking is often most effectively done when a clear context with parameters has been established. This helps to focus the group's thinking by setting boundaries and limits. I have found two preparatory exercises useful in helping to focus a group's creative work.

Formulating an Agreed Plan

A useful context for action planning is a framework of important issues or questions that must be resolved if the strategy is to be successfully implemented. It is essential that the group identify these issues before beginning to specify the work to be done in executing the strategy. A comprehensive list of issues relevant to a particular strategy can be generated by applying a simple three-step process. First, the group articulate their vision of how the operating system will work in the organization after the strategy has been successfully implemented. This vision should incorporate in no more than a paragraph the principal intended outcomes of the strategy, expressed as a description of how the operating system will work in the future.

With this scenario in mind, the group identify in the second step whatever major differences or gaps exist between their future vision and today's reality in the operating system. In the third step, the group identify the issues to be addressed by the strategy. These are the questions that must be answered or resolved in order to close the gaps between the future vision and the currrent situation. In Appendix 5 is a particularly good example of a list of issues prepared by an action planning group working to formulate a set of proposed actions for a cost reduction strategy in a manufacturing firm providing components for aircraft jet engines.

Another way to enhance the framework for action planning is for the entire planning group to identify potential obstacles to successful strategy implementation. Once the group have selected the strategies for their operating plan (Chapter 9), they can consider a number of typical obstacles that might hinder their ability to achieve the desired outcomes (Appendix 6). Those obstacles identified by group consensus as potentially significant problems should be considered by each action planning group as part of the framework for their creative thinking.

Once an action planning group have developed a list of issues and potential obstacles that must be addressed by the strategy, they have established a framework for their creative thinking about how best to define the specific elements of work or tasks required to resolve each issue and deal with the obstacles. A useful starting question to consider for each issue is, 'What will it take to resolve this issue or deal with this obstacle; what kind of a triggering event is indicated?' A triggering event might be a management decision, a group consensus, a redesigned process or system, a study or other kind of research, and the like. Once the triggering event is identified, the group can then address the question of describing the work required to lead up to it.

120

Each action step should be described in a way that communicates the scope of the task and its ultimate output or 'deliverable' clearly to anyone who reads the plan, even if that person did not participate directly in its formulation. Each task statement should begin with an action verb. There should be sufficient description to guide those who will actually execute the task to where they should direct their attention and energy. Each task statement should make explicit what outcome is expected. Examples of action statements and programmes can be found in Appendix 7.

An Analysis of an Action Programme

To conclude this chapter, here is my commentary on a typical action programme to clarify further some of the ideas suggested earlier. Four additional examples of action programmes from both manufacturing and service businesses are presented in Appendix 7. The action programme analyzed here was developed by a planning group representing an operating system that supports the desktop computer business of a major worldwide computer manufacturer. This operating system is focused both on the engineering design and manufacturing functions.

The operating plan strategy for which this action programme was developed reads:

Improve Engineering/Manufacturing/Marketing collaboration worldwide to develop and co-implement product criteria for lower total product costs, faster time-to-market, and higher levels of customer satisfaction and functionality.

Action programme

Step 1
Establish a formal process to get faster agreement
on new product specs (worldwide with change
controls), ensuring inputs and buy-in from
Marketing and Manufacturing.

(a) Describe what happens today and recommend outline of a more formal approach	9/30/87*
(b) Get support from Group General Manager	10/15/87
(c) Develop more formal approach	12/01/87
(d) Get buy-in and approval	12/24/87
(e) Implement	start 1/88
	[BH], CS, DV, WP, DL, TK, RL, JK

Comments

This is a macro step requiring several months to implement. It attempts to address several issues simultaneously. The planning group believed that a major cause for excessive new product development time was initial establishment of product specifications. Although these were often specified early on by Engineering, subsequent disagreements by Marketing and Manufacturing caused a series of revisions. The intent here is to change the entire process from a sequential series of presentations and reviews from Engineering to Marketing to Manufacturing, to a more parallel collaborative effort.

Step 2

To improve time-to-market (worldwide), get
agreement and commitment within the MS Group
to a single, disciplined, decision-focused new
product introduction/development process.
(Integrate/differentiate design reviews, readiness
reviews, programme reviews, checkpoint reviews,
project reviews; integrate with preparation of
documentation and manuals.)

(a) Describe current processes (purposes, who involved, what actually happens, meeting times)	9/30/87
(b) Get support from Group and our GM to invest in redesign effort	8/01/87
(c) Develop redesigned process	11/87
(d) Get buy-in and approval	12/87
(e) Implement	start 1/88
	[FJ], LB, DG, JR, GV

Comments

The group wanted early evidence of successful results from this strategy as a spur to sustain implementation momentum (Chapter 12). The group identified five separate, overlapping processes related to the development and introduction of new products. All five processes required regular meetings, often involving the same participants. It was intended to integrate these five processes into one, and free up significant amounts of managers' time within the first four months of implementation.

122

Step 3

Work with our MS Engineering group and	[CS], DV, JK
Corporate Engineering to ensure that emerging	plan direction
CAD strategy is appropriate to time-to-market and	10/01/88
customer satisfaction objectives, and is articulated,	implementation
sold and implemented in engineering groups;	ongoing
develop and integrate related manufacturing tools.	

Comments

Another macro step aimed at integrating computer-aided design technology into the new product development/introduction process and relating this to computer-aided manufacturing. An issue is gaining broad acceptance of this approach from a number of different engineering groups in various parts of the company. The people assigned to this task represent the major constituencies involved.

Step 4

Review I→L information and experience in Phase	[RS], AH, JC,
I→L(TTM) and identify and address opportunities	GG, TS, LA,
for improvement. (Goal 25 per cent improvement.)	start plan
	1/01/88
	implement after

Comments

This is another macro step aimed at streamlining the single process identified in Step 2 (the letters refer to new product development/introduction phases).

Step 5

Develop and implement a 'cost dynamics awareness'	[LB], LW,
training session (half day?) for key project, product	IG, RD
and engineering managers and key marketing and	design 9/05/87
sales managers.	implement

Comments

This is a more focused action to design and conduct a brief training session aimed at heightening cost awareness among key managers in the operating system.

123

Step 6

See Strategy III, action step 6, re improved
forecasting.

Comments

This is a cross reference to an action in another strategy that is intended
to contribute to this strategy.

Step 7

Determine desirability for value engineering capability. Develop and implement strategy.	[IM], CS, BF, J.Macklin study and recommend (plan) report 10/01/87 implement Q487

Comments

Another more micro step intended to assess the feasibility of undertaking
formal value analysis as a potentially useful process.

Step 8

Develop manufacturing cost model to counteract product proliferation tendencies in Engineering and Sales.	[LB], mgmt/sci finance 1/88

Comments

A sizeable effort to develop and employ a cost model to encourage product
designers to use more standardized approaches in their designs.

Step 9

Design process to ensure product team agreement on customer satisfaction criteria and integrate into action steps 1 and 2.	[DV], VM, VP, SH Europe rep.10/30/87

Comments

A relatively major programme to develop research-based criteria for
customer satisfaction and apply these in steps 1 and 2.

* The dates listed (in 'American' style) are the targeted completion times for each
task. The initials designate the managers assigned to work on the action step, and
the initials contained within brackets [] designate the manager accountable for
action step completion.

Clearly, this action programme is comprised of a number of diverse efforts, some focused and of relatively short duration, and others of more ambitious scope. The people assigned to work on each task were selected so as to represent all the key functions and departments both with relevant inputs to make and with substantial interest in the outcomes. The person whose initials are bracketed is the one accountable for task completion.

Action programmes such as these provide the managers responsible for execution with implementation roadmaps. In Chapters 11 and 12 I discuss several ways in which these roadmaps can be used.

Part V

Ensuring Implementation Success

11

Tracking Implementation Progress

In Chapter 3, 'The Anatomy of Implementation,' I made the following six points about the relationship between performance measures, monitoring progress and implementation success:

1 Every organization has in place a set of performance measures that have become established or institutionalized over time. Some of these measures are local − at departmental or functional level. Others are systemic, embracing groups of functions and/or work processes.
2 At any particular time, these established measures may or may not be aligned with intended future strategies.
3 Existing departmental or functional measures tend to perpetuate established behavioural norms and can constitute a significant barrier to achieving changes in the operating system.
4 A key issue in achieving successful implementation of any strategy and the changes it requires of the operating system, is how to institute a systematic process for tracking implementation progress and making mid-course corrections. Such a process depends heavily on a set of performance measures that are strategically driven and congruent with intended strategies.
5 Strategically derived measures are most effective when established congruently at three levels:

   (a) the SBU level focused on overall business performance relative to business strategy;
   (b) the operating system level focused on operating system performance relative to the operating plan; and
   (c) departmental or functional level focused on departmental performance in the context of the operating plan.

6 Departmental or functional measures are key to making operational over time the changes initially installed as a result of the operating plan.

In this chapter, I first discuss performance measures, and then how these are applied in a monitoring process.

The Dilemma of Measuring Performance Improvement of Complex Systems

Senior executives responsible for SBUs and operating systems need to know how to measure the impact on system performance of the changes and improvements instituted by the operating plan and its strategies. These top managers want to assess whether the investments embodied in their strategies (effort, time and resources) are in reality paying off in terms of the desired gains. This need is both legitimate and urgent. Executives need answers to the question, 'Am I getting the expected return on my investment?', in order to take remedial action when results are disappointing.

For this executive need to be met, there must be an ability to measure with reasonable precision, cause–effect relationships within complex systems in the context of performance improvement. Furthermore, such measures must be made at three levels: against business objectives; against operating system objectives; and against departmental objectives.

EXAMPLE

When millions are invested to introduce a new generation of computing hardware and software, a SBU general manager wants to know how this is helping to achieve her strategic objective of gaining three points of market share. With respect to the operating system, she also wants to know how this investment will speed time-to-market and reduce total cost-of-goods-sold. Key departmental managers, too, want answers to more parochial questions. What impact will the new computing technology have on computer-aided design, on computer-aided manufacturing, on computer-integrated manufacturing, on inventory reduction, on management information for decision support, and on transaction processing?

These executives and managers want and need answers that are precise, clear and reliable about return on investment. They also want unambiguous answers about accountability. And they want to know when they should consider modifying the strategy and action programme in order to take corrective action, and what specific actions to take.

When one considers realistically what is possible today in measuring cause–effect relationships in complex systems, results (alas) fall far short of meeting managers' wants and needs. There are three reasons for this. First, no one today knows how to measure precisely and clearly the impact of changes on the performance of an operating system — even when the change involves only a single element in the system. On the one hand, the interactive dynamics among the many variables in any operating system are extraordinarily complex; on the other hand, the state-of-the-art in measurement techniques is still quite primitive. Current efforts to measure the impact on operating system performance yield, at best, results that are impressionistic and often somewhat ambiguous. Consider the following examples.

EXAMPLE

In the classic Hawthorne experiments,[12] the Western Electric Company wanted initially to measure the impact on productivity of changes in illumination levels. A number of attempts to measure the effect on employee output of changing illumination yielded a consistent result. No matter whether the lighting level was increased or decreased, output continued to improve.

One early conclusion drawn was 'that light is only one, and apparently a minor, factor among many which affect employee output'. Another conclusion was that 'there were so many factors affecting the reactions of the workers that it was hopeless to expect to evaluate the effect of any single one of them.'

Later experiments revealed the existence of a subtle and complex web of personal, social, and informal organizational forces that affected system performance. These studies later formed one of the seminal cornerstones of a new discipline, organizational behaviour.

EXAMPLE

One of the world's largest food-processing companies was pursuing a strategy aimed at becoming the lowest cost producer to improve its competitive advantage in an intensely competitive marketplace. To achieve cost-reduction objectives for the operating system, each department was instructed to set its own cost-reduction objectives.

The Purchasing Department acted to meet its objective by introducing a plastic bottle as a substitute for the much more costly glass bottle used for the company's most popular, highest-volume product. This was done with careful attention to packaging requirements and specifications.

EXAMPLE continued

The new plastic bottle was introduced on the high-speed filling lines in Manufacturing with disastrous consequences. Output dropped abruptly from 400 bottles per minute to 40. Purchasing did not realize that the high temperatures of the sauce filling the bottle would cause a plastic bottle to react differently from a glass bottle. What promised to be a major contribution to lowered costs, in practice actually increased costs.

EXAMPLE

To implement a productivity improvement strategy, the management of one of the largest British tobacco companies decided to invest more than £20 million in a new generation of cigarette-making machinery. The new equipment not only operated at twice the speed of existing machinery, but also combined into one continuous operation, the two separate functions of making and packaging. The basis for management's approval of this large investment was an expectation that at least a two-fold improvement in productivity would result in a near-term payback.

After the new machines were installed and operating, the actual resultant productivity gain proved to be less than 5 per cent. Dismayed by this result, management acted to identify the underlying causes for the disappointing outcome. The answers that were uncovered proved both simple and complex. The simple cause for the meagre productivity gains was a large increase in machine downtime on the new equipment − downtime that was almost four times as costly in terms of lost production as downtime on the old machines.

But the factors that created this greatly increased downtime were multiple and complex. A major factor was that the business had fundamentally changed during the two years that elapsed between the initial capital budget request submitted for the new equipment, and its eventual installation. The justification for the capital budget request was written when the business consisted primarily of one very successful brand of cigarettes and two minor brands.

During the two years in question, the marketing strategy changed in order to target a number of special consumer 'niches' with specially designed brands. Each of these new brands had unique 'constructions' (e.g., tobacco blends, cigarette diameters and lengths, filters, etc.).

EXAMPLE continued

As a consequence, the nature of operations changed from long production runs of a few brands to short runs of many brands, each requiring a changeover of the equipment to accommodate the different constructions. These frequent changeovers created much downtime.

Another major cause of downtime was the existence of many restrictive practices that had developed over a decade in management's relationship with the union. In the cigarette business, a strategic imperative is the need to keep the shelves of retail outlets continuously stocked with the company's brands. This is because of the high cost of recapturing lost customers who switch brands when their preferred brand is unavailable and their taste buds adjust to substitute brands.

The strategic need to maintain an uninterrupted flow of cigarettes to customers caused the company to concede to the union's every demand. A shutdown or even a slowdown of production by union action was unthinkable. All this led to the institutionalization of a substantial number of restrictive practices, many of which contributed to machine downtime.

Finally, the greater complexity of the new equipment and their sophisticated electronic controls made the machines much more vulnerable to shutdowns. The company's failure to provide specialized training to operatives and maintenance mechanics in recognition of this fact, resulted in more downtime.

These three examples have in common the introduction into complex operating systems, of single-factor changes aimed at improving operating effectiveness and productivity. In each instance, certain gains were anticipated. But in all three cases, the actual gains realized were far different from those projected because a number of other unforeseen factors intervened. The hard truth is that at our current state of knowledge, we don't know how to measure precisely and unarguably, the impact of single-factor changes on complex operating systems.

A second factor that further complicates and contributes to the ambiguity of measuring performance in operating systems is that a major determinant in assessing performance is outside the system and beyond the reach of its management. This judge of performance is the buyer or user of the system's output. No matter how effectively the operating system functions, if buyers won't purchase or users won't use the system's output, the performance of the system can only be considered unsatisfactory. Thus the ultimate measure of any operating system's performance lies in its marketplace. When the system supports an SBU, that marketplace is outside the firm. When the system is focused on a support function within an organization (e.g., Human Resources, Finance, Maintenance, etc.), its marketplace is its internal clients.

Flaws in traditional measures

There is a third reason for the gap between management's need for precision and clarity in measuring system performance and anyone's ability to meet this need. All known approaches to measurement are flawed and often misconstrued by management. For example, almost every attempt to measure the performance of single elements within organizations, in actuality measures much more than it was intended to measure. Consider efforts to measure the performance of individuals within organizations. Even when the individual's job has a high degree of autonomy and independence, efforts to measure that person's performance encompass many other factors.

EXAMPLE

A job with a high degree of autonomy common to many organizations is a salesperson calling on prospective customers within a territory remote from the organization's offices. Clearly, that salesperson's performance depends heavily on personal initiative, judgement, energy, application, knowledge of products and customers, and persuasiveness. These factors are all directly associated with the individual. But in addition, the salesperson's performance is also affected significantly by a number of other factors that are related to the operating system of which s/he is a part. These 'external' factors include: how the salesperson's territory is defined; how the salesperson is compensated; how the salesperson is managed; how the salesperson was trained; the quality of the product or service itself; and how effectively the product or service is supported in terms of advertising, promotion, merchandising, and after-sales service. Thus, when the measure of a salesperson's performance is the extent to which sales goals are met, the salesperson who exceeds the goals reflects *both* high-level individual performance and high-level performance of the entire operating system of which s/he is a part.

Another flaw in many known performance measures is that the very act of applying a measure influences the outcome — sometimes in unintended, often unproductive ways.

EXAMPLE

The compensation system for senior-level managers in a large North American durable goods manufacturing firm consisted of two components – one fixed and the other variable. Because it was the intent of the compensation system to motivate good performance, a high-level performer could increase his/her fixed salary by as much as 100 per cent. The primary indicator of individual performance was improvements in return on assets measured at the close of each year. It was not unusual in this company for SBU general managers to exert every effort at year end to reduce inventory of finished goods as much as possible. Some of these executives achieved dramatic results (which were reflected in fat year-end bonuses) by emptying the finished goods warehouses. They accomplished this by loading finished products onto leased trucks, railcars and aeroplanes at year end, with instructions for these same vehicles to return for unloading on the first working day of the new year!

Another illustration of flaws in traditional approaches to performance measurement can be found in efforts to apply standards or goals to the quantity or quality of work output. What was intended as a benchmark often becomes, in practice, a constraint. Both work standards and goals are frequently translated into quotas or ceilings, to be exceeded by employees only at the risk of censure and sanctions imposed by their fellow employees and unions.

To date, all attempts to model complex systems so as to take into account subtle interrelationships and cross-impacts among variables, have involved unrealistic assumptions and substantial simplification. Thus, these models have limited usefulness in predicting the impact on system performance of changes in some elements.

What, then, can be done to resolve the measurement dilemma? Management want and need ways to measure with some precision the impact on overall operating system performance of changes introduced by the operating plan intended to achieve strategic outcomes. Yet, our current state of knowledge about how to accomplish this can at best yield only somewhat ambiguous impressions. Despite the reality of this dilemma, we must nevertheless find ways to track improvement of system performance, however imprecise these may be.

A Practical Approach to Measuring Performance Improvement in Operating Systems

A practical approach to measuring performance improvement in operating systems, for a start, requires an understanding of the dilemma posed above and an acknowledgement that it cannot be resolved entirely to management's satisfaction. This means that management at the outset must recognize the current limitations of measuring performance and cause—effect relationships in operating systems. They must therefore be willing to settle for something less than precise attribution of gains resulting from specific changes.

When management approach the question of measurement, they are most likely to make some headway when their outlook is based on the following three premises. First, it's unrealistic to expect precise answers to the question, 'If we make this change to the operating system, what gains can we anticipate in system performance?' Second, because of the current limitations in the state-of-the-art of measurement, we must be willing to settle for best efforts, even when these provide us with answers that are only suggestive. Third, best efforts at measuring the impact of changes on system performance mean a good deal of trial and error, before we can expect to come up with measures that tell us something useful.

Two factors help to lessen the intensity of the measurement dilemma. Measurement for the purpose of monitoring and tracking operating plan implementation, means measuring *improvement* in system performance, not absolute levels of performance. Reliable answers are more readily achieved in assessing improvement or change, than in measuring absolutes. This is because a reasonably accurate assessment of improvement can be achieved by applying the same measures before and after a change to the system. Although the measures themselves may be flawed, when applied consistently over time, the resulting trend will have more validity than the measures themselves.

The other offset to the measurement dilemma is that the usefulness and effectiveness of performance measures can be improved over time by trial and error. Seldom have I seen any planning group getting their performance measures 'right' from the start. Typically the measures adopted at the outset evolve and change with experience. Often the measures in use at the end of the first year of plan execution are quite different from the ones applied at the outset of implementation.

A Tailored Measurement Package

In my experience, there are two basic requirements for a realistic, practical approach to measuring any performance improvement in an operating system resulting from the implementation of an operating plan. One requirement is that a *package* of *different types* of measures be used, rather than attempting to focus on a single measure or even a group of the same kind of measures. When several different types of measures are applied and a clear pattern of improvement can be discerned from all or even most of them, one can be confident that the improvement is indeed real. This is because a consistent picture stemming from a multi-dimensional approach is more reliable than a similar picture derived from only one type of measure. Cumulative evidence of improvement drawn from a variety of different perspectives strengthens validity.

The other requirement is that the measurement package not be standardized, but rather tailored to and derived from the specific operating plan. Many managements make the error of trying to apply the same standard set of measures to many different operating systems. They do this because they believe they can develop comparative performance data and league tables just as for football and baseball teams. There is a fundamental flaw in this approach. Teams in a particular sport are identically structured and are pursuing an identical objective. This is not true of the different operating systems in a company.

Each operating system not only has unique characteristics, but is likely to be pursuing a strategy different from the others. When a measurement package is intended to provide feedback to a management group about how effectively they are implementing an operating plan, that package must reflect the objectives and strategies of that particular plan.

EXAMPLE

One SBU in a large US corporation manufactures and sells differential axles to automobile and truck manufacturers. There are three separate plants in this SBU. One of these is a relatively old unionized plant in the north producing large forgings. Another much larger plant, also located in the north and unionized, produces gears and other machined parts, some from the forgings supplied by the first plant. The third plant is new, non-union, and located in the south. There, finished axles are assembled from the components supplied by the other two plants.

137

EXAMPLE continued

The operating plans for these three plants have little in common. The plan for the forging plant addresses a serious productivity problem caused by union-imposed restrictive practices coupled with antiquated, unreliable equipment. The plan for the machining plant is aimed at sorting out unreliable delivery performance caused by quality problems and faulty planning and scheduling. The plan for the new non-union assembly plant focuses on making a success of an experiment with employee involvement and gains-sharing. Clearly, the measurement packages developed to track the implementation of these three operating plans are as different as the plans themselves. Each measurement package employs indexes that reflect the unique focus of each plan.

The tailored measurement package required to track operating plan implementation is developed by the planning group once they have completed the action programme for each strategy (Chapter 10). This package should contain four or five types of measures.

Global measures

One kind of measure is 'global' encompassing total system performance. When an operating system supports an SBU, some examples of global measures are: net sales revenues divided by total employees or by total person-hours worked; net sales revenues divided by total payroll cost; value-added sales revenues divided by total payroll cost; net sales revenues divided by total cost of labour and materials. When the operating system centres on a function that provides services within an organization, examples of global measures are more likely to focus on units rather than on revenues: net units processed divided by total person-hours worked; or net units of output (provided to 'client' departments) divided by total person-hours worked. Clearly these global measures are crude and impressionistic when applied over time to detect any improvement trends. They reveal nothing of cause—effect relationships within the operating system. Their only virtue is that they reflect gross changes in overall system performance.

Strategic performance gap (SPG)

Another kind of measure, based on a global measure, is focused on the identification of any Strategic Performance Gap (SPG) that may exist between the level of system performance required to meet strategic business objectives and the current level of performance. In Figure 12, the global measure of operating system performance used by this large manufacturer of durable goods was net sales revenues divided by the cost of goods sold plus depreciation. This ratio was computed over a five-year historical period and plotted on a trend chart. A least squares analysis converted the actual trend into a straight line whose slope represented the actual historical track record of performance improvement.

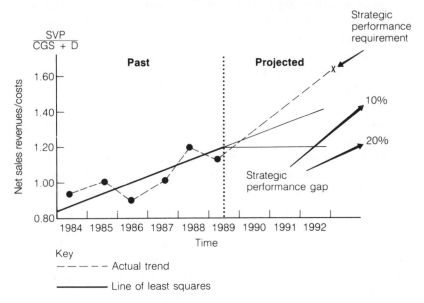

Figure 12   The performance gap.

From an analysis of the business strategy and operating plan and their objectives, a strategically required performance level was projected for the time when operating plan implementation would be complete. This required level of system performance was then compared with the current performance level. The required level was also compared with the projected level assuming continuation of the historical track record trend to the time when plan implementation would be complete. In Figure 12, if this assumption were valid, the SPG would be about 10 per cent. A more conservative assessment, based on an assumption that no further system performance would occur beyond today's level, would set the SPG at 20 per cent. Once the SPG has been established, measures can be applied to track progress towards closing the gap.

139

Targeted measures

A third type of measure essential for inclusion in the tailored measurement package is a set of targeted measures for each strategy in the operating plan. A targeted measure is the opposite of a global measure. While a global measure encompasses the performance of the operating system as a whole, a targeted measure focuses on a specific element (or group of elements) within that system. On the one hand, a global measure provides clues about improvement in total system performance with no detail about what specific aspects of the system may be causing this improvement. A targeted measure, on the other hand, illuminates improvements only in certain elements of the operating system. These improvements may or may not be related to any improved performance of the overall system. Thus, global and targeted measures are complementary. Only by combining information from both can one gain a more complete and valid understanding of how and why an operating system's performance may be improving.

A planning group can begin to develop a set of targeted measures for each strategy in an operating plan by reviewing the detailed action programmes. They ask, 'If we are successful in implementing these action programmes, where are we most likely to see any gains; what tangible improvements can we expect to be visible?' A list of possible answers to this question is generated. Typical answers may be: lower inventories, reduced staffing, more effective equipment utilization, reduced cycle times, an increase in repeat customers, a lower rate of personnel absences and turnover, fewer engineering changes, etc.

Once a planning group have identified the areas where expected gains will occur, it is usually a straightforward task to specify the particular targeted measure that will track the achievement of each expected gain. Many of these measures are already in use in the organization. The development of targeted measures for a tailored measurement package is more likely to require a selection from measures already in use, than the invention of entirely new measures.

Detailed action programmes

Another kind of measure for tracking operating plan implementation is the detailed action programmes themselves. A well developed action programme specifies tasks, 'deliverables', start and completion dates and accountabilities (Chapter 10). When actual accomplishment is monitored systematically against an action programme (see final section of this

140

chapter), management have an index of implementation performance, quite different and apart from the three types of measures already discussed. Performance against the action programme is a qualitative indicator of how reliably the commitments to perform planned work are actually met. The three measures already discussed are indicators of the extent to which the expected results from that work are actually being realized.

Global and targeted measures, the SPG and the detailed action programmes all belong in a tailored measurement package, as complementary means for tracking implementation progress. No one of these types of measures is sufficient. But collectively, they can provide management with meaningful evidence of accomplishment.

Cost systems and work standards

A fifth type of measure might also be added to the measurement package under certain conditions. This kind of measure is work and cost standards and variances. Tracking variances from both work and cost standards can add yet another dimension of measurement provided that the standards have some validity and have been well maintained. Unfortunately many firms which invest substantial funds and effort to install standard cost systems and work standards, fail to continue to invest in maintaining these standards over time. As changes are made in equipment, technology, materials, processes and procedures, and jobs, standards must continuously be updated and revised. Unless this occurs rigorously, once-valid standards can become meaningless, and thus useless as an instrument for measuring implementation progress.

Developing the Measurement Package

In developing the tailored package of measures for their operating plan, a planning group need to consider how they want to use these measures. My previous discussion focused on using the measurement package to track implementation progress. But there is another, quite different purpose to which the measurement package can also be directed. Measures can be a powerful force to enhance employee motivation.

Should management explicitly decide to utilize measures for motivational purposes in addition to monitoring, the measures must meet a set of special criteria. For measures to be used effectively for motivational purposes, they must be easy to understand and have a high degree of credibility. When measures are so complex that a sophisticated mathematician is required to translate them, or when measures depend on information widely perceived as unreliable or subject to manipulation, employees will simply view the information generated as suspect, and not take it seriously. Furthermore, the feedback from measures intended to heighten motivation must be more frequent than that used for monitoring implementation progress. Feedback for motivation should occur at one- to two-month intervals, while feedback for monitoring need occur only once every three to four months.

No operating plan can be considered complete without an initially defined tailored measurement package designed to track implementation progress. A planning group develop this package after they complete the detailed action programmes. They are aware that their initial effort is only a first cut, and that the quality and utility of the measures will be improved over time with systematic trial-and-error application. They decide at the outset whether they want to use the measurement package only for monitoring, or whether they want in addition to use it to enhance employee motivation.

To develop the measurement package, a planning group first review the action programmes and identify the source of expected gains. Next, they estimate the probable magnitude of these gains after the first and then the second year of plan implementation. These gains are defined in both particular terms (e.g., reductions in cycle time, cost, waste, etc.; improvements in responsiveness to customers, quality of service, etc.) and more systemic or global terms (e.g., sales per employee; value-added divided by labour and material costs).

Once a planning group have projected expected gains and identified their sources, they can select the global and targeted measures, and calculate the SPG. They determine a base period for computing the gains, set up trend charts for each measure, and determine the frequency for measurement. In Appendix 8 are some examples of tailored measurement packages.

The following questions can serve as a useful checklist against which to test an initially formulated tailored measurement package (those with an asterisk are especially important when measures are intended to enhance employee motivation):

- To what extent are these measures focusing on the areas that really count in achieving the desired changes to the operating system?
- How practical are these measures in terms of the relationship between the effort required (to apply the measures) and their expected value?

- To what extent have we taken all the key factors into account; are the measures sufficiently comprehensive?
- Will we be able to get performance feedback soon enough to help us make any needed mid-course corrections?
- To what extent do the numbers truly reflect what is within the control of management?
- To what extent are these measures easy to understand?*
- How credible will these measures be? Can we live with the margin for error?*
- How generally accepted will the measures and numbers be?*

Ensuring Congruence with Budgets and Rewards

In Chapters 2 and 4, I suggest that plans are most likely to be implemented successfully when there is a close alignment and linkage among the business strategy, operating plan and such established organizational systems as budgets and rewards. When budgets and/or the reward system are incongruent with the plans management are trying to execute, management's focus can be diverted or undermined with disastrous consequences to plan implementation. How can congruence be achieved?

Traditional budgets are developed annually by each department or function in isolation, most typically by extrapolating from past years' budgets and by larding in some contingency factors. There is seldom any explicit effort made to relate the budget to the demands made on each department by the strategies being pursued. When the approved budget fails to contain sufficient funds to meet the requirements of the business strategy and operating plan, there is conflict. In most organizations, the budget is a more deeply entrenched and respected system than strategic and operational planning. Thus it is the budget that prevails and the plan that suffers.

Since 1979, a few pioneering corporations[13] have begun to address this problem by radically changing their budget development process so as to base budgets on strategy. A strategy-based budget is derived directly from (and is therefore generated *after* and is tightly linked to) an SBU's strategic and operating plans and their action programmes. A strategy-based budget therefore avoids any possible conflict or incongruence with the business strategy and operating plan.

Strategy-based budgets

In a strategy-based budgeting process, each function or department carries out the following four steps.

1 It determines the *minimum* budget required for it to continue its existence. This 'readiness to serve' or baseline budget funds the minimum level of basic capabilities it must have in place in order to respond to the specific demands of *any* strategy. For example, a marketing department will require a basic, minimum-level market research capability in order to support any marketing strategy, whatever its particular demands.

2 It considers step-by-step the specific action programmes supporting the business strategy and the operating plan, and forecasts any demand each action step might make on the department for work. For each step, estimates are made for associated expense by line item, and any revenue that might accrue to the department.

3 For each strategy and its associated action programme, the department totals the expenses required by line item and offsets these with any anticipated revenues. The resulting net expense is then layered over and above its 'readiness to serve' baseline budget.

4 The budget from 3 (above) is converted into a line-item budget.

The resultant budget is thus organized around and derived from strategies and action steps rather than around line items extrapolated from past history with added contingencies. A strategy-based budget is a critical element of strategic management because it is a powerful force for integrating strategies and their implementation into the day-to-day operating fabric of an organization.

Reward system

Another important element of strategic management is the reward system. In order to ensure that strategy implementation is integrated into day-to-day operations, it is crucial that the reward system be congruent with the strategies being implemented. That is, implementation success or failure should trigger direct positive or negative consequences in both individual compensation and non-monetary rewards. For example, for each manager:

- *Merit increases* are geared directly to the extent to which s/he exceeds, meets or slips commitments regarding action plan implementation. Superior performance is recognized by merit increases that are substantially greater (or more frequent) than those awarded for average performance (e.g., 15−25 per cent per annum of base compensation vs 5−7 per cent). Any individual job or work objectives are derived from current strategies and action programmes; performance against these serves as the basis for merit increases.

- *Executive bonuses* are awarded on the basis of the extent to which specific strategic or tactical goals are achieved, exceeded or missed. Multiple (weighted) criteria can be specified annually, some geared to company-wide performance goals and uniform for everyone, and others geared to specific SBU goals and differentiated from one SBU to another.
- *Stock option* awards are based on performance against individual job or work objectives and/or commitments met in implementing strategies.
- *Advancement within the organization* is based on performance on strategy implementation.

Thus, by gearing personal rewards directly to the achievement of strategic objectives, everyone affected has a strong personal stake in achieving successful implementation outcomes.

Establishing a Systematic Monitoring/Plan Updating Process

Once a planning group have defined an initial measurement package tailored to track operating plan implementation and possibly to stimulate employee motivation, they must then put in place a process for systematically monitoring implementation progress and updating and modifying the plan when necessary. Such a process is a crucial element of strategic management.

No plan, no matter how soundly conceived, can be expected to remain valid for more than six to eight months after it was initially developed. Unanticipated events, both within the operating system and in the business environment outside the organization, can call for changes in strategy. Initial assumptions thought to be key to successful plan implementation may later prove to be invalid. Initially identified obstacles to achieving the required changes in the operating system may later prove to be more formidable than originally anticipated. Any of these developments may require substantial revisions to the initial plan. Management need both mechanisms and a process enabling them, throughout the period required to implement the plan, to identify the need to modify or revector the plan, and then to make the necessary changes.

In order for management to recognize any need to modify an operating plan, they require three things:

(a)   a clear delineation of the course they intend to take;
(b)   signals to inform them when they are no longer on that course; and
(c)   regular opportunities to take stock of the situation and decide what action to take.

Management's course during implementation is defined by the operating plan's objectives and detailed action programmes. The measurement package is a major generator of signals to inform management whether or not they are maintaining that course.

Signal generators

A planning group can implant three other signal generators in the operating plan to complement their measurement package. One of these is a set of explicit assumptions made by the planning group (and documented in the plan) on which successful plan implementation depends. These assumptions identify forces usually outside the operating system, that are beyond management's ability to control or influence, and that are necessary to support the execution of the action programmes. Here are two examples of such assumptions: 'The demands on the operating system required by the business strategy will remain essentially unchanged for the implementation period,' 'There will be no major economic recession.'

Another signal generator is a summary of the major qualitative changes that are expected to occur to the operating system once the operating plan is successfully implemented. Based on a review of the detailed action programmes, the planning group answer the question (and document in the plan in broad-brush stroke terms), 'If we do all these things as we intend, what major changes will become apparent in the operating system? What will be different from today in the way we operate? How will the *outcomes* of successful action programme implementation be manifested in changes of operating system behaviour?'

A third signal generator is an analysis and assessment of the risk that management will fail to implement the operating plan as intended. The planning group first identify and note any major obstacles to implementation success. Next, they assess the risk of failure by recording their consensus in answering the questions shown in Table 3.

Table 3   Risk assessment

Source of risk	Levels of risk		
	Low	Medium	High
1 Defined obstacles to successful implementation	(the greater the obstacles, the higher the risk)		
2 Probability that assumptions will hold throughout the implementation period	(the higher the probability, the lower the risk)		
3 Ambitiousness of plan objectives	(the more ambitious the objectives, the higher the risk)		
4 Management's familiarity with the strategies in the operating plan	(the more familiar the strategies, the lower the risk)		
5 Management's past track record in successfully changing the operating system	(the more successful the track record, the lower the risk)		
6 Depth of management	(the more thinly stretched is management, the higher the risk)		
7 Overall management competence	(the more competent in dealing effectively with unanticipated events, the lower the risk)		
8 Organizational responsiveness	(the more responsive the organization will be to management's demands, the lower the risk)		
9 Conflict with established culture	(the greater the conflict with the existing culture, the higher the risk)		
Overall risk assessment	*Low*	*Medium*	*High*

Progress Reviews

With their implementation course defined, and four signal generators implanted in the operating plan, management need to complete their monitoring/updating process by establishing regular opportunities to take stock of implementation progress and accomplishment and decide on any appropriate actions. A useful component of an effective monitoring/ updating process is the designation of a strategy manager/coordinator for each strategy in the operating plan. This person's role is to provide leadership, facilitation support, coordination and monitoring for all the tasks specified in the action programme for a single strategy. In my experience the time demand for this part-time role ranges typically from four to eight hours per week.

There are two ways in which management can take stock of their implementation process. The most effective method is a formal, full-day, progress review working session scheduled every three or four months during the implementation period. Essential participants in this session are the SBU (or functional) head, each of the strategy managers/ coordinators and each of the managers designated as accountable for the action steps in the detailed action programmes. In addition the Sponsor may want to attend, along with other members of the planning group.

Each full-day progress review session begins with a report on the status of plan implementation. Each strategy is reviewed in turn. The strategy manager/coordinator may want to make an overview/summary statement about the progress being made in implementing the strategy for which s/he is responsible. Then each manager accountable for an action step or task, reports on the following:

1 progress achieved in completing the task;
2 any problems and obstacles encountered;
3 any changes required to the timetable;
4 any suggested additional tasks that should be undertaken;
5 any comments about interdependencies with other action steps in the plan;
6 any learnings that should be shared.

After each accountable manager reports on his/her action step, the entire group may question and discuss the information presented. The time required for status reporting and discussion may take from three to five hours.

Next on the agenda of this formal progress review session is a presentation and discussion of the trend charts for each of the measures in the tailored measurement package. The group consider the charts individually and collectively to identify any meaningful patterns in the data. Afterwards the group should question whether each measure should continue to be applied, dropped or revised. Any specific accomplishments are noted.

In the final section of the agenda, the group first review the other signal generators in the plan. Are the initially stated assumptions still holding? Is there any evidence that the anticipated qualitative changes to the operating system are beginning to happen? What is their current assessment of risk; has it changed from the initial assessment, and if so, why?

Depending on what the group learn from their review of implementation status, action step by action step, and from the measures of outcome and other signal generators, they consider whether or not any changes are required to the plan. Does the timetable need to be modified? Are any additional action steps required? Is there a need to change priorities and/or direction? It is in these formal progress reviews that the operating plan is updated and modified.

In addition to the full-day progress reviews, there is another less formal opportunity for monitoring implementation progress. This is the SBU (or function) Head's regular staff meetings. Whether these occur weekly, bi-weekly or monthly, one to two hours should be allocated in one monthly meeting for progress reporting on the more critical action steps. This reporting can be done either by the manager directly accountable for that step or by the strategy manager/coordinator.

This process of systematically reviewing implementation progress accomplishes two things. When the directly accountable managers meet together to consider achievements against plan and the information presented by the signal generators, implementation momentum is sustained and fuelled. Communications flow freely about accomplishments and problems. Initial commitment and enthusiasm are refreshed and reinforced. This process also enables the group to maintain a relevant, vital plan by continuously injecting updates, additions and modifications. In this way the operating plan remains a vital mechanism for managing the enterprise.

12

Sustaining Momentum and Focus

When an operating plan is developed using the approach and process described in Chapters 5–11, by the time the planning group have completed formulating the plan, its members have generated high levels of enthusiasm and commitment to carry out the plan. Typically, this initially strong energy and determination remains a powerful force driving implementation during the first two to three months. Equally characteristic, however, other forces in the operating system soon act to weaken and dissipate this early enthusiasm and commitment.

At least during the initial stage of implementation, the work required to carry out the action programmes all too often is layered over and above the regular activities of managers. When day-to-day crises and pressures crowd in on a manager's time, it is the work on the operating plan that is most often deferred. Despite initially good intentions, commitments are postponed and timetables slip. Unless concrete steps are taken to address this conflict between the need to execute a plan on the one hand, and business-as-usual on the other, yet another example of implementation failure has occurred.

The critical issue I address in this chapter is how to sustain the focus and momentum of the entire management group throughout the period required to implement an operating plan — a period that may exceed two to three years. The participative process involving a planning group is powerfully effective in establishing among its members, a strong foundation of understanding and credibility regarding the operating plan coupled with the commitment to carrying it out. How can this initially powerful driving force for implementation not only be sustained but also extended to include all the other managers and supervisors in the operating system who did not participate in the planning group?

Management have only five means available for taking positive action to sustain over a several-year period both focus on the action programme and implementation momentum. I discuss each of these in the remainder of this chapter.

Early Successful Accomplishments

If an operating plan can achieve some visible early successes (within the first three to five months of implementation), these will help to sustain enthusiasm and commitment to continued implementation. It is imperative that these early successes be widely publicized, noting explicitly that they are a direct result of implementing the operating plan. When employees in an operating system see clear evidence that constructive achievements are indeed being accomplished by carrying out the action programme, the credibility and perceived value of the plan is widely reinforced and enhanced. This response helps to sustain focus, commitment and momentum in implementing the plan.

A planning group should not rely on serendipity to achieve early implementation successes. Rather, they should make a deliberate effort when developing the action programmes, to ensure that some early successes will indeed occur.

EXAMPLE

The Instrument Systems Division of a multi-divisional supplier of components to the worldwide aerospace industry had been averaging about one hundred engineering change notices (ECN) each month. These ECNs were both costly and disruptive to operations. Each ECN required some major or minor design change to the products, most of which were already being manufactured. Thus, a typical ECN required changes in manufacturing processes and methods, and often created considerable obsolete work-in-process and scrap.

When the planning group were formulating action programmes for a strategy aimed at cost reduction, they saw an opportunity for an early success. They included an action step establishing a cross-functional screening procedure for ECNs. Within the first three months of implementing the operating plan, the monthly average of ECNs dropped from 100 to 32, and continued to remain at this reduced level. The impact on operations and on costs was highly visible and dramatic. It served to reassure everyone in the operating system that management's efforts in developing and implementing their new operating plan were truly worthwhile.

EXAMPLE

The Finance function of one of the world's largest computer manufacturers formulated an operating plan aimed both at enhancing their effectiveness in providing business decision support to line managers in the sales organization, and at improving their own productivity in fulfilling their fiduciary responsibilities.

One strategy in their operating plan focused on improving the processes, systems and tools used for conducting business support and fiduciary functions. The planning group deliberately incorporated into the action programme for this strategy, an action step intended to achieve some 'quick wins' aimed at solving several nagging problems that impacted a large number of Finance staff.

An early success was the development of software that linked two accounting/control systems. This eliminated the need for considerable manual work. This achievement freed many Finance staff from a considerable amount of laborious drudgery, enabling them to apply more time to their business decision support activities. This single early successful outcome of implementing the operating plan stimulated broad support within the Finance operating system for continued longer-term efforts to carry out the operating plan.

Broadening the Base of Management and Employee Involvement

Another means that management can employ to sustain focus and momentum in implementing an operating plan, is to broaden the base of management and employee involvement in the action programmes. A fundamental concept on which this book's approach to making strategy happen is based, is the need to involve in formulating a plan, the managers and supervisors who must carry it out. Participation in plan formulation ensures that they understand it, believe in it and are committed to carrying it out. This concept underlies the notion of forming a planning group to develop the operating plan.

But even when a planning group consists of as many as 30 members, these managers and supervisors often represent only a fraction of the total management group in the operating system. Seldom do any non-managerial employees participate in a planning group. Typically, at the outset of implementation, the planning group represent only a core

152

group of managers and supervisors with the understanding and determination necessary to drive the implementation process successfully. To sustain implementation focus and momentum, it is critical that this core group be substantially extended.

I have found that certain action steps present the best opportunities for involving more managers, supervisors and employees, beyond those in the planning group. In Chapter 10, I note that action programmes tend to be comprised of a number of action steps of widely varying scope. While some action steps may be narrowly focused involving only a few people and requiring only a few weeks to execute, other more macro steps are programmatic, requiring many people working months to complete. In the initial formulation of the action programmes, the scope of the macro steps is outlined broadly, with only a core group of key managers identified who will be accountable and involved.

At the outset of implementation, a more detailed plan needs to be developed for executing each macro action step. The core group of managers initially designated can invite other managers, supervisors and employees in the operating system who did not participate in the planning group, to become involved in the work. The process of formulating a detailed implementation plan for a macro action step enables these newly recruited managers, supervisors and employees to develop a level of understanding, belief and commitment approaching that of the members of the planning group. These outlooks and feelings are sustained when the new recruits become involved in the specific tasks required to execute the macro action steps. Through such a process, the core group of 20 to 30 managers in a planning group can be extended to twice to three times the original number directly involved in plan implementation.

A Systematic Communications Programme

Another means of achieving broad employee involvement is a systematic communications programme designed to support the implementation of the operating plan. Such a programme should be designed to maximize the involvement of everyone in the operating system. The objectives of a communications programme are threefold:

(a) to inform everyone about the operating plan — its objectives, strategies, action programmes and supporting rationale;
(b) to provide opportunities for employees to question and discuss the plan; and
(c) to provide regular feedback about implementation progress and accomplishments.

Immediately upon completion of an operating plan, every manager and supervisor in the operating system is provided with a copy of the plan, showing the detailed action programme, measurement package and other signal generators. Management then conduct a series of meetings intended to familiarize everyone in the operating system with the plan. These meetings are designed to answer the following questions:

- What customer needs are being addressed by this plan?
- What is the plan intended to achieve and why?
- How and when do we plan to achieve the plan's objectives?
- What resources will be applied?
- What major changes in system and personal behaviour will be required?
- How will we be tracking and measuring progress?

It is desirable to prepare a handout that contains a condensed version of the essential highlights of the plan, for distribution to everyone at the initial implementation launch meetings. A handout that has proven especially effective is a plastic-coated card about 25 × 35 centimetres printed on both sides. On one side is a summary of the operating plan's overall objectives and supporting rationale. On the other side each strategy is listed along with its concrete objectives, and the measures to be used for tracking progress.´

In these initial meetings, time is allocated for employees' questions and discussion. Managers announce that after employees have had time to understand the operating plan, any suggestions regarding implementation are welcomed. Specific suggestions should be offered to immediate supervisors, who then forward the ideas to the appropriate accountable manager for the relevant action step.

When an operating plan addresses an operating system that is part of a larger organization, copies of the full plan or the specially prepared condensed summary are distributed to selected executives and managers outside the operating system along with a cover note explaining why they have been sent the document. The criteria for this special distribution include:

(a) internal 'clients' for the operating system's products and/or services;
(b) other groups in the organization which may have a stake in the outcome of successful plan implementation;
(c) other functions whose support will be needed during plan implementation; and
(d) other interested parties such as senior executives.

These initial distributions of the plan and initial implementation launch meetings are supplemented and reinforced with articles and news briefs inserted into existing in-house media, such as company magazines and newsletters. Consideration might be given to a special newsletter devoted entirely to the plan, mailed to employees' homes.

Once implementation is under way, an effective communications programme provides regular, systematic feedback on implementation progress. Information is given about both specific accomplishments and progress against objectives. A variety of media are employed.

Managers can meet with employees every three or four months immediately after the full-day progress review sessions described in Chapter 11. The information to be communicated is determined at the close of each of these review sessions, and distributed in written form to all managers and supervisors in the operating system. This information can include the more meaningful trend charts that track progress both against global and targeted measures, and against closing the Strategic Performance Gap (see Chapter 11). Some companies I have worked with post and update monthly copies of these trend charts in highly visible locations such as the entrance to the company cafeteria. Progress feedback meetings provide time for questions, discussion and suggestions.

Feedback on implementation progress and accomplishments is also provided in other company media. Articles in company publications, special newsletters and displays in building lobbies and corridors are all useful means for continuously reinforcing everyone's awareness and involvement in the implementation process. If the organization has professional communications expertise in its advertising or public affairs departments, these resources should be brought to bear on the systematic communications programme to ensure that it is designed and executed as effectively as possible.

Establishing and Maintaining a Climate of Accountability

A fourth means of sustaining implementation focus and momentum, is the establishment and maintenance of a climate of accountability. This means creating and sustaining the belief among all managers and supervisors accountable for meeting their action programme commitments, that implementing the operating plan carries a high priority and that commitments are being taken very seriously. This belief translates into an awareness that there are consequences when commitments are

155

either met or missed. These consequences are experienced most directly in how the reward system is applied. Those who exceed or meet commitments are recognized by substantially greater pay increases, bonuses and organizational advancement than those who fail to meet their commitments.

A key figure in creating and maintaining this climate of accountability is the Sponsor of the operating plan (Chapter 5, pp. 58−61). When the Sponsor is uninvolved in the planning group, s/he reviews and validates the operating plan before implementation is launched. Typically, this involves reviewing the proposed plan document and interrogating and interacting with a subset of the planning group until the Sponsor becomes comfortable with what is being proposed. In some instances, the Sponsor may require some modification to the plan before approving it. When the Sponsor is dealing with several proposed operating plans, and there are insufficient resources to fund every one of the proposed strategies, s/he must decide which ones to fund, which to cut back and which to defer. Such decisions require trade-off judgements. In my experience, when the Sponsor is concerned with only a single proposed plan, any modification seldom touches on fundamental issues. Typically, changes involve steps added to action programmes, alterations to task assignments and modifications to timetables. How readily and enthusiastically a Sponsor approves a proposed plan, especially its objectives, sends an initial signal of support and importance.

Once implementation begins, the Sponsor's continued behaviour substantially influences subsequent progress. An early opportunity for the Sponsor to signal the importance of carrying out the operating plan occurs when dealing with any issues raised by a planning group. Often in the course of their work, a planning group identify issues in the organization beyond their ability to influence, which require resolution for plan implementation to be successful. These issues typically fall into areas of company policy, practice and priorities. They are presented to the Sponsor for action.

EXAMPLE

One of the largest metal can manufacturers in North America, headquartered on the east coast, formed a planning group to develop an operating plan to improve productivity in the company's largest and poorest-performing plant. This west coast facility, located in one of the company's fastest-growing markets, had a long track record of being out of control. Both plant management and local union leaders had

---

EXAMPLE continued

been intimidated by a relatively small group of minority-group employees who were dealing in drugs and were dominating work practices. The planning group formulated a 2.5–3 year plan for management to regain control of the plant and improve productivity. They identified several issues for resolution by their Sponsor, a western regional vice president who did not participate in the planning group.

One issue had to do with the company's practice in developing its managers. For many years, Corporate Human Resources had been using this west coast plant as a critical proving ground for promising young managers on their way up the corporate ladder. Typically, a manager would be posted to a second- or third-level position in this plant for 14–20 months. If this manager survived the experience with no disastrous consequences, he would be moved to a higher-level position in another of the company's 150 facilities. Thus, there was little continuity or stability in this west coast plant's management. The planning group believed that this practice needed to be suspended long enough to permit the current management group to implement their proposed operating plan.

Another issue concerned an accounting practice. A key element in one of the proposed strategies was an investment in more equipment maintenance to redress long neglect of the can-making machinery in this highly mechanized plant. But current accounting practice dictated that quarterly budgets for maintenance must be proportional to plant throughput. In this highly seasonal business, the effect of this accounting practice was that in peak season months there would be ample funds for maintenance, but no opportunity to apply these because the plant was operating at full tilt. In the troughs of seasonal swings, when the equipment was available for maintenance, there was too little in the budget to achieve what was needed. Clearly, said the planning group, it was imperative to be exempted from this accounting practice, at least for a long enough period to catch up with needed maintenance.

A third issue for the Sponsor had to do with the company's inventory policy. The planning group reasoned that they could succeed in regaining control of the plant only with active support from the local union leadership. Their plan laid out a credible approach based on union-management cooperation. But to interest the union in working with management on this strategy, the planning group believed they needed to offer some initial inducement. The inducement was an offer to reduce the depth of workforce reductions in the seasonal troughs. To make such an offer, however, required that the company approve higher levels of inventory.

In this example, how the Sponsor acted to deal with these three issues so critical to the successful execution of the operating plan, sent a resounding signal to the plant's management about how seriously senior management were valuing and supporting their efforts.

Another way in which a Sponsor establishes a climate supportive to successful implementation is how s/he deals with extraordinary requests from the planning group for resources to improve the operating system's readiness to implement any improvement plan. Sometimes in formulating an operating plan, a planning group identify in their analysis of organizational readiness (Chapter 8, pp. 92–6), some serious deficiencies which could impair the organization's ability to implement *any* improvement strategy. For example, the information system is in shambles and requires substantial upgrading. Or first-line supervisors are weak and demotivated, in need of substantial attention and training. Addressing issues such as these often requires substantial investment. When a Sponsor is responsive to such needs, it becomes immediately clear to everyone that implementing the operating plan is a matter of the highest priority.

After the first two to four months of implementation, the Sponsor remains key to sustaining a climate of accountability. Appearances at quarterly full-day progress reviews signal continued interest and concern. Most important, however, is how the Sponsor deals with individual rewards and recognition. When these appear to bear little relationship to actual performance against the promises contained in the operating plan, the message is clear. Plan implementation is no longer important enough to warrant the efforts required. On the other hand, when the Sponsor substantially differentiates rewards and recognition between superior and average performing managers, and when these performance assessments relate directly to meeting action programme commitments, the message is equally clear. Plan implementation must continue to receive the highest priority.

Although a Sponsor's behaviour is a critical factor in sustaining implementation focus and momentum, all too often I find that Sponsors have difficulty in providing optimum, continuing support for the two to three years required to implement an operating plan. With the best of initial intentions, Sponsors often become distracted by other pressing demands and fail to provide the necessary ongoing, sustained attention to operating-plan implementation. Although the Sponsor is potentially one of the most powerful forces for keeping plan implementation on track, in my experience I have found that it is unwise to rely too heavily on this person. It is a rare Sponsor who is able to behave appropriately and consistently throughout the implementation period.

Establishing Strategically-Driven Performance Measures at Departmental Level

The most promising and powerful means for sustaining implementation focus and momentum is the institution of a set of performance measures in each department of the operating system that are explicitly aligned with and supportive of the strategies in the operating plan.

In Chapter 11, the measurements discussed with reference to the tailored measurement package are all directed to an entire operating system. These systemic measures are necessary for tracking implementation progress for an operating plan. But such measures are insufficient for relating each department's performance to the requirements of the operating plan. This is because there is a fundamental difference between the nature of business strategy and day-to-day operations. Business strategy is integrated and systemic. Its performance demands are on the organization as a whole and its operating systems. But day-to-day activities in any organization are fragmented, occurring primarily within each function or department. How, then, can an integrated effort be mobilized to achieve strategic objectives when most people's attention is focused by parochial departmental or functional priorities on achieving local agendas? These priorities and agendas tend to be formed and maintained by an accumulated collection of local measures instituted over time. These measures provide the day-to-day indices by which each department's managers and employees both determine the objectives and priorities for allocating personal time and effort, and assess the adequacy of both individual and departmental performance.

Consider four examples where top management depended on traditional, in-place measures to control strategy implementation, with resultant disappointing outcomes.

EXAMPLE

A large electronic company is pursuing a strategy to become one of the lowest-cost producers in the industry. Manufacturing set a goal for its US purchasing organization to lower purchase prices. Interpreting this to mean cost per component, Purchasing increased sourcing efforts in the Far East, buying in large bulk quantities (shipped by sea) to achieve volume discounts. Lead times were lengthened by six weeks. While the components were in transit, Production Planning reduced product requirements. At the same time, the assembly department modified the production process to include the automatic insertion of

---

159

EXAMPLE continued

components. Purchasing reported 'progress' against its cost goals. However, true costs surfaced in the factory. Longer lead times and lower production requirements caused manufacturing inventory to increase, with no improvement in throughput. Furthermore, delivery by Purchasing of components in bulk forced Manufacturing to postpone its implementation of automatic insertion (because this required components to be supplied on reels rather than in bulk). The apparent reductions in purchase cost were more than offset by rising inventory costs and continued manual insertion costs, with a net rise in total costs.

EXAMPLE

Two strategic business objectives of one company in a competitive hi-tech industry are to become both highly profitable and the product leader. To measure the performance of its R&D organization, management established as a strategic indicator of product leadership, the number of new products developed. An internal review revealed that in a sample of 20 new product introductions, 80 per cent missed first customer ship date − most by over a month. The resultant impact on Manufacturing was high costs to support these new products. This is because 30 per cent of the company's overhead costs stem from the logistical costs associated with change, material and load balancing transactions (engineering change orders, cancellations, etc.). Thus, performance against one strategic objective of product leadership was achieved at the expense of the other equally important objective of higher profitability.

EXAMPLE

To improve the timeliness of its services, a computer service bureau tried to reduce lead times for offering its message service to customers. It established a policy and implemented a process to accept verbal telephone orders. At first the new process appeared successful in reducing lead times to less than 24 hours. Later, an internal audit found a 70 per cent error rate in order entry. Some errors were caught by a manual, time-consuming reconciliation process. However, over 30 per cent of customers continued to dispute their bills and refused to pay. While timeliness did improve, quality and cost performances deteriorated dramatically.

EXAMPLE

As part of its strategy to lower total costs to support more competitive pricing, a company producing electronic components for the automobile industry is in the process of instituting 'just-in-time' (JIT) for Manufacturing. During the transition to JIT, the production process was streamlined to the point where it made no sense to start an assembly unless all the parts were available to complete it. An operational review of the Production Control function revealed that 'all is going well' because materials needed for production were in the 90 per cent range. Yet, production flow lines were frequently idle, waiting for material. Production Control was using a misleading measure that represented the *percentage of line items available*, believing that success meant having 98 per cent of the required parts available for production. However, if 2 per cent of the parts are missing, nothing can be built. Thus, Production Control's measure could show apparent improvement with no actual improvement in production throughput. This measure was irrelevant both to the 'delivery' and 'quality' dimension of performance as defined by Production Control's customer. The measure was therefore useless for monitoring the implementation of the JIT strategy.

What do these examples have in common? In every case, there was a disconnect between the intended strategy and what actually happened. Often the achievement of the desired strategic objective was subverted. The measurements used were inappropriate (i.e., not closely aligned) to the strategy being implemented. Action programmes were designed and implemented before appropriate performance criteria and measurements were instituted. Interdepartmental and intradepartmental goals were not integrated so that strategic objectives could be achieved.

Yet, performance measurement can be the most powerful single means to ensure implementation success. When these measures are customer-driven, strategically-aligned and integrated and instituted both at operating system and departmental levels, they provide both management and employees continuous signals as to what is most important in day-to-day work, and where efforts must be directed. Furthermore, strategically-driven departmental measures provide every employee with the means to identify with the success of the strategy, and track his/her contributions to its achievement. Thus, these measures can serve both as an informational and motivational tool. Unlike management attention and behaviour which can so readily be distracted and inconsistent, an 'appropriate' set of integrated measures at departmental level can provide a steadfast, continuous and highly visible signal to everyone engaged in making strategy happen.

Unfortunately, few organizations have yet to come anywhere close to establishing a strategically-driven performance measurement system that extends down to departmental level. Instead, most organizations have in place a hodge-podge collection of measures which have evolved over time. These may or may not be relevant to the current strategies being pursued. Some may even undermine successful strategy implementation because they focus attention at working levels on the 'wrong' issues. An example is forcing an undue emphasis on cost reduction when the crucial strategic requirement is speeding throughput time to improve time-to-market for new product introductions.

My colleagues and I have recently developed and implemented an operating control system called SMART (Strategic Measures, Analysis and Reporting Technique).[14] The SMART approach provides:

(a) a hierarchical framework for organizing measures;
(b) a method of tailoring and defining measures for each department; and
(c) a consistent reporting format.

SMART ensures alignment between day-to-day departmental measures and longer-term strategic objectives.

Linking strategic with operational objectives

A strategically-driven and aligned measurement system, SMART can be viewed as a three-tiered hierarchy of measures, working from the top→down (see Figure 13). Any operating system is generally too large and complex to serve as a practical link between the strategic business objectives of an SBU and the many functions and departments that comprise its operating system. We have found it useful to 'unbundle' the macro operating system into a number of Business Operating Systems (BOS). A BOS is related to a single strategy in the operating plan rather than the operating system as a whole. A BOS encompasses the primary flow of work and supporting functions, people, technology, work flows, policies and procedures, etc., required to execute a single strategy. For instance, a strategy to 'reduce time-to-market for new products' is supported by all the functions, people, etc., required to understand and meet a market need by bringing appropriate products to market. Another strategy (and BOS), might encompass the order-to-delivery cycle for existing products.

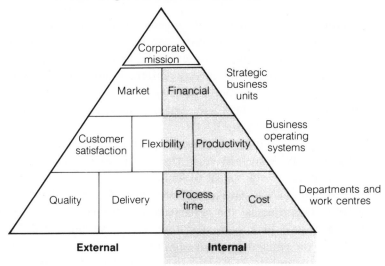

Figure 13   The SMART performance pyramid.

A BOS's objectives (and measures) can be defined in terms of:

(a)   customer satisfaction;
(b)   flexibility; and
(c)   productivity.

At the BOS level, customer satisfaction means how customer expectations are managed and met. Flexibility addresses the responsiveness of the BOS to the demands of a single strategy in the operating plan. Productivity refers to how resources (including time) are managed within the BOS.

But the operating system and its component BOS's systemic objectives and measures are insufficiently specific, detailed and close to managers, supervisors and employees at departmental level where most of the work in strategy implementation actually gets done. SMART addresses this issue by providing a tightly aligned linkage between measurements tailored to fit each local department, and the BOS's systemic measures. There are only four key departmental performance criteria for which specific local measures need to be determined: quality, delivery, process time, and cost.[15]

The bottom tier of the SMART pyramid holds the key to strategically relevant performance. High-*quality* products or services and regular on-time *delivery* are the paths to customer satisfaction. The combination of externally-driven *delivery* (when the customer wants to take delivery) and internally-driven *process time* (how to reduce the time to make it) defines flexibility.[16] Productivity goals can be achieved by reducing both *process time* and *cost*.

163

Quality is more than conformance to specifications; it should be defined by customers. Customers can be internal to the organization as well as in the marketplace. For example, an electronics firm might select a variety of *quality* measures for its different departments: 'plug and play' achieved in Final Assembly; parts per thousand accepted for purchased parts; and the percentage with which product features and performance targets are being met by R&D.

Similarly, each function should regard *delivery* as a goal to be met in ways uniquely defined by each department. *Delivery* relates to quantity and timeliness − the extent to which correct amounts are delivered on time both to internal and external customers. Consider these examples for different departments: the percentage of finished products delivered to the warehouse in a particular time frame vs the master production schedule; the percentage of all component parts delivered to an assembly line at the appropriate time; the percentage of engineering change orders completed on time; and the percentage of customer orders 'delivered' through credit checking vs the standard time for this activity.

Process time is the time required by a department to complete work from the time it is requested. Here are some examples: production throughput time from the request for an item; setup time in a work cell; time to design a product; and time to process an invoice.

In SMART, *cost* is not the traditional accounting cost for products, with all of the added allocations. Rather, it is any extra or excess costs incurred to satisfy the *quality* and *delivery* required by customers. In SMART, *costs* are considered to be 'waste'. The basis for this distinction is that costs are necessary, but waste is not. The best that any person or organizational unit can do is to minimize waste. Consider these examples: yield losses and subsequent rework in Manufacturing; rejected materials in Purchasing; inventory costs (if there is a belief in zero inventories); and the total costs associated with engineering changes (because the design should have been right in the first place).

Developing department measures

When an operating system and its component BOS's strive to improve responsiveness to customer requirements, not only must each department operate effectively, but also even more importantly, they must work together in an integrated way. It is important to understand the nature of this integration and, more specifically, how this impacts the four performance criteria at the base of the measurement pyramid (Figure 13). Departmental performance measures are either:

(a) *internal* (*process time* and *cost*), which are not directly perceived by the customer, but critical to the department's ultimate success; or
(b) *external* (*quality* and *delivery*), which are important to the department's customer.

For each department to maintain its strategic focus, each of the four performance criteria must be translated into a few selected local measures that describe how each criterion is manifested in that department.

In Figure 14 is shown the relationship between internal and external measures as the work flows from one department to the next. In this example, Department B measures its own internal performance with regard to *process time* and *cost*. Department C helps develop the measures and subsequent reporting on Department B's *quality* and *delivery* performance. It is the customer departments' perspective which counts when designing, developing and applying these external measures.

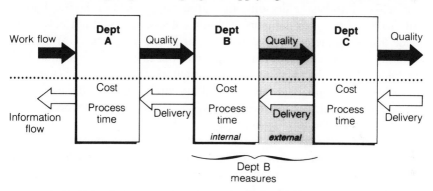

Figure 14 Internal and external departmental measures.

To ensure that each department's measures are in tune with those of the BOS and the business as a whole, it is essential to:

(a) understand workflow relationships;
(b) distinguish external from internal measures for each department; and
(c) involve both 'upstream' and 'downstream' suppliers and customers in specifying departmental measures.

The specification of local measures should start with the department closest to the external customer and work back the workflow towards the creation of the product or service. It then becomes possible to introduce a dynamic up-dating capability into the measurement system to ensure that it is tracking both current strategies and customers' expectations.

A department's performance measures take on a new look when supplier and customer work jointly to determine what specifically will be measured. For example, consider the new product introduction process in a BOS. Design Engineering is measured for *quality* of design and on-time *delivery* to their customer (Manufacturing). They are also measured against their own goals on the *cost* of their designs and *process time* to create them. Similarly, a support group such as Purchasing is now measured on percentage good parts procured and percentage materials available on time to Design Engineering or Manufacturing. Internal measures focus on targets for reducing lead times and lowering cost of ownership by customers.

When supplier and customer departments work together to develop performance measures for the supplier department, it becomes possible to resolve the often difficult issues of how to deal with any trade-off questions among the four performance criteria. Consider our earlier example of Purchasing deciding to source components in the Far East in bulk to lower cost per component. Such a decision would not have been made had Manufacturing been able to clarify two key issues: (a) the true meaning of cost is not cost per component, but rather total cost including inventories; and (b) plans to implement automatic insertion changes the specifications of the materials supplied by Purchasing. Once these issues are understood, the *quality* measure (components on reels) becomes more significant than the *cost* measure used by Purchasing.

There are immediate, additional benefits from applying this process, beyond those already noted. In our experience, even before data are collected and reported on the newly established measures, performance tends to improve because there is a clearer focus and improved real time dialogue between customer and supplier. With a focus on defining realistic expectations of *quality* and *delivery*, the two departments begin to understand one another's capabilities and problems. Each department can then take mutually beneficial actions of accommodation. Typically those actions involve two-way communication of specific information on a routine basis.

Priorities, performance comparisons and a new scorecard

The four major departmental performance criteria may not necessarily be equally important at any point in time. Furthermore, they will probably change over time. Shifts in strategy and management's focus on a particular area for improvement will cause changes in the relative importance of criteria. This requires emphasizing one criterion above the rest. This can be achieved by applying a weighting factor. For example, *delivery* may be critical for a time, but as the competitive environment changes, *quality* or *cost* may become a decisive factor with customers. There is also the possibility that there may be a significant gap between actual and desired performance for one criterion. Emphasis on that particular criterion will help close the gap; once closed, the emphasis will be shifted. For example, when *process time* is successfully reduced in a JIT project, the emphasis may then shift to *quality*. By emphasizing the criterion important to a change in strategy and/or an opportunity for improvement, the measurement system is sensitive to a business's performance requirements oriented to future needs. Priorities are thus communicated continuously to everyone in the BOS.

When there is a number of operating facilities to be managed, prioritizing takes on special significance. Measurement priorities can be structured to reflect each facility's mission or charter for a given period. If, for example, an operating plan requires one facility to introduce new products from R and D, process *quality* at the department level and customer satisfaction at the BOS level may be paramount. In a high-volume facility, where productivity may be paramount, the *cost* performance at departmental level may be the key requirement.

Tailoring and prioritizing measures may create a problem for senior executives who want to compare the performance of a group of departments or facilities with league tables. With SMART it is not possible to compare departmental performance against any measure. It is, however, possible to compare their rates of improvement.

SMART is designed to encourage continuous performance improvement. When emphasis is placed on improvement trends, rather than on performance to goals, the motivational impact is more likely to be that of positive reinforcement and encouragement.

In order for any measurement scheme to be effective, it is essential that senior managers have a succinct and visually simple control document. Figure 15 portrays a simple report format that can be used to summarize performance for a particular BOS or department over a period of time. Senior executives and managers can track performance of all the BOSs and their departments, relative to how effectively they are contributing to strategy implementation. Such control charts are dynamic. They are not a snapshot of performance frozen in time, but rather show how each BOS and its departments are moving through time.

167

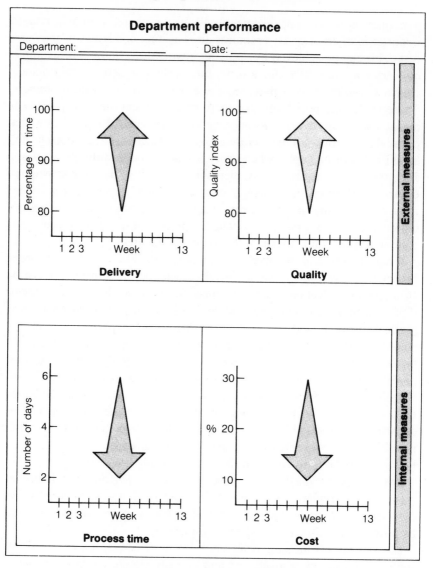

Figure 15   Sample report format.

SMART performance measures can thus be organized in an easy to interpret format. *Internal measures* (*process time* and *cost*) focus each department on doing more with less time and money. Improvement is then measured like golf, where improvement is going the same distance with less effort (less swings, less walking off course, and therefore less time). For these internal measures, a downward trend is desirable.

External measures (*quality* and *delivery*) are the opposite: the higher the score the better.

For a BOS, *cost* and *process time* measurements are derived by adding up all departments' performance against these criteria. *Quality* and *delivery* for a BOS are determined by the end customer and are therefore reflected in the external measures of the department that is furthest 'downstream', closest to the outside customer. For each department, *cost* is defined in terms of waste, *process time* refers to only the portion within the department's control and *quality* and *delivery* measures are defined from the viewpoint of the department's immediate internal customer(s). When departmental and BOS scorecards are given high visibility in each department in the BOS, this feedback and communication of implementation progress will enhance greatly the likelihood that an operating system and SBU will successfully achieve their strategic objectives.

The SMART approach promotes learning throughout the organization by continuously relating departmental actions and measures to strategic objectives. A major change occurs when SMART is instituted. Focus shifts from managing by the numbers at the top, to continuous improvement in activities at the BOS and departmental level. Thinking in systemic terms emphasizes the need to work across functional boundaries. With a horizontal perspective on the workflows that deliver value to the customer, management are encouraged to think and act more integratively, both with respect to functions and with respect to issues of balancing customer satisfaction, flexibility and productivity. As this perspective takes hold, it supplants the more traditional view of organizations as a collection of separate functions.

With SMART, it becomes possible to translate strategic business objectives, both financial and non-financial, into operational measures that are readily understandable within the operating system. This facilitates an early warning system for corrective action when strategies change. The same level of attention typically devoted to reporting company financial performance to the stockholder, is now focused on the needs of customers as well.

Thus, the SMART approach has the potential for being the most powerful force for sustaining the focus and momentum required to implement strategies fully. Sensitive to both internal strategic initiatives and shifts in customer expectations, SMART provides executives with a dynamic process aimed at continuous improvement.

13

Making Strategy Happen

In order for the management of an enterprise successfully to implement their intended business strategies and achieve their desired strategic objectives, they need to recognize at the outset the full implications for their organization. In most instances, implementing a strategy means instituting a number of substantial and durable changes in the operating system(s) that support each Strategic Business Unit. Achieving such changes depends on changing how functions and departments work and interact, and how the people in these departments behave.

Changing the workings of an operating system and the behaviour of people in it, is best accomplished first by carefully formulating a plan for change, and then implementing that plan in a systematic and rigorous way. An appropriate vehicle is an operating plan developed explicitly to improve an operating system's performance in support of an SBU's business strategy.

To set the stage for formulating an operating plan, decisions must first be made about its scope and Sponsor. Determining the scope of an operating plan means defining the operating system to be addressed by the plan. Every business engaged in by an organization depends on one or more operating systems both for its conduct and for execution of whatever strategies its management want to pursue. Defining scope is a matter of reaching a workable compromise among three different considerations:

(a) ensuring that the operating system contains all the key functions, workflows, supporting systems, policies, practices and procedures necessary to conduct the business;

(b) avoiding definitions of operating system scope so all-encompassing and complex as to be unmanageable in terms of effectively formulating and executing an operating plan; and

(c) ensuring that significant differences of place, technology, culture and other organizational characteristics within an operating system can be effectively addressed.

The Role of the Sponsor

The designated Sponsor for an operating plan is the senior executive who is accountable for the SBU's business strategy and/or is best positioned to address and deal with any interfunctional, policy and practice issues that may require resolution so as to facilitate implementation of the operating plan. The Sponsor sets the stage for operating plan formulation by validating the definition of scope and formation of the planning group, and legitimizing the participation of the members. The Sponsor may or may not be an actual member of the planning group. If not, the Sponsor reviews and validates or modifies the plan proposed by the planning group.

Once plan implementation begins, the Sponsor plays a key role in helping to ensure that focus and momentum are sustained. S/he is the driving force to resolve any issues identified by the planning group, to provide necessary resources and to create and maintain a climate of accountability for the managers and supervisors who are key to implementing the operating plan. This means ensuring that individual and group rewards and recognition are based on how well managers perform in meeting the commitments of the operating plan. Significant differences in performance are reflected by significant differences in rewards and recognition.

The Planning Group

The operating plan is formulated by a group of managers and supervisors in the operating system, each selected because s/he:

(a) is responsible for an important function or department in that system;
(b) is capable of contributing significant inputs to the formulation of the plan; and
(c) will be in a critical position to implement the plan.

The planning group include representatives of all key functions and departments in the operating system, and may be comprised of from 20 to 30 members. This group work together using a structured process to achieve consensus on the key elements of the plan.

It is important that such a large group of managers and supervisors be directly involved in developing an operating plan for two quite different reasons. One is that they are able to bring to bear both breadth and depth of knowledge and expertise about the dynamics of the operating system on the one hand, and the operational detail of the system's elements on the other. When all the significant functions and departments of an operating system are represented, and these managers work together for sustained periods of time, the application of their collective knowledge results in the development of a superior-quality, highly credible operating plan. A high level of plan quality is assured because the requisite knowledge is applied to identifying the highest leverage opportunity targets to be addressed by the plan, assessing realistically the organization's capabilities for plan implementation, selecting appropriate strategies and formulating workable action programmes.

The other reason for employing a large number of managers and supervisors in a planning group is to establish a strong foundation for successful implementation of the operating plan. A high-quality, credible plan is necessary but not sufficient to assure that desired outcomes will actually be achieved. Also required is a substantial majority of the management group with full understanding of the plan and its implications coupled with a strong commitment to carrying it out. The most effective way to develop this understanding and commitment is through direct involvement in formulating the plan. By such participation, each manager not only comes to understand the plan's details and underlying rationale, but also develops a feeling of ownership in the plan. It is this feeling that fuels commitment. In larger organizations, the up to 30 managers and supervisors involved in the planning group may not constitute a substantial majority of the entire management group in the operating system. They do, however, constitute a core which can subsequently be expanded to a majority when implementation begins.

Planning Group Working Sessions

A planning group is usually able to formulate a proposed operating plan by employing a structured process in a series of three full-group working sessions held off-site, away from distractions and interruptions: two two-day sessions followed by a one-day session, each spaced about four to five weeks apart (see Figures 16 – 19).[17] These sessions are most productive when they are conducted by someone outside the operating system who is objective and who is skilled in leading group processes. Such a person might come from a corporate function such as Strategic Planning, Human Resources or Organizational Development, or might be an outside consultant.

Before the planning group meet for their first two-day, off-site working session, two critical inputs are prepared by whomever is conducting the plan formulation process (Figure 16). One of these inputs is a 'straw-person' situation characterization. This is a proposed description of the operating system that lays out in detail:

(a)   the context in which the system operates;
(b)   its component elements; and
(c)   how the system works in its entirety.

This proposed situation characterization is developed from research based on interviews with representative managers, supervisors and employees in the operating system, and on study of relevant documentation about system performance. The other input is an analysis of demands made on the operating system by the business strategy, and how these demands are being perceived (in terms of priorities) by operating system managers.

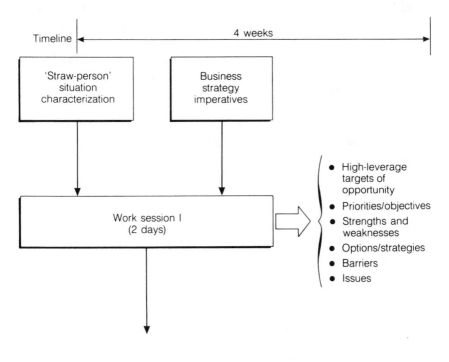

Figure 16   Operating plan formulation process I.

Initial working session

In their initial working session, the planning group devote most if not all of the first day to reviewing, modifying and validating the 'straw-person' situation characterization. As they do this, they also generate a list of potential high-leverage targets of opportunity. These targets are elements or aspects of the operating system which if changed appropriately and successfully, will exert a powerful force toward improving system performance in ways that better support the business strategy. Immediately prior to adjournment on the first day, each member of the planning group individually and anonymously completes an Organization and Management Readiness Assessment (OMRA) questionnaire so that their responses can be analyzed (by whomever is conducting this session) before they resume work on the second day.

The second day of the planning group's initial work session typically begins by developing consensus on what priorities should be driving the operating system in its support of the business strategy. The input on business strategy imperatives prepared prior to the working session, is used to stimulate this discussion. Once the planning group determine the priorities for the operating system, these are applied to prioritize the list of possible high-leverage targets of opportunity generated on the previous day. The highest priority targets are then translated into objectives for the operating plan.

Most if not all of the rest of the morning of the second day is devoted to assessing the capabilities of the operating system's management and organization to implement successfully any strategies for improving system performance. The group first identify, analyze and critique recent efforts to improve system performance. From this review of past system change efforts, the group try to draw some general conclusions that could illuminate future improvement efforts. Next the group discuss the feedback from their responses to the OMRA questionnaire, and try to conclude what these data suggest about overall implementation readiness and specific areas of strength and weakness. Finally, the group generate a specific list of operating system strengths and weaknesses in the context of achieving substantial improvements in system performance.

Once the planning group have completed the three pieces of analysis outlined above, they devote the remaining time on the second day of their initial working session to selecting the strategy options on which to base their operating plan. By limiting their choice to fewer than six options, they ensure that the operating plan will be sharply focused. The strategies selected collectively describe the general routes by which the management group intend to achieve the strategic objectives set for the operating plan.

Prior to adjournment, the planning group identify any major obstacles that might interfere with implementing the strategies selected. For each strategy in the operating plan, a small task group are formed from volunteers. Their task is to develop in the four- to five-week interval prior to the planning group's second working session (Figure 17), a proposed sequence of action steps specifying the work required to implement each strategy.

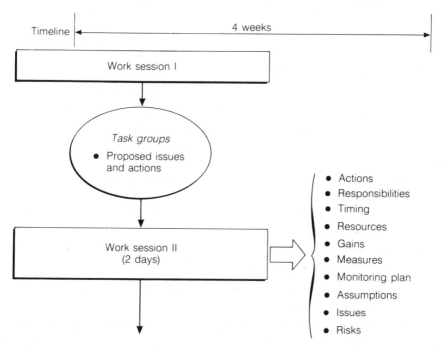

Figure 17   Operating plan formulation process II.

Second working session

About two-thirds to three-quarters of the second off-site working session is devoted to formulating detailed action programmes. Using the task groups' proposals as a point of departure, the planning group agree on a specification of the tasks, deliverables, and possible management assignments for the work required to implement each strategy in the operating plan. Then the planning group develop a tailored measurement package and a plan for monitoring so that implementation progress can be tracked for the operating plan as a whole and for each of its component strategies. Finally, the planning group complete the plan by:

(a)   identifying any issues they want help from the Sponsor to resolve;

(b)   noting the assumptions they are making that must hold in order for the plan to be implemented successfully;

(c)   summarizing how the operating system will change qualitatively after successful implementation of the plan; and

(d)   identifying and assessing the sources and extent of risk that the plan will not be implemented successfully.

Final working session

In the three- to four-week interval prior to the planning group's final working session (Figure 18), three tasks are completed by small groups formed for this purpose. One task is the preparation of a draft Proposed Operating Plan Summary document containing the elements of the plan already agreed to by the planning group in their two working sessions. A second task is the estimation of the expected quantifiable gains that will be achieved upon successful completion of the action programmes, along with the Strategic Performance Gap, an element of the tailored measurement package. The third task is the completion of the action programmes. This involves an integration of the separate action programmes for each strategy into a master action programme that:

(a)   takes into account of any interdependencies among tasks;

(b)   specifies start and completion dates for each action step; and

(c)   specifies managerial accountability for each task along with assignment of other appropriate managers and supervisors to work on task completion.

In their final one-day working session (Figure 18), the planning group review and complete the draft Proposed Operating Plan Summary document. The group make any necessary additions and modifications to the plan/document to ensure that it:

(a)   accurately reflects the group's consensus;

(b)   communicates clearly the plan and its supporting rationale; and

(c)   is complete from the standpoint of providing a clear roadmap for implementation along with the bases for signalling when implementation is off course, requiring modification to the plan.

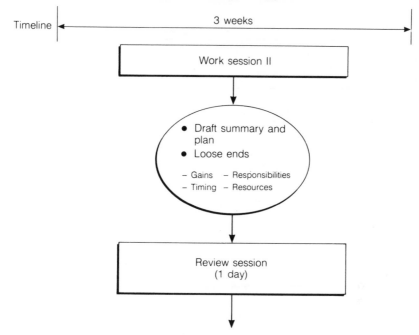

Figure 18   Operating plan formulation process III.

Sponsor approval and plan implementation launch

After this final working session, a final revised plan document is prepared and submitted to the Sponsor for review and validation or modification (Figure 19). This step is necessary only when the Sponsor has not participated directly in the planning group. Once validated, the operating plan document and/or condensed summary is distributed to managers and supervisors in the operating system and to selected executives and managers elsewhere in the corporation when appropriate. Meetings are held with all employees in the operating system to explain the plan, its requirements for changes in behaviour, and its rationale. Implementation begins.

Implementing the Operating Plan

In the initial stages of implementation, the Sponsor begins work to resolve any issues critical to implementation success. Managers accountable for macro action steps recruit additional managers and supervisors from within the operating system and involve them in

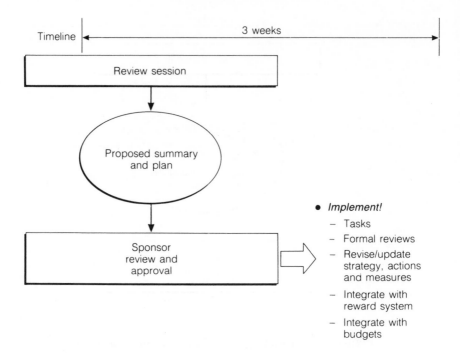

Figure 19   Operating plan formulation process IV.

formulating more detailed action plans to implement these more programme-like steps. By increasing the number of managers and supervisors involved in specifying the work required to carry out these larger elements of the operating plan, the original core group of managers and supervisors with the requisite understanding and commitment to carry out the plan successfully, is substantially extended. A majority of the management group now believe in the plan and are determined to achieve its objectives.

As implementation proceeds, managers key to carrying out the action programmes meet formally for a full day every three or four months to review progress and make any necessary modifications to the plan. Specific accomplishments and trend charts showing changes relative to base period measures are communicated widely throughout the operating system, using a variety of media. Any early successes are given special emphasis. Every month between the formal progress reviews, time is allocated in regular executive staff meetings to review and discuss implementation progress on key action steps.

Supporting Management Trends

This systemic, participative and dynamic approach to formulating and implementing operating plans that are designed explicitly to support business strategy not only makes strategy happen, but also resonates with four significant recent trends in management. Increasingly, senior-level executives have been concerned with how to deal with the problem of organizational fragmentation. Organizations have been growing in size, complexity and dispersion. Few enterprises now conduct only a single business. Most are comprised of several, often quite different businesses, each with its own characteristics, dynamics and demands on the organization. Also, often in response to external forces, the number of specialized organizational functions have proliferated. Each of these tends to develop its own concerns, agendas and priorities. As organizations grow, they often expand geographically with facilities scattered first across a single country and then throughout the globe. With such fragmentation, how does a senior executive get these diverse, often self-interested pieces to play together, especially in the interests of executing a business strategy?

The approach I advocate here provides senior-level general managers with a powerful tool for achieving organizational integration. By addressing strategy implementation as a problem of changing large-system behaviour, and by involving all key functions in that system in formulating how such changes are to be achieved, the resulting approach is integrated. In order to formulate a workable, credible operating plan, a planning group comprised of representatives from many different functions can do their job only by subordinating any parochial interests to the superordinate demands of the business strategy. Few steps in a typical action programme can be completed by a single function working in isolation. Most tasks in action programmes call for interfunctional and interdepartmental teams to work together. As they do this and achieve successful outcomes, typical 'walls' between functions break down. Managers discover the power of interdepartmental collaboration and integration. Repeatedly, I have seen this process ultimately change the culture of organizations with a long history of functional autonomy and parochialism.

Another management trend served well by the approach described in this book, is that more and more top-level executives are strangers to the organizations they are directing. In the past, top executives rose to their positions after a long climb up the management ladder, if not in a single company, then at least in the same industry. By the time an executive

179

had reached a top-level position, he had accumulated a great deal of detailed knowledge about the industry and about his firm. Because he already knew many of the answers, these provided the basis for his decisions.

Today, with far greater executive mobility, a top executive is as likely to have come from another company in another industry as from the same company s/he is now directing. S/he has not had the accumulated experience that provides ready answers when decisions are required. Instead, top executives who are strangers to the businesses they are now conducting must manage by questioning. They need to be skilful in asking appropriate questions so as to bring out the information needed to make effective decisions.

When a Sponsor and/or general manager who is a stranger to the business participates in a planning group, s/he learns a great deal about the details of how the operating system functions. Many such Sponsors and general managers have told me after this experience, that their involvement in the work of the planning group greatly accelerated their learning about the organization. They felt they came to understand things about the operating system within three to four months that would otherwise have taken them over a year to learn. When such a Sponsor is not part of the planning group, the act of reviewing and interrogating a proposed operating plan summary document also provides her/him with a great deal of detailed information about the operating system. This also facilitates the framing of further questions for interrogating the planning group prior to making decisions to validate or modify their proposed plan.

A third management trend relevant to my advocated approach to strategy implementation, is the growing frustration with 'managing by the bottom line'. Increasingly, executives are finding that such bottom-line business performance measures as growth in market share, return on assets and investment and profitability come too late to provide them with tactical guidance in implementing strategies. What they want and need is performance feedback that is continuous and sufficiently targeted so as to suggest when and what kind of mid-course corrections are required in order to achieve desired strategic objectives.

An operating plan of the kind I am advocating contains detailed action programmes coupled to a tailored measurement package, and such off-course warning-signal generators as identified key assumptions, expected operating system changes, implementation obstacles and other sources of risk. When reviewed frequently and systematically, all these indicators provide senior managers with the kind of continuous in-process performance feedback they need to decide whether and what kind of modifications to make to action programmes. This kind of information is far more useful in guiding strategy implementation than more traditional bottom-line measures.

Finally, the past two decades have seen the emergence of middle managers who are better educated and prepared than their predecessors to handle their jobs. This new breed of manager is more demanding, initiating and ready and eager to take on increasing amounts of responsibility and challenge. They are particularly keen to understand the larger context of what they are doing.

Repeatedly, I find that middle managers experience participation in a planning group as especially exhilarating and gratifying. Many tell me that they learn a great deal in the process. They say that for the first time, they understand the business strategy, how the operating system relates to this strategy, and how they can contribute to its successful implementation. Furthermore, their involvement in the planning and implementation process provides opportunities for them to push beyond the boundaries of their defined responsibilities and demonstrate what they can contribute to conducting the business. These opportunities occur in two areas. One is the opportunity to contribute creative inputs and insights both in the course of the planning group's working sessions, and in the various task groups that develop inputs for these sessions. The other opportunity is to demonstrate leadership as a strategy manager/coordinator or as the manager accountable for completing assigned action steps.

In my experience, when the process described in this book for formulating and implementing operating plans is used as a primary means for ensuring successful business strategy execution, management derives three distinct benefits. This process provides a highly relevant, continuous, engaging and significant management-development experience for middle managers and supervisors. It also meets top executive needs for a way to foster organizational integration, for detailed understanding about the operating system, and for an alternative to managing by the bottom-line. Finally and most important, this process provides the means for substantially enhancing the probability that business strategies will indeed achieve their intended outcomes. With this approach, management can truly make strategy happen.

Appendix 1

Sample Operating System Characterization

1 Scope

CMD has been conducting two somewhat different businesses

- *Construction* (new and modification/upgrades) and *Maintenance* (major overhaul/replacements during outage shutdowns):

		CMD workload allocation % (based on labour $)				
		1985	1986	1987	1988	Budget 1989
Construction	Fossil	1.5	4.8	8.4	10.5	20.4
and	Nuclear	58.2	28.2	16.0	11.2	6.8
modification	Bad Creek	3.4	7.7	14.2	22.1	22.8
(Capital $)	Other	3.3	4.7	4.1	3.5	8.0
	Sub Total	66.4	45.4	42.7	47.3	53.0
Maintenance	Fossil	11.1	10.6	11.9	10.5	10.4
(O&M $)	Nuclear	20.6	41.6	41.1	37.7	32.7
	Other	1.9	2.4	4.3	4.5	3.9
	Sub Total	33.6	54.6	57.3	52.7	47.0

Highlights

- Fossil construction/modification workload allocation has increased dramatically.
- Fossil maintenance workload percentage appears to be flat.
- Nuclear construction workload percentage continues its steep decline.
- Nuclear maintenance workload was essentially level 1986–1988, but will decline as responsibilities are reallocated.
- Overall, after the end of nuclear construction in 1985 and with the beginning of Bad Creek, the allocation of work to construction has remained relatively steady through 1988.

After a restructuring at end of 1988, CMD's role in maintenance is primarily that of outage support. NPD and FPD have primary responsibility for day-to-day maintenance (see Figure A1).

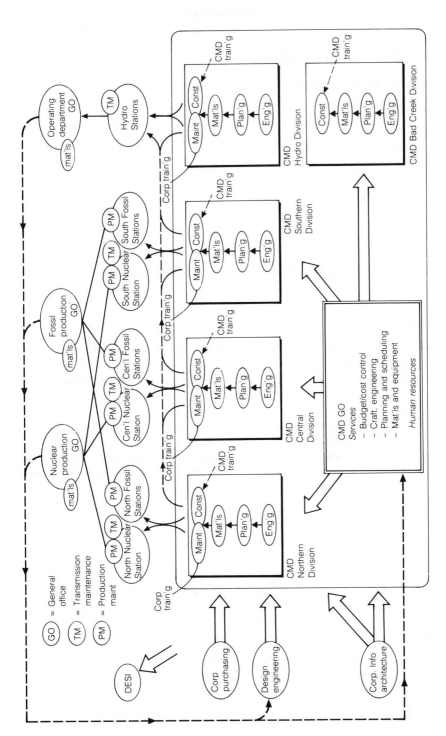

Figure A1 The CMD operating system.

2   Business Context

Electric utility industry

- Size (1987 proj.):

Market segments	Total industry Revenues ($ billions)	%	Unit sales (000 M Kwh)	%
Residential	63.2	41	840	35
Commercial	46.8	30	655	27
Industrial	40.6	26	830	34
Other	.2	3	87	4
Total	155.8		2,412	

Electricity accounts for about one-third of the energy consumed in the US

Growth

- Overall growth 1980 to 1987: revenues, 7.3 per cent; unit sales, 13.5 per cent.
- The ratio of electricity use to GNP rose 50 per cent between 1960 and 1976. It peaked in 1976 and in 1986 (per 1986 data) reached the lowest level since 1971.
- Most of the growth in power demand in recent years has gone to heating and cooling of buildings.
- Gradual introduction of more efficient technologies could lower future electricity growth rates from 2−3 per cent to less than 1 per cent annually.

Structure

- Past/present:
    - vertical monopolies;
    - horizontal (regional) fragmentation;
    - highly regulated at state level.

- Future unbundling distribution, transmission and generation with:
    - distribution as a regulated monopoly;
    - generation (at least new capacity) deregulated and competitive;
    - transmission unclear.
- The nature and pace of structural change is politically sensitive.

Sample Operating System Characterization

Technology: generation/production

- New technologies are not likely to contribute significantly to the US electricity supply short-term (next decade).
- Longer-term, a number of developing electric power generating technologies are beginning to show some promise as future electricity supply options.
- Photovoltaics may show the most promise in the medium term.

Prices

- Since 1970, the average price of electricity has risen more than 50 per cent in real terms, following decades of steady or declining rates. Recently, average industry prices have declined slightly.
- Many utilities' rates are well above (and continuing to grow against) alternative options available to an industrial client (e.g., Canadian power, co-generation).

Capacity

- Although recent demand forecasts predict an upswing in demand growth over the next decade, there remains some excess capacity in most regions of the country, but near shortages elsewhere.
- Few new (base capacity) plants are now being planned.
- Very big seasonal and time-of-day fluctuations in demand.

Financial operating characteristics

- Very high capital intensity.
- Average profit margin: 10.2 per cent (Q2 1988); no company (out of 52) lost money.
- Economies of scale are no longer greater with larger stations.
- Utilities have not yet cut costs as have deregulated industries.

Major industry trends

- Increasing competition.
- Unbundling (separating generation from distribution).
- Restructuring.
- Divergent trends in regulation.
- Market orientation within utilities is widespread and growing.
- Third-party producers are broadening and diversifying the generation base.
- Investor-owned utilities are to a degree losing control of the industry to new producers of power.

- Increasing flexibility in the way electricity is sold (volume, off-peak, quality).
- Changing relationship to the capital markets.
- Some utilities diversifying into non-regulated, non-utility businesses.
- Most new construction in the next decade will be in peaking and co-generation.

Competitive Analysis

- *Utilities are competing with:*

    1 one another;
    2 other types of power producers (including clients); and
    3 other energy supplies (alternative fuel).

- *Factors driving competition are:*

    1 increasing client options;
    2 excess generating capacity;
    3 rate disparities;
    4 shifting regulatory rules;
    5 changing utility cost structure;
    6 new technologies;
    7 entrepreneurial spirit;
    8 market structures;
    9 question of transmission access;
    10 changing Federal energy policy; and
    11 internationalization of marketplace.

- *Bases of competition* (will vary by unbundled segment) are:

    1 price;
    2 distribution channels and ready access;
    3 reliability/service;
    4 quality (e.g., line surges);
    5 product/service customization;
    6 capital; and
    7 emissions.

- *DPC's competitive position is currently strong.*

	DPC	Industry
Earning/share	$4.29	$2.57
Price/earnings	10:1	9:1
Return on equity	13.2%	11.7%

- *DPC is a low-cost builder and supplier of electricity.*
- *DPC is regarded in the industry as one of the best managed, with superior expertise in design, construction and operation.*

3   The Corporate Context

DPC's corporate objectives, strategies and imperatives

- Five-year profit/price objectives:

  1 prices + 5 per cent;
  2 assumed inflation + 15 per cent; therefore
  3 real prices − 10 per cent.

- Profit and price objectives to be achieved by:

  1 off-peak sales (including sales to neighbouring utilities);
  2 improving non-regulated earnings; and
  3 reducing operating costs (limit increases to 4 per cent/year; limit capital to $800 million/year).

- To meet cost objectives, DPC's top management has implemented a programme to identify/eliminate least essential work activities and reduced the workforce.

- Key assumptions:

  − 3 per cent annual inflation over next five years
  − 2.5 per cent client growth rate
  − slower industrial revenue growth

- DPC's top management intend to change the company's culture.

Old	New

− Give best possible service
− Operate efficiently
− Increase revenues through rate
  increases
	− Deliver a quality of service
	  even better than we have had
	  before
	− Think/act like a non-regulated
	  entrepreneur
	− Be client-driven
	− Focus on cost containment/
	  reduction
	− 'One-company concept'

- 'One-company concept' progress has been widely misunderstood.
- DPC as a whole has yet to learn how to operate in a more austere way.
- Current five-year plan has defined budget and financial objectives.
- No explicit strategic plan for DPC as a whole or for most major departments.

DPC's capacity and new construction

- In 1988, 64 per cent of electricity generation is nuclear, 34 per cent fossil and 2 per cent hydro.

- Electricity generated growth rate of 10 per cent/year in 1950s and 1960s has slowed to 2.5 per cent/year growth (current and projected until 2000).
- Some additional peak capability will be required over next ten years.
- No need seen for new baseload until after 2000; no new nuclear plants planned.
- Possible addition of 2−3 new fossil units and 1 new hydro station by 2010.
- Possible new joint venture (fossil) plants.
- Bad Creek will be completed in 1992.
- Next pump storage (Coley Creek), twice the size of Bad Creek, identified; getting licence, but not yet committed.
- Older hydro and fossil stations now being rebuilt rather than phased out.
- Twenty units of combustion turbines needed over the next ten years for peak loads (CMD's role regarding construction/installation is not yet clear).

DPC's maintenance

- Increased $ and effort required to comply with increasingly demanding regulations: environmental, hazardous waste, nuclear and skill qualifications.
- Increasing costs to maintain aging stations.
- Little progress in standardizing equipment-related maintenance procedures; some progress in administrative and programmatic procedures.
- The details of CMD's role in nuclear and fossil maintenance are being defined.

4   CMD's Situation Characterization (11/88)

(Based on interviews conducted in the summer of 1988 by GJH consultants with members of CMD and managers and executives in DPC.)

CMD's role and mission

- CMD is chartered by DPC to provide an in-house construction capability and management skills to build power plants and support facilities.
- CMD provides modification and some maintenance services.

Organizational structure

- GO functional groups interact with three geographical operating divisions, each having a parallel functional structure; Bad Creek construction division.
- CMD divisional characteristics vary significantly.

Sample Operating System Characterization

Characteristic	Northern	Central	Southern	Bad Creek	Hydro
Geographic Scope	> 130 miles to most distant station	70 miles to most distant station	90 miles to most distant station	N/A	180
Stations served Nuclear Fossil Hydro	1 5 9	1 2 10	1 2 8 (+ Bad Creek)	1	26
Staffing (approved 1989)	1045	945	930	757	75
Nuclear station Equipment Cooling Years on Stream	Westinghouse Lake 7	Westinghouse Cooling Towers 3	Babcock & Wilcox Lake 15	N/A	N/A
Use of outside contractors	Extensive	Minimal	Moderate	Very extensive	Very little
NPD maintenance organization	Highly developed	Developing	Highly developed	N/A	N/A
Proximity to CMD GO	Close	Close	Distant	Distant	Close

- Four organizational levels (five interfaces) between VP, CMD and crafts-people (general supervisor level eliminated November 1988).
- *Both CMD and corporate departments* believe that there *should be* more emphasis on costs than there now is.

CMD's maintenance 'business'

- No consensus among *CMD's managers* about current priorities, or what they should be (some increased emphasis on quality and cost).
- *CMD's clients* are very confused about CMD's current priorities; many believe that the top priority *should be* quality (no real consensus).
- There is a clear consensus among *Corporate departments* (other than CMD's clients) that quality is now and should continue to be the most important priority, and that costs should be given considerably more weight.

* Cost, quality, short-cycle delivery, delivery reliability, fixed-asset utilization, volume flexibility and service characteristics flexibility.

Cross-functional collaboration

- Good inter-functional collaboration within CMD's Divisions, but much less so among Divisions.
- Considerable interaction/collaboration between GO functional groups and each Division.
- 'We're excellent in crises; otherwise the walls and fences come back up.'
- There is a widespread perception in CMD that there is a need to learn how to understand and use skilled people more flexibly across CMD's Divisions — to rise above local parochialism and prioritize work at a broader/higher level.

189

First-line supervision

- Ratio of supervisors to supervised (1/89): 1:10.3 (1:10.7 excluding Hydro maintenance).
- Craft supervisors spend 56 per cent of time supervising; 23 per cent paper; and 21 per cent communicating.
- Almost all of the 410 first-line supervisors (hourly or salary) have been promoted up from the ranks.
- CMD's management has been concerned for several years about the quality/effectiveness of first-line supervision and the need for upgrading their skills and achieving closer identification with management.
- CMD has believed that its first-line supervisors should be focused on managing people. Its clients (especially NPD) believe that at least equal weight should be given to technical guidance.
- Non-supervisory professionals in CMD's Divisions believe that their 'supervisors are too far removed from the work'.
- First- and second-line supervisors in CMD and Production Departments are good at working out problems among themselves.

Workforce

- Age distribution (all employees): 1 per cent less than 25 years; 32 per cent 25−35 years; 39 per cent 36−45 years; 21 per cent 46−55 years; 7 per cent more than 55 years.

Age and stability of management

	Avg.	< 40 yrs	Age 40−50	50−60	60+
Senior management	42	11%	56%	22%	11%
Middle management	43	31%	52%	15%	2%
	Avg.	< 10 yrs	Time on job 10−20	20−30	30+
Senior management	3.6	100%	−	−	−
Middle management	2.4	84%	15%	1%	−

- Considerable movement by middle managers position to position.
- Middle managers' churn is widely perceived by subordinates as having some adverse effect on organizational effectiveness.

Management style/behaviour

- Senior DPC management behaviour is widely perceived as wanting to remain above the fray, not wanting to take an active role in resolving touch issues, and in not responding or being sluggish in responding to initiatives from below ('hands off; let them fight it out' at department level).

- CMD is widely perceived (both internally and externally) as being very structured, doing everything by the book and being very rule-oriented.
- CMD's senior management is perceived by other corporate departments as being tough, willing to fight for CMD's turf and 'rights', willing to make the hard decisions.
- CMD's top managers' style is perceived by many in the department to be somewhat autocratic.
- There is a perception in CMD that the VP relies on the GM and is removed (and missed) from day-to-day managing and interaction with his staff.
- The GM is widely perceived in CMD as decisive but at times somewhat unpredictable; some people are a bit afraid of him.
- Strong top−down emphasis in CMD on achieving standardization and consistency on how people are treated, working practices and procedures, organization, equipment, etc.
- There is a widespread perception by middle- and lower-level CMD managers that consistency efforts are being carried too far, resulting in some inappropriate arrangements and stifling innovation.
- Most in CMD believe that its managers are at their best in crises.

Priorities* (management perceptions)

CMD's construction 'business'

- There is no clear agreement *within CMD*, either on what are the most important current priorities, or what these priorities should be.
- CMD's *clients* are confused about CMD's current priorities; most believe that the top priority *should be* quality.
- *Corporate departments* believe that CMD's top construction priority *is currently* quality; they do not agree on what CMD's top priority *should be*.
- Seniority (all employees): 0 per cent less than 2 years; 8 per cent 2−5 years; 46 per cent 6−10 years; 28 per cent 11−15 years; 18 per cent more than 15 years.
- Job categories (number of employees in each category):

	Caucasian		Minority		
	Male	Female	Male	Female	Total
Senior managers	8	1	0	0	9
Middle managers	107	1	3	0	111
Professionals	125	16	4	5	150
Supervisors	389	5	16	0	410
Technicians	528	110	39	13	690
Clerical	109	216	21	39	385
Crafts	2438	28	294	8	2768
Operatives (semi-skilled)	106	5	31	0	142
Labourers (unskilled)	7	1	9	4	21
Total	3817	383	417	69	4686

Appendixes

- Employee distribution: 15.6 per cent exempt, 84.4 per cent non-exempt.

Function/section	Headcount %
Planning and schedule	5.1
Materials and equipment	10.1
Engineering	9.5
Human resources	2.2
Construction craft (Bad Creek)	8.0
Maintenance	62.2
Hydro maintenance	1.1
General office	1.8

- Change in the workforce (as of 12/31 of year):

Section	1984	1985	1986	1987	1988
Central	3258	1404	1493	1399	1016
South	1022	1016	1110	1108	932
North	751	1504	1288	1311	928
Bad Creek	18	193	354	594	744
General office	53	53	80	80	61
Hydro maintenance*	0	56	60	68	72
SMS*	0	639	0**	0	0
Total	5102	4855	4385	4560	3753

* Merged with CMD on January 1, 1985.
** Absorbed into Divisions.

- The skilled craft workforce is aging; 94 per cent take early retirement (when possible); 17 per cent are likely to be gone in five years, and 50 per cent by 2003.
- Some say CMD is broadening their specialized craftspeople to be more flexible generalists. Others say there is a switch from craft specialist to task specialist (turbines, boilers, valves, etc.).
- Some in CMD perceive that some of the best construction craftspeople are in maintenance.

Training and development

- Differences in nuclear plants require different maintenance procedures and operating rules; a person qualified for a job at one plant may not be really qualified for another plant.
- Front-line supervisors go through same training as crafts.
- CMD recognizes the need for training in maintenance and has been pursuing it since early 1986.

- At least 10 per cent of CMD craftspeople in the divisions may be unable to be trained in maintenance, especially regarding nuclear training (INPO).
- In 1987, CMD logged 255,010 work hours of training at a cost of $5 million.
- There have been two qualification programmes (ETQS and EQP); these are now being coordinated administratively.
- No job-posting system (craft/other non-exempt).
- Clerks perceive that job transfers within CMD (to other Divisions) and into other DPC departments are impossible and the process doesn't work.
- Management development and training accounts for 0.7 per cent of the training hours.

Work climate

- In general, morale is high at craft level.
- Supervisors believe that craftspeople seem to be accepting the change from construction to maintenance and that their morale is high.
- Some supervisors suggest that craftspeople like maintenance better (better security than construction).
- Lots of rules have been quite rigidly applied in CMD that might have been more appropriate to the construction regimentation: e.g., whistles for lunch and break; no coffee pots (or refrigeration); the numbers of rules are being reduced.
- CMD supervisors perceive there is too much bureaucracy (except in crises).
- Good team spirit within CMD and across departments according to supervisors: 'We get along well together . . . everybody falls in and does the job.'
- Craft supervisors believe in quiet collaboration: 'We don't believe in over-emphasizing consistency. It hampers innovation and creativity. . . . Divisional people keep creative things hidden.' 'We keep our good working relations at lower levels quiet.'
- According to some CMD supervisors, there is an atmosphere of pressure and tension due to layoff prospects, training/qualifications tests and differences in personnel practices between CMD and stations (e.g., 4−10).
- One group of supervisors was exceptionally proud of their Division: 'top people gravitate to our Division: management values teamwork and openness (important in performance assessment); performance is rewarded; emphasis on innovation, creativity, risk taking.'
- Many in CMD and their client departments believe that CMD is being asked to do more than it can handle.

CMD operational planning

- Overall, CMD managers perceive the planning process as valuable/beneficial.

- Some problems were perceived by a number of CMD's managers: too internally focused; lacks new ideas; lacks hard facts; too much word-smithing; too many strategies and actions; not enough emphasis on making the plan happen; not enough communication of the plan to the supervisors; 'career suicide' if you say the wrong thing.

Work planning and scheduling

- Three different computer-based systems (e.g., Primavera, Project II, Quicknet) involved in work planning and scheduling are not integrated; there is no DPC-wide consensus on which one(s) should become the standard.
- CMD senior management is committed to PCS.
- There are many different views about PCS in CMD; many believe that PCS is a good system that people don't know how to use (philosophically and technically), and that in order to work, PCS requires teamwork and a commitment to the process (by DED, the production departments and CMD). Others believe that PCS is inappropriate for their work (e.g., nuclear modifications; maintenance).
- Many people in CMD Planning and Scheduling Group came from the craft ranks.
- Some CMD general supervisors and clients believe that CMD does unnecessary and over-elaborate planning.
- Many CMD general supervisors believe work planning and scheduling is ineffective (inexperienced staff; inflexibility in coping with unanticipated problems).
- Optimum staffing levels have never been established (based on the balance between the cost of outage duration vs the cost of maintaining an in-house capability to handle any outage rapidly).

Management information

- FIS's substantial potential value (enabling CMD managers to set up accounts to manage their own work) has not been realized; implementation to date has been weak.
- 'Our MIS gives us information six weeks late.'

Communications

- CMD uses a variety of communications mechanisms:
  1 Employee Forums employees meeting with management;
  2 a weekly printed News Brief; and
  3 a monthly employee newspaper.
- Many in CMD perceive the Forums as useless; some issues are taboo and there is no feedback on issues discussed.

- Long range plans are not communicated broadly except within GO.
- 'Communicating decisions in CMD tends to be sluggish and sometimes ineffective.'
- Lower levels in CMD are generally unaware of priorities, new programmes and projects.
- Some believe that CMD's management prefers to divulge only what is absolutely necessary.
- When one CMD Division finds a way to work that is more effective, information is shared; the actual change is often slow in being implemented by others.

Rewards and compensation

- Pay structure for hourly personnel is based on a cost-of-living adjustment and satisfactory performance.
- Pay for salaried personnel is based to some degree on performance.
- Compensation levels are relatively high for the area.
- In the exempt classification, there are 84 different positions, each with its own defined pay range ($\sim$40 per cent spread).
- In the craft classification, there are 14 different scales, each with an 8.5 per cent spread.
- In the clerical and technical classification, there are ten grades, each with a 10 per cent spread.
- Pay scale differences between GO staff positions and the field line positions make job rotation/transfers difficult.
- CMD has a very limited range of options to recognize substantial differences in individual performance: no bonus system; 2–3 per cent point difference in the annual increase between low and high performance.
- Like most DPC departments, CMD in the past has not been effective in dealing with poor performers; few have been terminated.
- A major motivator in CMD is personal pride; CMD recognizes and enhances this pride through many awards, dinners and speeches.
- Women in CMD doubt that there's any future for them in CMD.

Relationship with clients (1/89)

- CMD's clients are all DPC's generating stations: 3 nuclear, 9 fossil and 27 hydro. Differences in design, operating characteristics and culture are significant.
- Client satisfaction criteria: (1) quality and timeliness (includes minimum disruption to client operations); (2) CMD's productivity and costs.

- Clients are generally well satisfied with CMD's work but complain about CMD's being too high, especially indirect charges (110 per cent), and minor annoyances (house-keeping).
- Who does what between CMD and station is clear on construction work, less clear on plant modification and unclear on maintenance where stations have own maintenance staff.
- CMD believes it must consider more than just what the client wants (like a contractor). 'We're ratepayers and shareholders in the Company ... we must take *both* our clients' needs and DPC's interests into account.'
- In general, clients have very different views about how their relationship with CMD works or should work.
- NPD, FPD and CMD supervisors collaborate effectively.
- There are redundant warehouses: CMD Divisions and fossil and nuclear plants.
- Some CMD Division staff perceive that the pendulum has swung too far toward service and pleasing the client.
- CMD/Client Relations vary by Division and production departments:

	Nuclear	*Fossil*	*Hydro*
North	• formal	• informal • controversy • improving but still problems • FPD tries to manage CMD people • at high levels	• comfortable
Central	• polite cooperation • guarded • more receptive to measures and controls	• good service • clients manage jobs, not CMD people • some tension • not most efficient or productive relationship • extremely happy with CMD	• comfortable • excellent
South	• good relations • partnership	• excellent service • fairly good relations • good support	• comfortable
General Office	• good relations • understanding is developing	• CMD/FPD GO relations poor	• good
In general	• good at lower levels; worse at higher levels • severe conflicting marching orders with CMD • maintenance is increasingly specialized	• good at lower levels; worse at higher levels • severe conflicting marching orders with CMD • 'CMD supplies craft' • 'Orange Book not needed'	• Hydro is simple • CMD 'overkill' • movement of management to/from CMD/Hydro

Relations with Corporate departments other than clients

- There is variation in how Corporate departments view CMD:
  - Some Corporate managers believe that CMD is not busy, duplicates the effort of others, over-staffed, and a burden to the Company.
  - There's a perception that CMD takes too long to get something done, for example, 'CMD has craftspeople instead of plumbers ... the plumbing for a water fountain will be a work of art.'
  - Others believe CMD is better at maintenance than the stations, and that CMD has now become quite responsive, after overcoming growing pains.
- Current CMD to DES goal: sell 60,000 work hours annually (professional, skilled craft), to fill in 'valleys' in cyclical nature of CMD's work.
- Supporting DES is difficult; CMD has problems freeing up the (best) managers/professionals and the economics of moving large numbers of craft.
- CMD's relationship with DED is close and generally positive.
- There is a need to define how much information is needed in engineering drawings and establish a consensus between CMD and DED.
- There is some 'overkill' and 'nuclear mindset' in DED's designs for CMD.
- When CMD loses a bid, DED can hire an outsider to supervise the project, while CMD people stand idle.
- CMD's relationship with TD is workable but testy at times, because of TD's lack of planning and inability to give stations support in outages.
- CMD/DPC comparison:
  - 'DPC people go to great lengths to be non-confrontational; however, when CMD feels confronted, they're very defensive, think everyone's out to get 'em, paranoid.' – Corporate Manager
  - 'CMD is now "mainstream" in the Company. We used to be a separate entity as a construction company (independent).' – CMD Manager
  - 'Smith sent out an "Attendance Monitoring System" and had to rescind it. It was the management who objected, they didn't want to do it. Yet, we enforce it in CMD. Why?' – CMD Supervisor
  - 'CMD has "corrective action" procedure and policy, which is not consistent with DPC's policy.' – CMD Supervisor

CMD's performance

- CMD's nuclear construction performance relative to industry was spectacular (Watalba at $1580/kW vs Industry $3200/kW).
- A key CMD measure is conformance to budget ($+/-$). In DPC, performance under budget can be criticized as much as coming in over budget.

- CMD has recently introduced performance indicators to measure quality, cost, schedule, radiation exposure, safety, attendance, budget, materials and equipment and profitability.
- CMD has been asking its clients to complete a Client Satisfaction Questionnaire that measures quality, safety, cost, schedule and cooperation.
- In construction, performance measures are relatively clear (meeting specifications, cost and due dates).
- CMD managers' attitudes toward quantitative measurement vary: some high-level CMD managers want to be trusted to perform, not measured; many believe that 'figures lie'.
- The construction capability and reputation of CMD varies widely by Division, according to DED which keeps score.
- CMD's efforts to track idle time have failed.
- CMD has no control over overhead charges (fluctuate widely during year).
- 1987 turnover ranged from 3 per cent in the Southern Division to 9 per cent in Central. In 1988, turnover is projected to be 11 per cent in Central and 8 per cent in the Southern.
- Absenteeism has been steadily declining from 4 per cent in 1985 to 2.9 per cent in 1987 and 2.8 per cent estimated for 1988.
- Sick pay has steadily dropped, from 3.6 per cent of base payroll in 1985 to 2.7 per cent estimated for 1988.
- CMD's clients must use CMD up to its availability. However, they do not pay directly for CMD's services.
- On some jobs CMD's price quote is three times that of outsiders.
- CMD's cost estimates are driven by:
  1 uncertainty about doing small jobs;
  2 estimates to cover the inevitable changes;
  3 DPC fringe benefits and higher labour costs; and
  4 travel time.
- CMD and its clients have different indirect charge structures (allocation of direct/indirect − 12 per cent at stations vs 110 per cent in CMD).
- CMD's clients have difficulty understanding CMD's budget process.

5 CMD's Culture

- CMD's traditional culture is very different from the new (required) cultures of maintenance and moderate-sized construction projects.
- CMD's culture is in transition with regard to its maintenance support business.

Sample Operating System Characterization

Most CMD managers and executives behave as if they believe:

- The culture is changing:

Issue	From	To
Business perspective	Secure defined role	Competitive positioning
Organizational position	Proud independence	Interdependence
Quality	Perfection	Exceed specifications
Cost	A secondary concern	A primary concern

- There is not a lot of praise, not a lot of punishment.
- There's a balance between consistency and customized service.
- 'We are well organized and plan everything we do.'

Appendix 2

High-leverage Targets of Opportunity (Prioritized)

1 *CMD must continue to cut costs.*
2 *How can CMD resolve the 'turf', pride, control, competition issues in providing maintenance and modification services to clients?*
3 *How can we resolve/work with philosophical differences between CMD and our clients re: technical/managerial responsibilities of supervisors?*
4 *How do we deal effectively with poor performance and encourage superior performance, using the reward (and disciplinary) system we have?*
5 *How can we deal with conflicting measures (culture) between production, operating department and CMD?*
6 How can we accommodate increasingly restrictive operating regulation while positioning ourselves to benefit from less restrictive transmission and generation regulations?
7 How do we maintain aging stations and returned PMP units with decreasing resources and funds?
8 How can we achieve standardization of maintenance among plants?
9 While CMD's basic charter remains the same three tasks, how do we resolve the confusion from constantly changing emphasis within these?
10 How do we resolve the difference between clients' desires and corporate priorities?
11 Why is CMD perceived to be better in crises than in the day-to-day, routine tasks?
12 Does CMD's top management sufficiently understand the 'realities' and difficulties of maintenance work?
13 Are we missing the mark by trying to standardize process and not dealing with differences in philosophy among CMD managers?
14 How can we improve inter-divisional collaboration in the interest of better standardization, accelerated learning, improved productivity, etc.?
15 Who is our competition and how should we be addressing them?
16 Do we need to replace the skills that we'll be losing over the next five years through retirement? If so, how?
17 What to do about the 10 per cent of divisional crafts who appear to be 'un-trainable'?
18 Are we getting our money's worth on our $5 million training investment, and how can we measure?
19 How do we overcome corporate's perception that CMD has excess 'overhead'?

20 How can we work with other departments to balance cost of outage vs cost of resources to handle outage?

21 How to plan and execute cost-effective outage support?

22 What is it about work planning which makes it less than accepted by the supervisors?

23 How do we manage advancement of women and minorities?

24 What should we do to change attitudes about CMD at the corporate department head level?

25 How can we reduce our indirect charges?

26 How can we get our clients to understand our budgeting process?

Appendix 3

Organization and Management
Readiness Assessment Questionnaire

Key to Interpretation

To determine overall quadrant position:

1 Apply following weightings to questionnaire responses:

Forms	Columns
A and C	5 4 3 2 1
B and D	1 2 3 4 5

2 Determine a total score for Forms A, B, C and D by multiplying the responses in each column by the appropriate weighting.

3 Add the total score of Forms A and B. Calculate an average score for the planning group. This should be applied to the horizontal axis of the OMRA grid. The range of individual scores should be shown.

4 Add the total score of Forms C and D. Calculate an average score for the planning group. This should be applied to the vertical axis of the OMRA grid. The range of individual scores should be shown.

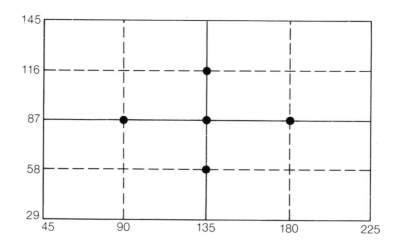

202

To identify potential strengths and weaknesses

For discussion

1 Identify those questions where at least a two-thirds *majority* of responses were in either columns 1 and 2 or 4 and 5.
2 Correlate questions identified in 1 above by related topic or issue (e.g., adequacy of management information, capability of first-line supervision, etc.).

OMRA* QUESTIONNAIRE:
Form A
Operating System Characteristics

The way I see things operate in our organization . . .	Almost always true	Usually true	As often true as not true	Seldom true	Almost never true
1 Our business strategies are developed by *all* major functional heads (e.g., marketing, engineering, operations, finance, etc.) working together in *joint discussions*, not by a single executive integrating separate functional inputs.					
2 We try to resolve issues and problems at *whatever level* is closest to the facts, rather than push them all up to the top.					
3 First-level managers and supervisors see their jobs as *more than overseeing the work* and following prescribed procedures; they also feel responsible for *improving* things wherever possible.					
4 Before important decisions are made, *everyone* who ought to be heard has a chance to make inputs.					
5 *Decisions* important to our business may be primarily influenced by one major function but are not final until we reach a consensus based on the interests of the organization as a whole.					
6 We regularly use *group meetings and committees* to *make sure information is widely shared.*					
7 In communicating with our employees, we use other means in addition to *official communications and announcements.*					
8 We formulate long-term business strategies through a *regular planned participative* process.					
9 The information a manager needs for making decisions is *reliable and timely.*					
10 Budget variances are used *more* to diagnose problems and improve future performance than for placing blame and punishing people.					

* Organization and Management Readiness Assessment©

OMRA Questionnaire

	Almost always true	Usually true	As often true as not true	Seldom true	Almost never true
The way I see things operate in our organization . . .					
11 My rewards — salary, merit increases, promotions — depend *at least as much* on how well the *company* performs as on my personal performance.					
12 We encourage our managers to work out disagreements *where they occur*, if possible, and not to push them higher in the organization for resolution.					
13 Rewards for salaried people are *fair* and *reasonable*, all things considered.					
14 Our employees show lots of *initiative* and *energy* at work.					
15 Communications are good in *every* direction: top-down, bottom-up, across department lines.					
16 Managers are *good at settling differences* in ways that *take account* of the *various interests involved*, and the *overall needs of the firm*.					
17 Relationships with our employees are positive, based on *mutual respect*.					
18 Rewards for performance take account *both* of individual effort and the *person's impact on others* in the department and beyond.					
19 Managers of different departments *work cooperatively with each other* to solve problems.					
20 Rewards for hourly-paid employees are *fair* and *reasonable*, all things considered.					
21 We use *special committees* and *task forces* to help solve major problems.					
22 Relationships with our unions are based on *mutual respect* and the belief that *both* parties can and should be winners.					

205

OMRA* QUESTIONNAIRE:
Form B
Operating System Characteristics

The way I see things operate in our organization . . .	Almost always true	Usually true	As often true as not true	Seldom true	Almost never true
23 Managers and supervisors try to *maintain very tight control*; they closely oversee and question subordinates.					
24 Nearly all problems migrate to the top of the organization for resolution — even unimportant ones.					
25 Our business strategies are centred on our *technology, as interpreted by our technical experts*.					
26 First-level managers and supervisors have a hard time seeing themselves as part of management; they feel *closer to the workforce*.					
27 Managers and supervisors are expected to have *immediate and detailed answers* to any questions asked of them — not to rely on others.					
28 It's hard to get the *information you need* in the form you want it, when you want it.					
29 Management and supervisory meetings are used for *briefings and information exchange*, not for solving problems or exploring issues.					
30 Our technical experts really *call the shots* here. Everyone else pretty much has to fall into line.					
31 First-level managers and supervisors spend their time *expediting, dealing with technical matters, maintaining discipline, and doing paperwork*.					
32 Our long-term business strategies are *inside the CEO's head*; it's hard for the rest of the organization to know where he's going.					
33 Our business strategies are determined mainly by marketing and financial considerations.					

* Organization and Management Readiness Assessment©

OMRA Questionnaire

The way I see things operate in our organization . . .	Almost always true	Usually true	As often true as not true	Seldom true	Almost never true
34 Management relies on *the written word* as its primary means of communication, preferring this to face-to-face interaction.					
35 The data furnished to management is *too late* and *too aggregated to be useful*. Personal 'little black books' and rules of thumb are in common usage.					
36 When the performance of our employees in operations is measured, it's in the form of *variances from engineered or cost standards*.					
37 When you come right down to it, *rewards mean dollars*.					
38 Our levels of *absenteeism, employee turnover, accidents and complaints* are *high* in comparison with other similar companies.					
39 Rewards for *salaried* people are based mainly on *seniority*; it's one way of *treating people alike*.					
40 Rewards for *hourly-paid* employees are based mainly on *seniority*; this is a way of *treating people alike*.					
41 The working climate here is *hostile* and *mistrustful*, with plenty of *conflict* and *tension*.					
42 When it comes to performance, we concentrate on what can be *quantified*.					
43 Even when situations call for a *broad, organization-wide view*, managers prefer to *concern themselves with their own areas* of expertise.					
44 When we measure how effective our organization is, we look at the sum of *individual* performances.					
45 Union/management attitudes are *hostile* and *mistrustful*, with plenty of *conflict* and *tension*.					

OMRA* QUESTIONNAIRE:
Form C
Management Orientation

As I reflect in general on my personal views, I believe that . . .	Strongly disagree	Partly disagree	Neither agree nor disagree	Partly agree	Strongly agree
46 Strategy should be centred mainly on *market offerings*.					
47 In effective organizations, *each function sets its own goals* and *does the best it can* to meet them.					
48 The essence of management is *control*, down to the details.					
49 Having *prompt, detailed answers* to questions asked by upper management is a key to being seen as competent.					
50 Our technical functions are the *most important* part of our organization. Ultimately, it's our *technological capabilities* and *performance* that should determine our future strategy.					
51 Motivating people is a matter of applying the right *combination of carrots and sticks* and of encouraging a competitive attitude.					
52 When it comes to pay, it's better to treat people *uniformly* than to get into hassles about trying to recognize differences in performance.					
53 Information is power. Managers should be careful about how much they give out. People should be *told only what they need to know*.					
54 Strategic planning is a *luxury* that only large, mature companies can afford. We need to devote all our energies to staying on top of the changes in our markets and technology.					
55 When we evaluate performance, we should try to measure as *precisely* as possible *each individual's contribution*.					
56 Management is paid to do the *thinking and directing* and to keep *employees satisfied enough* to minimize disruptions.					

* Organization and Management Readiness Assessment©

208

OMRA Questionnaire

As I reflect in general on my personal views, I believe that . . .

	Strongly disagree	Partly disagree	Neither agree nor disagree	Partly agree	Strongly agree
57 A first-level manager's and supervisor's job is to *carry out orders* and *get results*. S/he should be technically superior and a good troubleshooter.					
58 Our payroll — hourly and salaried — is a *variable cost* just like other expense items.					
59 Unions are for the most part an *obstacle* to more effective operation. If we can't avoid unionization, we should try to control the unions we're stuck with, offering them no more than we have to.					

OMRA* QUESTIONNAIRE:
Form D
Management Orientation

As I reflect in general on my personal views, I believe that . . .	Strongly disagree	Partly disagree	Neither agree nor disagree	Partly agree	Strongly agree
60 In formulating our business strategies, we should aim to make *careful trade-offs* among the interests of technology, marketing, finance, operations and human resources.					
61 People are motivated when *their own interests coincide* with the *company's*. Money may be key, but people are interested in lots of other things.					
62 Those in the organization *best* able to solve a problem should be *provided* with *whatever information* they need to do this.					
63 In effective organizations, *all functions* work together *cooperatively*. Departments must be prepared to *compromise* if that is what serves the best interests of the *firm*.					
64 Long-term strategic planning is *critical* to our continuing *viability* as a firm.					
65 Pay should reflect *individual differences* in *performance*, even though this is difficult to do in a way that seems and is fair.					
66 The effectiveness of our operations depends on how well we develop and encourage the *fullest possible utilization* of our *employees' skills and capabilities*.					
67 Accomplishing *planned results* is a true measure of control.					
68 No single discipline or function should automatically dominate our planning for the future. Our long-term success depends on how effectively *all* our functions can pool their thinking and work together.					
69 Knowing *what questions to ask* is *more* important for a manager than having a ready answer to every question.					

* Organization and Management Readiness Assessment©

OMRA Questionnaire

As I reflect in general on my personal views, I believe that . . .	Strongly disagree	Partly disagree	Neither agree nor disagree	Partly agree	Strongly agree
70 Our first-level managers and supervisors are a *key resource* who can make or break our effectiveness.					
71 Performance assessment should take into account *all the organizational factors* that affect that performance.					
72 We should think of and deal with our human resources as *capital* not expense, requiring investment and conservation.					
73 Performance measurement is a key to motivation; we should be *prepared to sacrifice precision* if need be, to keep from arousing defensive reactions.					
74 Unions are an important element of industrial life. They provide employees with *safeguards* against unjust and arbitrary actions, and provide them with a means to influence their conditions of employment.					

Appendix 4

Generic Strategy Options

Emphasis Options

1 External emphasis

The business we are in is at the stage where the most important things are happening outside the company, in the marketplace where our customers and competitors are. If we are to maintain or increase our share of the market, we have to be successful in playing a fast-moving highly competitive game in which we can take full advantage of quick turns and opportunities at the right moment. For example, our products and services have to be either in tune with what customers want, or available when wanted, or noticeably better than the competition's, or all of these − even if it increases the challenges internally.

2 Internal emphasis

The business we are in has settled down to the point where either our position in the market is acceptable and reasonably secure and stable, or where there is little opportunity to improve our position. We need to put more emphasis on how well we function internally, improving our controls, costs and margins, as well as the consistency and smoothness of our operations. This kind of productivity improvement is now the main part of our business plan.

3 Mixed external and internal emphasis

The business we are in is at the stage where we have to pay close attention to *both* external and internal affairs. Our internal operating effectiveness is the key to keeping our margins up, but that alone is not enough to ensure success. We also have to be alert and responsive to changes in the marketplace if we are to remain competitive. This situation requires continual trade-offs between internal and external considerations.

Thrust or Theme Options

1 Improve quality of products/services

The main thrust should be to improve the conformance to customer requirements of our product/service quality. If our customers can see and value our superior quality, we can improve our competitive position in the marketplace by bettering the level and/or uniformity and/or reliability of our quality.

2 Improve fixed-asset utilization

The main thrust should be to improve the utilization of our facilities and equipment by:
- Improving the layout of our facilities
- Improving planning and scheduling
- Making use of idle capacity/wasted space
- Reducing downtime caused by breakdowns, setups and changeovers of equipment
- Increasing throughputs
- Redesigning equipment

3 Increase flexibility for changes in products and services

The main thrust should be to improve the organization's ability to respond quickly and flexibly to market requirements for product/service innovations ... introducing market-oriented improvements and features that meet requirements of time, cost and specification.

4 Reduce costs

The main thrust should be to cut all our costs to the lowest practical level. This will either improve profit margins, or allow us to adopt new pricing strategies aimed at improving our market share.

5 Increase flexibility for changes in volume (capacity)

The main thrust should be to improve the organization's ability to respond flexibly to market requirements for substantial changes in volume for products and/or services. This includes managing our capacity in relation both to growth demands and to seasonal and cyclical changes.

213

6 Improve ability to meet schedule commitments

The main thrust should be to improve the organization's ability to deliver existing products/services with reliable predictability − on time, in accordance with promises to customers and planned schedules.

7 Increase capability for short-cycle delivery

The main thrust should be to improve the organization's ability to respond very quickly and flexibly to customers' requirements for product/service delivery cycles shorter than the 'normal' cycle for manufacturing or service response to customers' orders. This includes both increases and decreases in volume and unexpected demands for 'specials'.

8 Improve materials utilization

The main thrust should be to improve the utilization of materials by:
● Reducing scrap, waste and obsolescence
● Improving process yields
● Recycling
● Redesigning products, services and packaging

9 Improve people utilization

The main thrust should be to improve the utilization of employees' capabilities, with particular emphasis on:
● Management style
● How decisions are made
● Communications
● Ways of resolving conflicts
● Training and development
● Rewards
● Motivation
● Selection and placement
● Clarifying and simplifying roles, accountabilities, and interrelationships

Strategy Options

1 Simplify the product line and/or range of services

Invest in narrowing the product line/range of services and/or in standardizing products/services and components. Prune out products and services; reduce the number and diversity of market offerings so that efficiencies can be realized in:

- Marketing
- Selling
- Processing
- Operations
- Inventories
- Distribution
- Servicing
- Accounting

2 Upgrade existing physical facilities

Invest in improving existing physical facilities in order to:

- Improve product/service quality/reliability
- Improve the work environment so that employee motivation might be enhanced
- Reduce operating costs

3 Improve equipment and processing technology

Invest in better equipment or processes to:

- Improve product/service performance/quality/reliability
- Increase throughput and yields
- Increase flexibility for product and/or volume changes
- Reduce set-up and changeover costs
- Reduce labour intensiveness
- Reduce maintenance costs

4 Increase mechanization

Invest in substituting machines for people employed wherever possible and economically attractive, in order to:

- Reduce payroll costs
- Achieve better, more consistent quality

5 Increase capacity

Invest in increasing capacity by expanding the plant, increasing throughput or expanding service capability in order to:

- Increase responsiveness to market demand
- Provide more comprehensive services or service coverage
- Reduce overtime
- Reduce wear and tear on equipment
- Improve plant layout and housekeeping
- Increase economies of scale

6 Optimize make/buy mix

Either invest in making or providing materials, components and/or services currently being purchased in order to:

- Increase value added
- Improve quality/reliability
- Reduce total costs
- Use available capacity

- Improve material/component/ service availability for planning and scheduling

or increase amount of work/materials/services purchased from vendors in order to:

- Decrease value added
- Improve quality/reliability
- Improve material/component/ service availability

- Reduce total costs
- Free up capacity
- Reduce overtime

7 Improve vendors' quality

Invest in working with vendors of materials, components and services to improve the quality of purchased goods and services in order to:

- Improve the quality of market offerings
- Improve reliability/predictability of purchased goods and services
- Reduce total costs
- Improve delivery reliability

8 Improve distribution

Invest in reshaping product/service distribution network policies and practices to:

- Increase responsiveness to the market and/or coverage
- Focus on highest profit outlets
- Reduce inventory, transportation and warehousing costs
- Improve productivity of the distribution system

9 Improve energy/utilities efficiency

Invest in improving energy/utilities efficiency by:

- Replacing existing facilities and equipment with more energy/utilities efficient facilities and equipment
- Reducing energy/utilities losses by insulation, recycling, etc.
- Instituting/refining control systems
- Converting to lower-cost energy sources

10   Reduce material losses

Invest in systems, procedures and methods to:

- Reduce scrap and waste
- Reduce material obsolescence
- Lower purchased material costs

11   Improve work methods and procedures

Invest in improving work methods and procedures to streamline and increase the efficiency of how work gets done by applying:

- Industrial engineering concepts and techniques
- Manufacturing engineering concepts and techniques
- Operations-research concepts and techniques
- Group technology

12   Improve equipment utilization

Invest in improving the utilization of existing equipment to increase throughput and return on investment by:

- Improving planning and scheduling to achieve longer runs and fewer changeovers
- Coordinating with marketing/sales to improve use of any excess capacity
- Ensuring conformance to operating standards
- Arranging for shared use
- Introducing or upgrading preventive maintenance

13   Increase standardization in operations

Invest in standardizing operations to:

- Simplify operating processes, procedures and practices
- Reduce inventories
- Improve quality and reliability
- Improve responsiveness to customers
- Reduce maintenance costs
- Increase flexibility in moving product among manufacturing facilities

14   Improve information handling

Invest in improving efficiency of information handling and data processing by streamlining methods and procedures in order to:

- Reduce clerical costs and errors
- Improve response time between data inputs and outputs

15 Improve design of product/service

Invest in developing new or modified designs for products/services that will:
- Improve responsiveness and conformance to customer requirements
- Improve quality and reliability
- Lower total costs (design, manufacturing, marketing, delivery, packaging, distribution, warranty, repair)
- Increase market acceptance

16 Improve management information, financial and operating systems, controls and reports

Invest in systems design and information technology to improve the relevance, comprehensiveness, accuracy and timeliness of management decision support information including:
- Business models
- Budgeting, planning and control
- Market research/industry and competitive analysis
- Forecasting
- Purchasing/procurement
- Inventory control
- Operations planning and control
- Quality control/assurance

17 Apply rewards and penalties

Invest in improving employee motivation by systematically and consistently:
- Encouraging desirable activities by incentives and rewards (cash, prizes, citations), and
- Discouraging undesirable activities by penalties (discipline, layoffs, shutdown).

18 Improve communications

Invest in improving employees' understanding of what they are doing and how this fits the company's goals and needs by:
- Making goals, priorities, decisions and instructions more clear and specific
- Opening up new vertical and lateral channels
- Listening more attentively

The investment may be to improve:
- Media (newsletters, closed circuit TV, audio-visual presentations, etc.)
- Development of content
- Meetings

19   Develop a workforce with multiple, flexible skills

Invest in sharpening employee selection procedures and methods and in enhancing and upgrading employees' skills and understanding in order to:

- Decrease employee specialization and optimize the ability to use employees flexibly
- Develop multiple skills
- Increase knowledge of technology, products, operating methods and processes
- Increase potential for higher, knowledge-based pay

20   Improve selection, training and development of managers, supervisors and employees

Invest in improving selection procedures and methods, and training and development activities, for management and supervisory personnel in order to:

- Upgrade overall quality and competence of people
- Increase particular skills and skill levels
- Develop new skills
- Increase knowledge of technology, products, operating methods and processes, and of other organizational functions
- Increase potential for advancement

21   Reduce lost work time

Invest in the development and improvement of policies, systems, procedures and the manner in which these are implemented to minimize the time employees spend away from their jobs for such reasons as:

- Illness (personal and family)
- Accidents
- Personal reasons
- Grievances and complaints
- Union business

22   Redesign jobs

Invest in the redesign of jobs to make them more challenging and satisfying by either or both:

- Enlarging the number/range of tasks and responsibilities
- Incorporating functions being handled by other groups

in order to:

- Reduce total costs
- Improve quality

- Enhance employee motivation
- Increase organizational responsiveness and flexibility

23 Improve performance of individual departments

Invest in improving the quality of personnel, organization, and/or operating methods and procedures and measures in each department (or in selected departments) in order to:

- Upgrade the effectiveness of the organization as a whole
- Strengthen a particular function in the organization

24 Change organizational structure design/focus

Invest in restructuring the formal organization by:

- Changing the relative status of functions
- Regrouping functional responsibilities
- Eliminating organizational levels
- Clarifying chains-of-command
- Reducing spans of control

in order to:

- Enhance market responsiveness
- Improve organizational effectiveness
- Reduce total costs
- Provide more business focus

25 Improve integration among departments/functions

Invest in breaking down walls between departments/functions in order to:

- Improve coordination and cooperation among departments
- Provide ways for functions to reconcile conflicting interests, goals and criteria
- Establish common goals and language
- Improve how interdepartmental processes function (e.g., new product introductions, new business proposals, programme/project management, etc.)
- Upgrade the effectiveness of the organization as a whole

26 Improve union–management relations and chip away at workforce-related productivity problems

Invest planning time and managerial and supervisory effort to improve union-management relations, chipping away at workforce-related productivity problems little by little by:

- Placing on the contract bargaining agenda items that can improve productivity, achieving gains through normal bargaining, and/or
- Attempting by direct management action to eliminate or modify restrictive practices that have developed over time

27 Shorten time-to-market for new products/services

Invest in designing processes, systems and procedures to shorten the time required from the initial concept of a new product/service to its delivery to the first customer, so as to improve responsiveness to market needs and opportunities. This may involve:

- Improvements in crystallizing product/service specifications
- Better design methods and tools
- Closer collaboration among marketing, technical groups and operations
- Simplifying and making more efficient the sequence of steps required
- Using autonomous task teams

28 Shorten order-to-delivery time for existing products/services

Invest in designing processes, systems and procedures to shorten the time required from the placement of an order by a customer to the delivery to that customer of the product or service, so as to improve responsiveness to customers and reduce inventory costs. This may involve:

- Redesigning work units and workflows
- Simplifying and making more efficient the sequence of steps required
- Closer collaboration among relevant functions
- Improvements in equipment and processes
- More standardization
- More flexibility in the workforce
- Instituting just-in-time operations processes

29 Shorten provisioning time

Invest in redesigning internal processes and in working with a reduced number of suppliers of materials, components and services to minimize the time between provisioning and actual need, so as to minimize inventories and throughput time. Institute just-in-time purchasing and delivery of materials and components.

30 Engage in productivity bargaining

Invest in preparing a comprehensive, one-shot 'this-for-that' bargaining package to eliminate/modify either/both formal contractual provisions or informal 'custom and practice' understandings to open up new opportunities for productivity improvement based on specific activity changes by the work force:

- Price potential gains: offer to pay out some when achieved in order to induce the union and employees to agree to desired changes
- Invest in developing management's capability (including supervisors) to capitalize on the opportunities created by the changes achieved

31 Establish a programme for total quality control/ improvement

Invest in developing, training for, and applying systems, procedures and methods aimed at:

- Establishing that everyone is responsible for quality (not only quality control/inspection)
- Achieving maximum employee involvement in pursuing 'perfection' with regard to quality
- Applying such techniques as statistical process control

32 Encourage employee involvement

Invest in setting up and training joint voluntary employee/management councils (or 'quality circles') to identify and recommend changes both in the way work is done and in the work environment so as to:

- Improve the 'quality' of the time spent working
- Improve the quality of the product
- Improve productivity
- Increase employee satisfaction

33 Institute employee involvement with productivity gains-sharing

Invest in establishing an on-going formal programme (e.g., Scanlon or Rucker type plan or Improshare) to generate labour cost (and related) savings through voluntary participative problem-solving groups involving both employees and management.

Share frequently the cash benefits, if any, with everyone in the entire unit (including support functions) on the basis of a formula agreed upon with the unions and/or employees involved.

Appendix 5

An Example of a List of Issues to be Addressed by a Strategy*

Strategy — to reduce total costs of products, improve:
- Product design
- Manufacturing equipment and processes
- Work methods, procedures and standards
- Material costs

I Product Design

A   How can the design specification from the customer be clarified in a timely manner?

1 Up-front negotiation — a clear understanding of requirement.
2 Customer requested changes.
3 Schedule and cost impact.
4 Force (gently) customer to document request.
5 How to do it and remain responsive.

B   How do we achieve commonality of parts?

1 No catalogue of parts.
2 Do we desire to staff for this purpose?
3 What savings would be realized?
4 What training would be required?

C   How do we improve design reviews?

1 Emphasis is on producibility, not cost.
2 Review the present procedure for adequacy.
3 How do we enforce the procedure?
4 How to add Cost Estimating to the Design Review earlier.

---

* The action plan derived from these issues is shown in Appendix 7, Example A.

D   Should the documentation system and flow be improved, and if so, how?

1 Review the system for adequacy.
2 Can it be streamlined?
3 Train the people to understand and use the system.
4 What system should we use for Engineering change control?
5 Can initial change implementation be expedited for pre-production?

E   Should we train new people who are in contact with the customer?

1 Customer-relations course with extra emphasis for engineers.

F   Should the design personnel be grouped for technology, not customer interface?

1 Is there a significant benefit?
2 Is the climate right?

G   How do we fully utilize a design-to-cost strategy?

1 May not be used in all instances because cost goals are not understood.

II   Manufacturing Equipment and Processes

A   Should all manufacturing equipment be reviewed for obsolescence?

1 Which areas should receive priority?
2 Does new equipment support future growth areas?

B   Should we adopt the policy of more assembly line flow as opposed to individual assembly?

1 Where would it be applicable?

C   What approach should we take to processing/process sheets?

1 Concern here is the age of the workforce.
2 What level of detail should be provided in processing?
3 What is the payback?
4 What are the resources constraints?

D   How do we address robotics in a job shop?

1 Should it be justified on economics or as a learning experience?
2 How do we identify the areas?
3 How do we address the issue with the bargaining unit and the supervisors?

E How can we look to other areas for the use of automated processing and testing?

1 Do we have the resources to undertake it?
2 How do we train people to recognize opportunities?

F How does Statistical Process Control (SPC) fit in with other cost-reduction efforts?

1 Is everyone committed to SPC?
2 How extensive should our involvement be?

G How do we take full advantage of the information generated in the pre-production process?

1 Is the present information system adequate?
2 Is it timely?
3 Does it interface well with Manufacturing and Engineering?

H How do new manufacturing technologies get transmitted to Engineering?

1 Is there a system?
2 How do we improve communications so everyone gets the 'word'?
3 How does Engineering transmit new manufacturing process technology to Manufacturing?
4 Who is responsible?

I How do we implement Computer Aided Manufacturing in the manufacturing areas?

1 Do we have a strategy?
2 Does it require a task team?
3 Do we have the resources?

III Work Methods, Procedures, and Standards

A Are the work methods as definite as they should be?

1 How definitive must they be?
2 Do we observe the work centre guidelines?
3 How do we encourage operators to follow the process sheet without deviation?
4 Should the role of the Engineering Standard Procedure be increased or diminished?

B How can we improve upon the present work methods and procedures?

1 How can we guarantee that the drawing and process sheet are compatible?
2 Can we standardize the drawing information?

C   Under the pressure of shipping requirements, can we still maintain economic methods?

1 Does the customer schedule allow us to achieve this?
2 Can we control it?
3 What is an economic lot size?

D   Can we achieve better schedule control?

1 Is the customer a major part of this problem?
2 Are we meeting the schedule by the most economic means?

E   Do we have capacity control?

1 How do we define capacity?
2 How do we measure our capacity?
3 How do we determine what our true capacity is?
4 How do we best utilize our capacity?

F   What use do we intend for the standards?

1 What are they used for?
2 Can the standards be improved without better work method definition first?
3 Should they be used for performance measurements?
4 Should the standard be the accepted production norm?

G   What are the supervisor's responsibilities for day-to-day operations and training?

1 Are the supervisors knowledgeable of the technical aspects of their areas of responsibility?
2 Are the supervisors aware of their total responsibility?
3 Are the supervisors' workloads too heavy?

IV   Material Cost

A   How can we specify critical parts to allow second sourcing?

1 Is second sourcing precluded by customer mandate?
2 Is second sourcing precluded by ESD Engineering mandate?
3 How do we assure second sourcing is considered in the design?

B   How do we ensure multiple sourcing of non-critical items?

1 Is there too much internal control on non-critical items?

Example of Issues Addressed by a Strategy

C   How do we control components when they are second source? (Traceability, etc.)

1 Do we issue too large an order to an initial source before proof of his capability?

2 Can we achieve adequate traceability economically?

D   Can we improve our awareness of material cost in design?

1 Should there be a formal interdepartmental interface among Cost Estimating, Purchasing, Engineering, Manufacturing Engineering?

2 Design-to-cost?

E   How do we keep a second source current and on-board?

1 Do we split orders on a percentage basis to ensure second-source continuing capability?

Appendix 6

Some Typical Obstacles to Successful Strategy Implementation

1 *Declining work ethic*

Improving the way we operate here is stymied by what has happened to the work ethic — it's gone, or nearly gone. Most people just don't care as much as they used to.

2 *Poor management information*

Our state of knowledge about ourselves is so incomplete, so inaccurate, and so untimely that we couldn't be sure whether, or by how much, the effectiveness and efficiency of our operating system might have (or be) improved.

3 *Poor employee—management relations*

The employee—management relations climate around here is too sour to allow much hope for any kind of cooperation on improving the way we operate.

4 *Inadequate first-line supervision*

For a variety of reasons our first-line supervision is too limited in number, unknowledgeable, unskilled, or demotivated to handle the pressures and provide the day-to-day leadership for any serious improvement efforts.

5 *Restrictive work practices*

We are so hemmed in by formal and informal restrictive work practices that the implementation of an operating improvement strategy has two and a half strikes against it from the start.

6 *Scarcity of professional/ technical/ managerial resources*

Implementing any significant improvement effort is constrained by our lack of sufficient professional and/or technical and/or managerial resources. Our staffing is too thin and we are missing some vital, needed skills and know-how.

7 *Low levels of employees' intelligence and skill*

The levels of our employees' education, intelligence and skill here are too low for us to expect an effective response to any requirements for substantial changes in behaviour.

8	*Weak middle managers*	Our middle-level managers are too weak for us to count on them for much help in implementing any kind of significant operating improvement strategy.
9	*Scarcity of funds*	It's unlikely that we'll be able to get the funds needed to support what we want to do. Either company funds are being allocated elsewhere, or capital is too scarce — both inside and outside the company — for us to make the necessary front-end investment for a meaningful improvement effort.
10	*Inexperienced workforce*	Our workforce has many young people with very little experience in our industry. They lack basic skills and know-how. It is difficult for us to consider undertaking any kind of improvement effort.
11	*Policy strait-jacket*	They* probably wouldn't let us step out of line with a programme that might conflict with established policies and procedures, or set a precedent. (*For example, Division, Group or Corporate headquarters.)
12	*Union Roadblock*	The union (either at the local or international level) would never accept local initiatives that deviate from the norm.
13	*Out on a limb*	How much real commitment for this is there at the top? Are we walking out on a limb?
14	*Conflict with our company culture*	What we are considering is too much in conflict with company traditions, norms and practices for it to succeed. It's against the grain. The 'anti-bodies' in our company culture will surely kill it!
15	*Too much on our plate*	We are already doing so many things that we can't possibly take on anything additional.
16	*Wild card*	Any other obstacle not suggested in 1−15 above.

Appendix 7

Examples of Action Programmes

Example A

(For a components manufacturer in the aerospace industry.)

Strategy

To reduce cost of products, improve:

- Product design
- Manufacturing equipment and processes
- Work methods, procedures and standards
- Material costs

(this action programme was developed from the list of issues in Appendix V)

Action programme

1 Create a formal process for design specification review and control, based on new and existing product categories. This process will include: role of project engineer; bid/no bid authority; participation in decision on cost and timing issues; and understanding of specifications.

[JDG]*, LS, RB, JY
start 6/1/85
outline 6/30/85
procedure 12/86

2 Develop a programme for establishing a parts catalogue (mechanical/electrical and manpower needs/benefits).

[GB], JM, KT, JF
start 6/1/85
programme 7/30/85
implement start 9/1/85

3 Review and update present design review procedures; add cost estimating into process; include design-to-cost

[NG], GRB, RP, SB
start 6/1/85
report: 7/30/85

4 Review, update, improve the present production release documentation system/flow and engineering change control

[BF], JF, BD, DS,
EC, DB
start 6/1/85
initial plan 8/30/85
final plan 10/30/85
implement start 11/15/85

5 Develop a programme for raising design-to-cost awareness; programme for training in design-to-cost methodology (include materials awareness).

[GW], DD, RP, DB, AD, outside resource
start 6/1/85
plan 7/31
implement start 8/15/85

6 Develop a master plan for manufacturing technology, equipment and processes, linked to business plan. To address: assembly lines; robotics; automated processing and testing; energy; preventive maintenance; CAM.

[FM], DH, JS, JD, AM, JB
start 6/1/85
initial plan 10/31/85
final plan 12/31/85

7 Develop statistical process control (SPC) programme.

[FM], DH, JS, JD, AM, JB
start 6/1/85
initial plan 10/31/85
final plan 12/31/85

8 Evaluate desirability of value engineering effort.

[RS], MW, DB, GW
start 6/1/85
report 9/30/85

9 Review and improve information feedback from pre-production (coordinate with steps 3 and 4).

[EM], RH, WI, DM, DLP
start 6/1/85
review 7/31/85
complete 9/30/85

10 Develop criteria for defining need for detailed work methods (get ISD input; analyse soft spots) and propose approach.

[WL], CC, PP, GRB
start 7/1/85
complete 9/30/85

11 Review schedules vs capacity vs quoted lead times vs economic lot sizes; develop appropriate policy/procedures or revisions.

[DL], MW, RP, RH
review by JJC, JBF
start 7/1/85
complete 9/30/85

12 Evaluate and improve techniques for planning and control of capacity.

[AS], WL
start 7/1/85
report 9/30/85

13 Complete specifications for and implement automated shop-floor control system.

[WL], RD, AS, LJ, DL
start 6/1/85
complete specs 9/30/85
start implement 1/86

14 Study labour standards trends; clarify uses for labour standards and develop policy/procedures.

[RP], JBF, TES
start 6/1/85
report 8/30/85

231

15 Develop policy and procedures for multiple sourcing; including vendor relations.

[LO/MC], AD, RF, WS
start 6/1/85
report 8/30/85

16 Develop more visibility regarding product costs in pre-production area.

[EM], JFP, RD, RB
start 6/1/85
report 9/20/85

17 Refine productivity measures and establish system to collect data and record measures on ongoing basis.

[TES], CL, JM
start 7/1/85
report 9/30/85

* The initials signify all individuals representing key functions assigned to execute each task. The accountable person is the one whose initials are in square brackets.

Example B

(For an electric utility the construction and maintenance function (scope of operating system: the construction and maintenance division with all its relationships with internal 'clients' and corporate departments).)

Strategy

In order to ensure that the quality of our services achieve consistently high levels of client satisfaction, we will refocus our services so as to exceed their expectations, improve our planning, scheduling and implementation to meet schedule commitments and maintain the required level of technical competence and qualification among our employees and supervisors.

Action programme

1 *Determine each client's perspective on quality of our service*

[DLF], VA, LMC, JH, HDL
start 1/5/89
report 6/30/89

(a) Review all existing data (such as Deb Morris' report) and prepare a summary of client satisfaction criteria.
(b) Define role and establish craft managers as point contacts for the stations we support.
(c) Craft managers review with stations their apparent desires.
(d) Determine how individual stations measure their own performance and identify our impact.

Examples of Action Programmes

2 *Establish a top-to-bottom client-driven*   [ARH] BC, DLF, JKL,
   philosophy in our division   DHS
(a) Define the parameters within which we will   start 1/5/89
    be client-driven.   report 9/30/89
(b) Establish department performance indicators
    and standards which clearly reflect our
    client-driven philosophy.

3 *Develop a commitment to client satisfaction* [TBB] BC, RLM, HW
   throughout the organization   start 3/1/89
(a) Develop client interface flow charts to show prototype 8/1/89
    us how to use consistent methods and still   test 11/1/89
    provide tailored client services.   T&Q plan 3/1/90
(b) Use the client interface flow charts to
    educate personnel on how to interact with
    clients.
(c) Implement a training and qualification plan
    (T&Q) that meets client needs.
(d) Continue to involve our clients in
    discussions on long-range planning in order
    to determine what's best for the company
    as a whole.

4 *Establish client satisfaction feedback*   [HDL] BC, LMC, JH,
   process   LW
(a) Provide performance indicator data and   start 1/5/89
    solicit feedback to improve quality of   progress report 5/1/89
    service.
(b) Establish ongoing people-to-people interface
    with clients.

Example C

(For a major computer company (scope of operating system: the financial function supporting US sales and services).)

Strategy

In order to enhance the overall business results for the company, we will lead the development and implementation of integrated US business models and metrics which optimize our business planning and decision-making processes.

233

Action programme

1 *Identify and analyse existing business models*
    [RR, MW]*
    start 9/1/89
    completion 11/1/89

(a) Survey existing US business models (Line or Finance models):
  - Headquarters
  - Areas
  - Districts

(b) Identify other applicable geographic business models.

(c) Establish Finance teams to review models.

(d) Review functionality, use and audience for key models.

(e) Review allocation methodologies for consistency.

2 *Present modelling direction and approach to gain senior management support for this strategy for model development*
    [JT, TH]
    start 11/1/89
    completion 12/1/89

(a) Obtain line representation in teams developing the approaches to model development.

3 *Develop US business model*
    [RR]
    start 11/1/89
    completion 6/1/90

(a) Review model logic and key drivers.

(b) Resolve/elevate business parameter issues to senior management.

(c) Validate total US business model with senior line management.

4 *Develop supporting models that are integrated with the US model*
    [CR, EK]
    start 7/1/90
    completion 9/1/90

(a) Design architectural parameters for model logic:
  - Time
  - Business dimensions
  - Geographic applicability
  - Etc.

(b) Establish modelling teams to create different views of US (headquarters):
  - Industry focus
  - Channel focus
  - Unique (e.g., government)

(c) Establish parameters/directions for
    'bottoms-up' modelling process:
- Account
- District
- Area
- Etc.

(d) Develop models for 4C: start 9/1/90
- In key accounts   completion 7/1/91
- All districts
- All areas
- Etc.

(e) Review all models to compare results

5 *Develop a formal plan and provide project*   [VP, GN]
   management leadership for implementation start 7/1/90
   of the business modelling process, including completion 9/1/90
   linkage with IS and IS strategy

6 *Develop and provide training to finance*   [BK, GC]
   personnel, reviewing qualitative and   start 9/1/90
   quantitative aspects. (Emphasis should be completion 4/1/91
   on consulting and the translation of results
   and actions)

7 *Develop and provide training to line*   [BK, GC]
   management, emphasizing the qualitative start 9/1/90
   aspects of business models   completion 4/1/91

8 *Establish reporting, control, and*   [BC, GN]
   communications processes to manage the start 7/1/90
   deliverables consistent with expectations completion 9/1/90

9 *Define consistent metrics and measurements* [CR, EK]
(a) Review business models in light of   start 8/1/90
    identified desired behaviours (see Strategy completion 9/1/91
    II) and hierarchical interdependencies.
(b) Identify the relationships and inconsistencies
    between functional metrics and
    measurements with US models.

(c) Identify and assess key metrics and
measurements by function in light of:
- Desired behaviours on both a
  hierarchical and interdependency basis.
- Highlighted need for greater goal
  congruence.
- Assessment of competitors and other
  environmental considerations.
- Long- and short-term goals.
- Controllability, or ability to influence.
- Simplicity.
- Other factors as deemed appropriate.

10 *Establish a measurement process for*   [JCB, BHP]
   feedback of results   start 4/1/91
(a) Form a cross-functional group of line and   completion 10/1/91
    finance managers to articulate integrated
    measurements to optimize the US
    organization.
(b) Propose and implement a regular review
    process to ensure discipline and
    accountability for established measurements.
(c) Take leadership (with Human Resources,
    etc.) to couple a reward and recognition
    system which is based on the key
    measurements.

* Here only the accountable managers are listed. Others who will work on these
  tasks are to be recruited and added from within the organization.

Example D

(For a regional US insurance company (scope of operating system: the entire
company).)

Strategy

Improve service quality. Provide improved customer-oriented, quality service.

Action programme

1 *Improve service effectiveness of the entire*   [MNS]*
  organization by enhancing supporting tools,
  systems and procedures

(a) Identify and document tasks (workflow) involving multiple people and/or departments for completion.

start 3/1/89
completion 7/31/89

(b) Review points of contact (moments of truth) for duplicating functions crossing department lines.

start 8/1/89
completion 9/29/89

(c) Analyze strengths and weaknesses of each task and point of contact.

start 10/2/89
completion 10/31/89

(d) Recommend changes to support improvement in organizational effectiveness.

start 11/1/89
completion 11/30/89

2 *Clarify responsibilities and accountabilities*

[EWG]

(a) Identify major activities accounting for 75 to 80 per cent of time for each position.

start 3/1/89
completion 5/31/89

(b) List present measures of functional performance.

start 6/1/89
completion 7/31/89

(c) Analyze strengths/weaknesses of present performance measures in the context of how effectively these encourage a high-quality service orientation.

start 8/1/89
completion 9/29/89

(d) Recommend more relevant standardized measures and reporting mechanisms to achieve common goals within and across departments.

start 10/2/89
completion 10/31/89

3 *Improve head office services by standardizing quality controls, emphasizing to each employee the importance and need for consistently excellent quality service*

[RWR]

(a) Develop a company standard of what quality service is to be.

start 3/1/89
completion 4/28/89

(b) Develop quality controls (directed toward accomplishing company objectives) for each department that has contact with, or provides services to, our customers.

start 5/1/89
completion 7/31/89

(c) Review these quality controls and standardize across department lines to ensure that company objectives are being met.

start 8/1/89
completion 8/31/89

(d) Develop methods of measuring and determining if quality of service is being met. Establish methods of reacting when service standards are not being met.

start 9/1/89
completion 11/30/89

(e) Develop and implement ways to make people constantly aware of the need for quality work, and for having quality controls.

start 12/1/89
completion 12/29/89

4 *Improve head office's ability to resolve errors quickly. Make problem solving/resolution a priority*

[SFA]

(a) Develop problem-solving techniques for each department and individual.

start 3/1/89
completion 4/28/89

(b) Identify problem areas that may need special attention or resources.

start 5/1/89
completion 5/31/89

(c) Develop a feedback programme that will move towards preventive activities (vs fire fighting).

start 6/1/89
completion 8/31/89

(d) Develop and implement ways to determine how our customers perceive our ability to resolve their problems.

start 9/1/89
completion 9/29/89

(e) Include, in performance appraisals, ability to solve problems.

start 10/2/89
completion 12/29/89

5 *Develop a telephone system which makes it easy for customers, and field employees to receive fast and accurate responses to their calls from employees trained in proper customer service techniques*

[KSB]

(a) Install sufficient trunk lines to minimize busy signals.

start 3/1/89
completion 3/24/89

(b) Train all employees receiving calls in proper customer service techniques; monitor calls to ensure high-quality responses.

start 3/27/89
completion 4/7/89

(c) Install automated attendant and other telephone software to enhance our professional image and ability to provide effective telephone service.

start 4/10/89
completion 4/17/89

(d) Provide rewards to support our commitment to high-quality telephone service.

start 4/18/89
completion 5/31/89

6 *Provide the tools and procedures needed to make data accessible to support consistently excellent customer service*

[LWA]

(a) Feasibility plan to eliminate CFO processing.

start 3/1/89
completion 12/29/89

Examples of Action Programmes

(b) Move CFO policies to MP System.

start 3/1/89
completion 12/29/89

(c) Automate CFO Rejected Payment System.

start 1/2/90
completion 4/30/90

(d) Install AS400 to improve the keying of batch receipts.

start 3/1/89
completion 2/28/90

(e) Improve PAC procedures and handling of returned cheques.

start 3/1/89
completion 2/28/90

(f) Automate Annuity Commissions.

start 1/2/89
completion 6/29/90

* Here only the accountable managers are listed. Others who will work on these tasks are to be recruited and added from within the organization.

Appendix 8

Examples of Tailored Measurement Packages

Example A

(From the operating plan for the design and manufacture of desktop computers (see the action programme analysed in Chapter 10).)

Global Measure

Net sales revenues divided by total payroll cost.

Targeted measures and Strategic Performance Gap (SPG):

For strategy	Targeted measure	SPG End 1st year implementation	End 2nd year implementation
I	Time-to-market: total product cycle time from initial design work to commitment date for delivering first lot of particular product.	17%	35%
	Customer satisfaction, defined to include: • time from order placement to actual delivery • system free of defects • conformance to specifications • installation is problem-free • order is complete • reliability (mean time between failures)	10%	25%
II	Total costs by system product	15%	30%

[Strategies III and IV support Strategies I and II]

Example B

(From the operating plan for an SBU that designs, manufactures and markets components to aircraft manufacturers.)

Major sources of expected performance improvement gains

- Product designs that will cost less to make.
- Reduced inventory of parts.
- Reduced scrap and rework everywhere.
- Better proposals at lower proposal costs.
- Increased credibility with Corporate.
- Faster new-product introductions.
- Lower material costs through dual sourcing.
- Reduced warranty costs.
- Reduced cost of quality.
- Fewer Engineering changes.
- Reduced backlog overdue.
- Reduced overtime.
- Reduced pre-production costs.
- Shorter manufacturing cycle time and reduced work-in-process.
- Reduced engineering costs
  - increased net sales $ per employee $ (not including benefits)
  - reduced loss of business from customer second sourcing
  - enhanced image/reputation with customers
  - more new business proposal wins
  - improved management/employee relations

Total required performance improvement (SPG):
net $ sales/$ payroll

Implementation year 1: 10 per cent
Implementation year 2: 15 per cent

Measurement plan

Broad system measures
- Net sales $/employee $
- ROA

Targeted measures
- Improvements in estimated cost of manufacture for comparable designs.
- Proposal wins as percentage of total proposals submitted.
- Cost of inventory.
- Scrap and rework.
- Average Engineering changes/month.
- Cost of quality.
- Warranty costs.
- Customer overdue.
- Overtime hours/straight time hours worked.
- Actual/scheduled time for new product introductions.
- Pre-production cost/sales.
- $ Work-in-process/$ sales.
- Sustaining engineering costs/$ sales.
- Ability to meet programme milestones throughout programme (percentage milestones made).
- Purchasing department expense/total $ material.
- Department expenses/$ sales.

Example C

(From an operating plan for the Construction and Maintenance Department (CMD) for a large electric utility.)

Measures

Strategy

I Improve cost competitiveness

- Estimated cost (work plans) vs actual cost*
- CMD cost vs competition's*
- Cost percentage mix (by function) by project plan*
- Number of projects lost (percentage) vs bids/available*
- $ value projects/CMD employee
- Number of products/CMD employee or total payroll $
- Overtime rate
- Percentage direct workers
- Percentage direct charge
- Number of contract hours used
- Hours of training/worker
- $ training/worker
- $ value of cost-reduction ideas by crew

Strategy

II Improve client satisfaction

- Client feedback form asks for: quality rating; schedule; safety; cooperating; housekeeping*
- Commitment of starts/completes on time vs actual*
- Frequency of incident investigation reports (NPD)*
- Number of people returned or complained about as 'unqualified'*
- Number of projects with client feedback as percentage of number of projects
- Number of client complaints per supervisor
- Number of rework occurrences within 30 days startup
- Formal annual client survey
- Response time to unscheduled requests
- Planned training profile vs actual

Strategy

III Achieve functional integration

- Percentage of modification work done by CMD
- Arguments about fossil modification (number of incidents or time in meetings)
- Number of violations of CMD jurisdiction statement

Examples of Tailored Measurement Packages

Strategy

IV   Enhance people utilization

- Number of transfers as percentage of total CMD employees (in/out of CMD)*
- First-line supervisor offers accepted as percentage of offers made*
- Percentage minorities and women in supervision*
- Attendance*
- 'Unsatisfactory' performers (increasing)*
- Safety incidents*
- Voluntary turnover percentage early retirement
- Participation in self-study programmes
- Number of employee recourses upheld

* Key strategic measures.

Objectives and expected gains

Strategy I

A   Reduce percentage of overhead cost $\left(\dfrac{\text{support group charges}}{\text{total changes}}\right)$ by 5 per cent in 1989 and an additional 5 per cent in 1990.

B   Improve total project cost performance to within 7 per cent of estimate for 1989 and to within 5 per cent of estimate for 1990.

Strategy II

A   Increase the number of client feedback forms received by 20 per cent in 1989 and 20 per cent in 1990.

B   Improve average score on client feedback forms by 5 per cent in 1989 and 5 per cent in 1990.

Strategy III

A   CMD jurisdictional statement issued and communicated by WHO, HBT and WOP.

B   Number of CMD complaints to NPD/FPD management about jurisdiction reduced to 5 in 1989 and 2 in 1990.

Strategy IV

A   Achieve 50 per cent of the needed qualifications for CMD workers in 1989 and 75 per cent in 1990.

B   Increase the amount of supplemental workforce that is 'temporary' rather than 'contract' by 10 per cent in 1989 and 10 per cent in 1990.

Notes

1 A commonly used term to denote a separate, relatively autonomous business within a multibusiness corporation is 'Strategic Business Unit' or SBU. This term is applied when the business is capable of formulating and executing its own strategy, quite independently of the strategies being pursued by other business units within the same corporation.

2 Survey by Phillippe Haspeslagh of INSEAD ('Portfolio Planning: Uses and Limits'), *Harvard Business Review*, Vol. 60, pp. 59-73 (1982).

3 Almost all of this research is analysed, interpreted and discussed by my partner Daniel H. Gray in his article, 'Uses and Misuses of Strategic Planning,' *Harvard Business Review* (Jan.–Feb. 1986).

4 For an extensive discussion of changing the behaviour of individuals and small groups, see Judson, Arnold S., *Changing Behaviour in Organizations*, Basil Blackwell, Oxford, forthcoming.

5 Judson, Arnold S., 'The Awkward Truth About Productivity,' *Harvard Business Review*, Vol. 60, pp. 93-7 (Sept.–Oct. 1982).

6 The relationship between a 'customer' within an organization and the support function that provides it with services should be viewed somewhat differently from a relationship between the organization and its external customers in the marketplace. With external customers, there is but a single objective, namely achieving consistently high levels of customer satisfaction. With internal customers, there are two, sometimes conflicting objectives: (a) customer satisfaction; and (b) doing what is in the best interests of the corporation as a whole (not only the 'customer').

7 Leonard, F. L. and Sasser, W. E., 'The Incline of Quality,' *Harvard Business Review*, Vol. 60, No. 5 (Sept.–Oct. 1982).

8 Vail, P. B., 'The Purpose of High-Performing Systems,' *Organizational Dynamics*, Vol. 11, No. 2 (Autumn, 1982).

9 Hayes, R. H. and Wheelwright, S. C., 'Link Manufacturing Process and Product Life Cycles,' *Harvard Business Review*, Vol. 57, No. 1 (Jan.–Feb. 1979); also Skinner, W., 'Manufacturing – Missing Link in Corporate Strategy,' *Harvard Business Review*, Vol. 47, No. 3 (May–June 1969).

10 Notions of traditional/undeveloped vs avant-garde/sophisticated are based on my interpretation of contemporary research and writings on management practice and organizational behaviour.

11 An excellent analysis and discussion of creative thinking by groups can be found in William J. J. Gordon's *Synectics*, Collier Books, Macmillan Company, New York, 1968.

12 Roethlisberger, F. J. and Dickson, W. J., *Management and the Worker*, Harvard University Press, Cambridge, Mass., 1947.

13 Texas Instruments Company was probably the first large corporation to transition to strategy-based budgets about 1979–80.

14 Cross, Kelvin F. and Lynch, Richard L., 'The "SMART" Way To Define and Sustain Success,' *National Productivity Review*, Vol. VIII, No. 1 (Winter 1988–9); also Cross and Lynch, 'Accounting for Competitive Performance,' *Journal of Cost Management*, Vol. III, No. 1 (Spring, 1989). A detailed exposition of this approach appears in a book by the same authors, *Measure Up! Tailoring Performance Measures to Suit Your Business*, Basil Blackwell, Oxford 1990.

15 These criteria are found in many recent contributions to the fields of operations management and cost management. A good example is: Howell, Robert A. and Soucy, Stephen R., 'Operating Controls in the New Manufacturing Environment,' *Management Accounting* (October 1987).

16 Cross, Kelvin F., 'Making Manufacturing More Effective by Reducing Throughput Time,' *National Productivity Review* (Winter, 1986–7).

17 This description of the process for formulating and implementing a typical operating plan represents a synthesis of hundreds of experiences with companies in a wide range of industries and businesses. In actuality, the two processes are exactly alike because of the unique characteristics in each situation.

Index

accountability, 20, 26, 111, 113–14, 118,
140, 148, 176
climate of, 39, 45, 51, 155–8, 171
action detailing (or planning/programming),
22, 25–7, 31, 36–7, 49, 101, 108,
110–25, 138, 172, 175
action programme, master, 117–19, 130,
140–4, 146, 147, 148, 150–4, 156,
172, 176, 179–80, 230–9
advancement, organizational, 145
assessment, self, 24–5
asset utilization, 81, 84, 100
assumptions, 11, 21, 22, 27, 65, 71, 74–5,
83, 145–7, 176

base period (for measuring improvement),
136, 142, 178
behavioural change, 11, 15, 35, 37, 154, 170
bonus, executive, 145
bottom-line management, 20–2, 180
brainstorming, 96, 115, 119
budgets, 4, 31–2
capital, 4, 31–2
expense, 4, 31–2
strategy-based, 31–2, 143–4
zero-based, 10
business definition, 15–17
business operating system (BOS), 162–9
business strategy *see* strategy, business
buyer *see* customer satisfaction

capabilities, organizational *see* strengths and
weaknesses
capacity, 81, 84, 100
capital
budgets *see* budgets, capital
markets, 29
utilization, 84
card deck tools
obstacles, 228–9
operating plan strategy options, 105–9,
212–22
'straw-person' description of operating
system, 74–5
career development, 181
cash, 84
cause–effect relationships (in operating
systems) *see* operating system

centralization/decentralization, 10, 17, 30
changes (to operating system), 35–40,
90–2, 130–5, 145, 154, 170, 176–7
behavioural *see* behavioural change
installation, 36–7
operational, 36–7
qualitative, 146, 176
climate, socio-economic, 65
climate of accountability *see* accountability
collaboration, cross-functional, 68, 102, 179
commitment, 27–8, 38, 40, 61, 113–14,
119, 141, 150, 152, 155, 158, 171–2,
178; *see also* ownership
communication, 27, 69, 112, 120–1, 149,
151, 153–5, 167–9, 176–8
compensation *see* reward systems
competition, global, 6
competitive
dynamics, 8, 17, 23, 68
environment, 8, 19–20, 22–3, 33, 65,
114
position, 23, 24, 50, 68, 84
reactions, 27, 30
competitors, 19, 23
computers, 32
conflict, 29–30, 93
with culture, 147
conglomerates *see* multi-business
corporations
congruency, 30–5, 38, 45, 93, 95, 143–5
consensus, 58, 60, 65, 80–4, 88, 99, 100,
101, 104–9, 120, 171, 176
constraints, 60
consultants, management, 8, 62, 172
consumer behaviour, 4, 6, 7
control
financial, 4, 12, 31–2
management, 30
systems, 30–4, 45, 92
corporate
departments, 61–2, 70, 172
face-off, 29–30
strategy *see* strategy, corporate
costs, 6, 142, 163–9
capital, 6, 7
control/reduction, 79, 81, 84, 100
energy, 6, 7
goods sold, 139

246

labour, 6, 7, 138
material, 6, 7, 138
structure, 7, 79
total, 80–1
creative thinking 113, 115, 119
credibility
of plans, 21, 40, 44, 61, 151, 172, 179
of performance measures, 142–3
critical mass, 27
culture
American business, 10–11
beliefs, 24–5, 88, 93
company/corporate, 10, 36
operating system, 70
customer satisfaction, 133, 163, 169
customers, 22–3, 163–9
cycles
short *see* responsiveness
time, 140, 142

decision-support *see* information systems
delegation 50, 92
deliverable, 36, 111, 114, 120, 140
delivery flexibility (short cycles), 81, 84,
100, 163–9
reliability, 81, 84, 100, 163–9
depreciation, 139
design engineering, 166
differentiation, 30
distribution channels, 19
diversification, 10
documentation, 72, 154, 173, 176–7, 180

economic forecasting, 4
economies of scale, 19–20
employee involvement, 102, 152–5
employee–management relations, 93
energy
cost *see* costs, energy
utilization, 84
engineering changes, 140, 164
entitlements, 7
environment, 6, 8
economic, 6, 8, 79
regulatory, 6, 8, 65
environmental impact, 6
equipment utilization, 140
exchange rates, 6
executives
experience, 180
mobility, 180
top, 8, 179–80

facilitation support *see* process facilitation
facilities, 55–6, 72, 170
fads in American business, 3, 10–11
feedback, performance, 137, 142–3, 153,
155, 161, 180
financial controls *see* control, financial
flexibility (of operating plan), 79
focus (of operating plan), 99–109, 150–69
fragmentation, organizational *see*
organization(al), fragmentation
fringe benefits, 7
functional
autonomy, 179
bias, 83
operating system centred on, 56, 138
specialization, 7, 179
functional integration *see* integration,
functional

gains, 39, 40, 49, 110, 117, 130, 133, 136,
140, 142, 176
Gantt charts, 3
General Electric Company (USA), 18–19
generic options *see* options, strategic
goals
operating plan *see* objectives, strategic
work, 135
growth opportunities, 4
guideline statement (Sponsor's), 59–60

Hawthorne experiments, 131
high-leverage
opportunity targets, 47, 65–75, 85–7, 96,
99, 101, 105, 111, 113, 172, 174,
200–1
history (learning from), 48, 90–2, 174
human resources, 62, 172

implementation
failures, 9–11, 12–34, 35–40, 150
focus, 150–69, 171
momentum, 150–69, 171
improvement, measuring *see* gains;
measures, performance
industry
characterization, 66
maturity (life-cycles), 22–3, 33–4, 84
inflation, 6
information systems (management
information), 6, 32, 69
inside → out perspective, 6, 22–3
integration, functional (organizational), 30,
50, 102, 164, 169, 179
interest rates, 6
interfunctional relationships, 93, 102, 114, 179
interrogation, 156, 180
interviews (individual and group), 71–2
intrapreneuring, 10
inventories, 140, 164
issues, key, 32, 37, 38–9, 60, 120, 156–8,
171, 176, 223–7

Index

just-in-time provisioning, 10, 167

knowledge (of the business and operating
system) *see* understanding,
management

labour relations, 6, 93
leadership, 58–62
of planning group, 61–2
learning (management, organizational), 21,
148, 169
from history *see* history
life cycles
industry *see* industry, maturity
product/service, 7
long-range planning *see* planning,
long-range

management
competence, 147
depth, 147
development, 14–15, 181
by objectives (MBO), 3, 10
style/behaviour, 11, 68
track record, 147
manager
functional/departmental, 113–14, 118,
150, 154, 173, 177
general/SBU, 58, 148–9, 180
senior, 8, 113–14, 117, 130, 154, 167
managerial grid, 10
manufacturing *see* operations
market(s)
marketplace, 17, 22–3, 134
penetration, 84
share, 84
marketing, 4
material utilization, 6, 84, 100
matrix management, 10
measurement package, tailored, 137–43,
154, 175, 180, 240–3
measures
departmental, 37–8, 129, 159–60
flaws, 134–5
global, 138–9, 142, 155
performance, 26, 36, 37, 69, 129, 145,
148, 154, 159–69
system, 129, 159, 163
targeted, 140, 142, 155
media, company, 155, 178
meetings, staff, 73
merit increases, 144–5
minority rights, 6
mission (of operating system) *see* operating
system, mission
models (of operating system behaviour), 135

monitoring, 26, 36–7, 49, 111, 142; *see
also* tracking performance/
implementation progress
motivation
employee, 49, 141–3, 161
management, 33–4
multi-business corporations, 7, 8, 29–30, 53
multi-national corporations, 7

norms, behavioural, 129
not-for-profit organizations, 101
numbers-driven plans, 20–2, 29; *see also*
performance, business

objectives
departmental, 130, 159
operating plan, 48, 76–86, 96, 99, 101,
105, 113, 130, 137, 147, 154, 156, 174
strategic, 22, 24, 50, 130, 139, 145, 162,
169, 170
observation, 22–3
obstacles, 26, 120, 129, 145, 147–8, 174,
180, 228–9
OMRA grid *see* organization and
management readiness assessment
operating plan, 43–51, 76, 101, 130,
139,143, 149, 150, 154–6, 170–9
model, 46
number of, 43–4, 52–6
strategies, 47, 49, 96, 99–109, 137, 162,
174, 214–22
structured process for developing, 172–8
updates, 49, 145–6, 149
validation, 59, 60, 110–18, 171, 176
operating system, 35–6, 39, 43–51, 65–75,
129, 130, 133, 161–2, 170–3
capabilities *see* strengths and weaknesses
cause–effect relationships, 73, 75, 130,
136
changes (improvements) to, 35–40, 47,
57, 60, 84, 85, 89, 90–2, 130–6, 170
mission, 68
priorities *see* priorities, operating system
responsiveness *see* responsiveness
scope, 48, 52–6, 66, 170
thrusts/themes, 101, 213–14
validation, 59, 73–5, 110, 156
operational planning 26, 39, 43–51, 143
operations, 39, 164, 166
options, strategic, 99–109, 214–22
order-to-delivery cycle, 162
organization(al)
arrangements/characteristics, 11, 102, 170
change capabilities *see* strengths and
weaknesses
fragmentation, 7, 159, 179
organization development, 62, 172

Index

organization and management readiness
assessment (OMRA), 92–5, 102, 158,
174, 202–11
organization structure, 17–20, 68
organizations as systems, 35–6, 65–70
outside → in perspective, 22–3
ownership (of operating plan), 27

participation (management and functions),
27–8, 56–8, 59, 60, 150, 152, 172,
181
people utilization, 84, 100
perceptions see assumptions
performance
business, 20–2, 68, 129
departmental, 37, 129, 159
measures see measures, performance
operating system, 37, 65, 70, 86, 100–1,
129–30, 131–45, 159, 173
promises, 29–30
pyramid, 163
reporting, 167–9
personnel absences and turnover, 140
planners, staff, 3, 8, 9, 11, 14, 62, 172
planning, 69
budgets, 4, 5
cycle,
long-range, 4–6
operational see operational planning
strategic, 5, 8–11, 12, 13–15, 33–4, 39
planning group, 27–8, 47–9, 52, 56, 62,
65–6, 73–5, 88, 90–6, 99–109, 110,
138, 140–6, 150–3, 156, 158,
171–8, 180
policies and procedures, 35, 52, 53, 162,
170
portfolio management, 10, 30
price, 18
priorities
departmental, 159
operating system, 8. 37–8, 48, 51,
76–86, 96, 99, 101, 105, 155–6,
166–9, 174
worksheet, 80–4
process facilitation, 61–2
process time, 163–9
processes (work/business), 35, 52, 55, 114
product design, 6, 84, 164
product/service flexibility, 81, 84, 100
productivity, 33–4, 49–51, 133, 163, 169
progress reviews, 36, 147–9, 155, 178
profit, 33–4, 84
psychological testing, 10
purchasing, 164, 166

qualitative elements of plans, 22
quality, 18, 79, 81, 100, 142, 163–9

quality circles, 3, 10
quantitative elements of plans see numbers-
driven plans
quantitative management, 10
quick-fixes see success, early

readiness, organizational and management
see organization and management
readiness assessment
readiness-to-serve (budgeting), 144
reconciliation (SBU vs. corporate), 29–30
regulation, government, 6, 65
reporting performance see performance,
reporting
research, 23, 167
operating system, 70–3, 173
resistance to change, 44
resources
allocation, 8, 30, 47, 84, 111, 154, 156,
171
requirements, 26, 29, 39, 110, 113, 115,
117, 156, 158
responsiveness (of operating system), 48,
79, 81, 100, 142, 147, 163–4, 169
restructuring, 10
return on investment, 130, 142
revenues, sales, 138–9, 142
reward systems, 33–4, 70, 144–5, 156, 171
monetary, 70, 158, 171
non-monetary, 70, 158, 171
rework, 164
risk analysis, 26, 30, 146–7, 176, 180
roadmap, implementation, 111

scenario see vision
schedule, master, 117–18
sensitivity training, 3, 10
share of market see market, share
signal generators, 146–8, 154, 176, 180
skills
group process, 61
SMART (strategic measures, analysis and
reporting technique), 162–9
social values see values, social
sponsor, 52, 58–61, 111, 156–8, 170–1,
176–7, 180
actions required, 58–60
mindset of, 60–1
staffing, 140
standards, performance/work, 135, 141, 155
stock options, 145
strategic
business unit (SBU), 17–20, 29–30,
44–5, 47, 51, 52, 53, 55, 66, 129,
130, 134, 138, 162, 170–1
business unit definition, 17–20
competition for resources, 29–30

imperatives, 48, 68, 76, 79–84, 86
management, 5, 34, 45, 145
performance gap (SPG), 138–9, 142, 176
strategic planning/plan, 3, 8–11, 12, 13,
   33–4, 43, 66, 68, 143
   formulation, 8–11, 13–34
   responsibility for, 8–11, 13–15, 39
strategy
   business, 8, 22, 24, 45, 47, 48, 51,
      52–3, 55, 76–86, 100, 101, 114, 139,
      145, 161, 170–1, 173–4, 179
   corporate, 8, 29–30
   feasibility, 26
   manager/coordinator, 147–8
   operating plan *see* operating plan,
      strategies
   quality of, 27
straw-person characterization (of operating
   system), 66–75, 173–4, 182–99
strengths and weaknesses, 6, 22, 24–5, 48,
   88–96, 99, 101, 105, 113, 172, 174
successes, early, 117, 151–2, 178
suggestions, employee, 154
supervision, first-line, 57, 68, 93, 114, 150,
   152, 154–5, 171–3, 177
system analysis, 48, 65
systems, organizational, 30–4, 45, 52, 92,
   102, 170; *see also* organization(al),
   arrangements

task groups, interfunctional, 26–7, 115–18,
   175–6
tasks, specification of *see* action detailing
technology, 4, 6, 66, 162, 170
time frame/timetable, 117–18, 149
time-to-market, 162
total quality control, 10

tracking performance/implementation
   progress, 39, 49, 111, 120, 136,
   140–2, 145–9, 154–5, 167–9, 175–6;
   see also monitoring
trade-off analyses/decisions, 14, 26, 30, 52,
   58, 156
training and development, 69
trend charts, 136, 142, 148, 155, 178
trial-and-error (performance measures), 136,
   142
triggering event, 120

understanding, management, 27–8, 38, 40,
   58, 61, 65, 79–80, 112–14, 119, 147,
   150, 152, 171–2, 178, 180–1
union-management cooperation, 102
unions (trade), 101
user *see* customer satisfaction

validation, operating plan *see* operating
   plan, validation
values, social, 6
variances, cost, 141
vision (of implementation outcomes), 120
volume flexibility *see* capacity

waste, 50, 142, 164
womens' rights
work climate, 69
work force, 7, 69, 114
   blue collar, 7
   professional, 7
work satisfaction, 7
work to implement a plan, *see* action
   detailing
workflow, 35, 52, 55, 162, 165, 169, 170

yield loss, 164